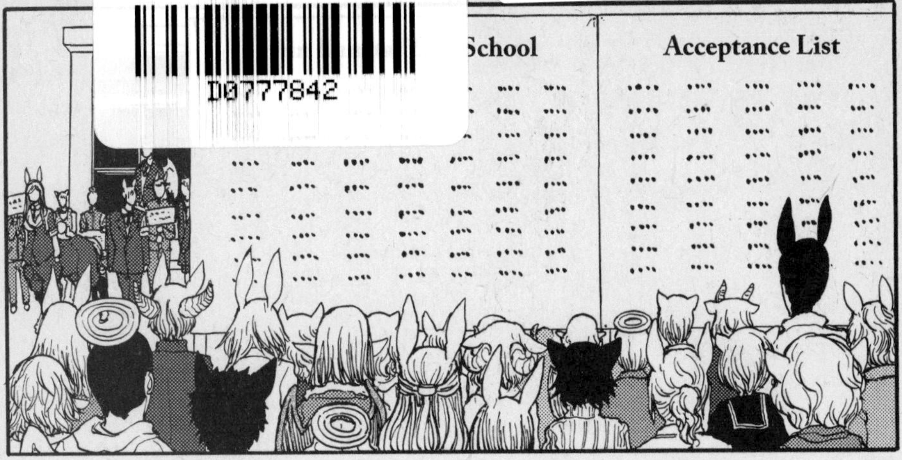
School
Acceptance List

CHAPTER 69

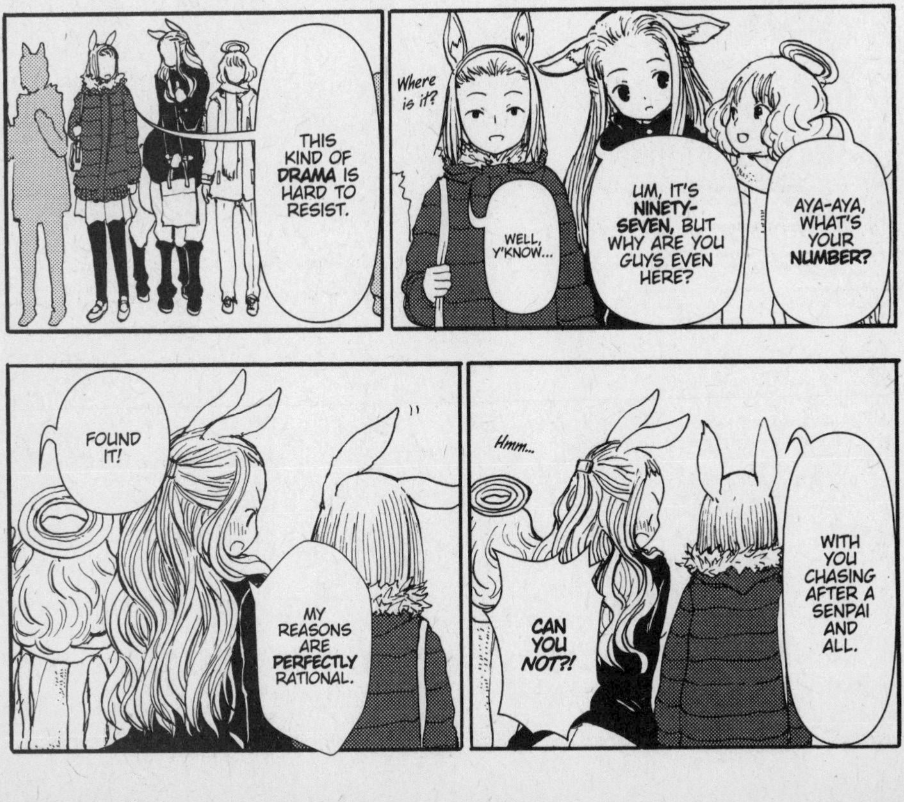
Where is it?
AYA-AYA, WHAT'S YOUR NUMBER?
UM, IT'S NINETY-SEVEN, BUT WHY ARE YOU GUYS EVEN HERE?
WELL, Y'KNOW...
THIS KIND OF DRAMA IS HARD TO RESIST.
WITH YOU CHASING AFTER A SENPAI AND ALL.
Hmm...
CAN YOU NOT?!
FOUND IT!
MY REASONS ARE PERFECTLY RATIONAL.

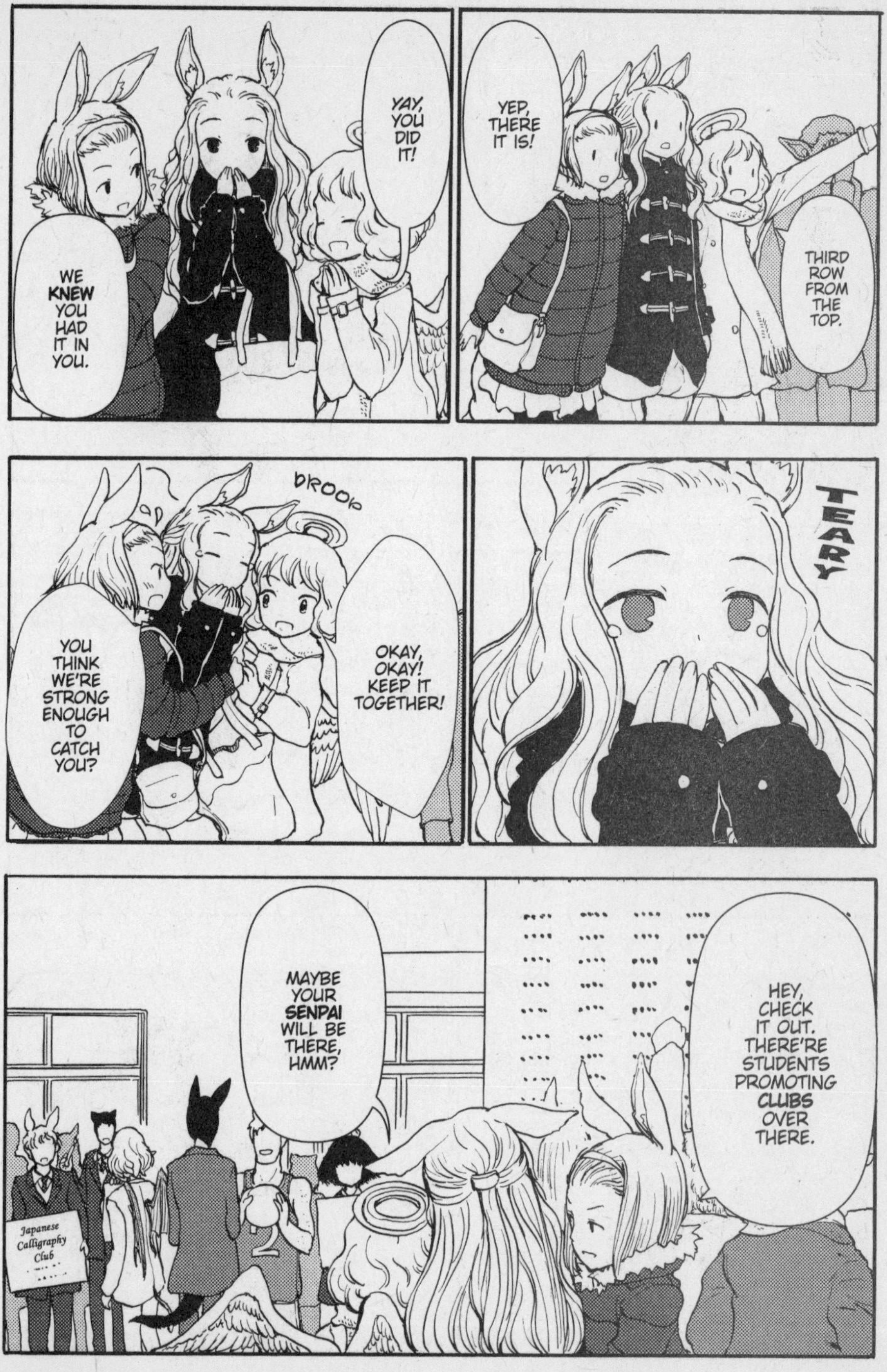
THIRD ROW FROM THE TOP.
YEP, THERE IT IS!
YAY, YOU DID IT!
WE KNEW YOU HAD IT IN YOU.
TEARY
DROOP
OKAY, OKAY! KEEP IT TOGETHER!
YOU THINK WE'RE STRONG ENOUGH TO CATCH YOU?
HEY, CHECK IT OUT. THERE'RE STUDENTS PROMOTING CLUBS OVER THERE.
MAYBE YOUR SENPAI WILL BE THERE, HMM?
Japanese Calligraphy Club

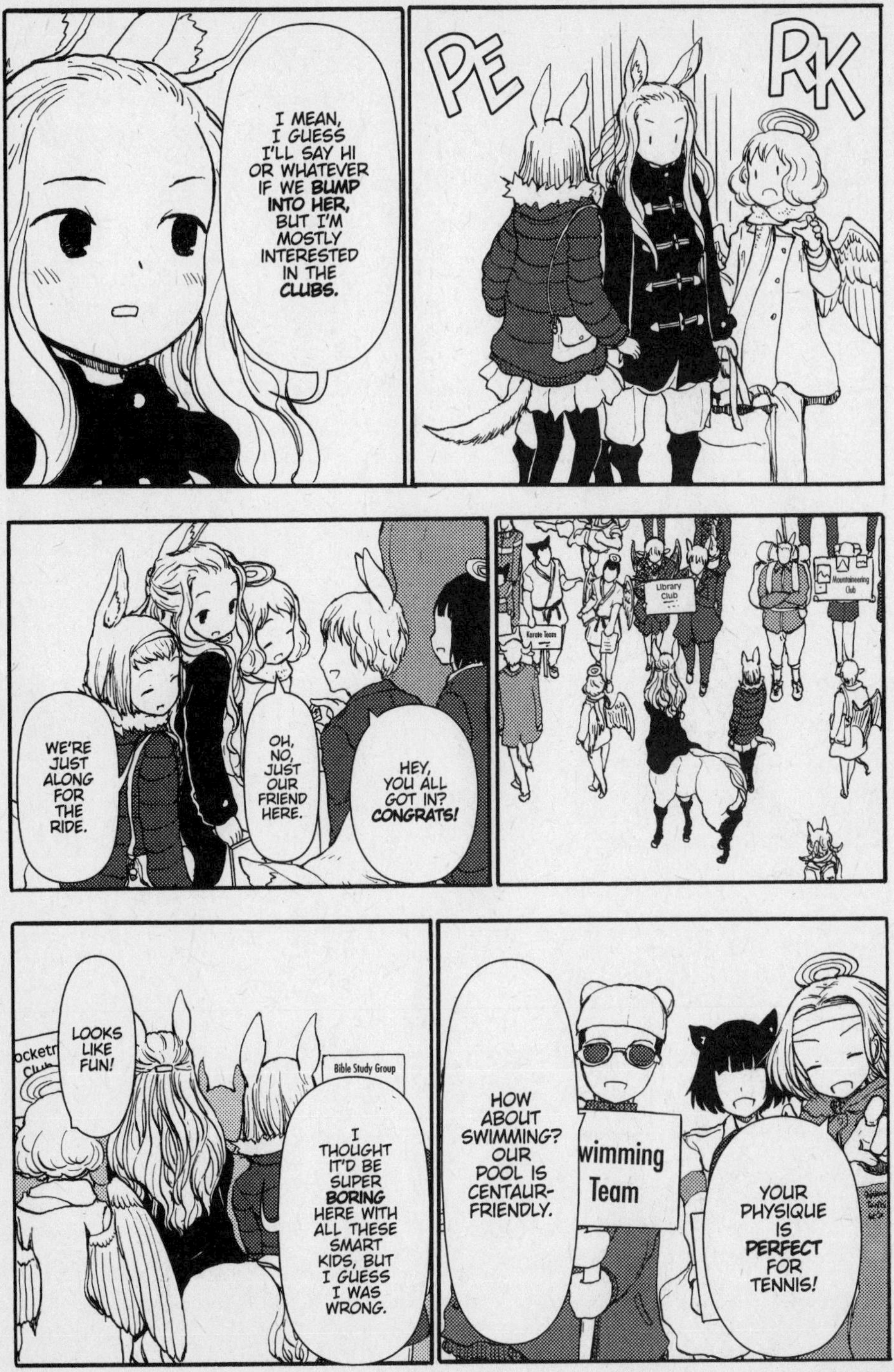
PE RK
I MEAN, I GUESS I'LL SAY HI OR WHATEVER IF WE **BUMP INTO HER,** BUT I'M MOSTLY INTERESTED IN THE **CLUBS.**
Mountaineering Club
Library Club
Karate Team
HEY, YOU ALL GOT IN? **CONGRATS!**
OH, NO, JUST OUR FRIEND HERE.
WE'RE JUST ALONG FOR THE RIDE.
YOUR PHYSIQUE IS **PERFECT** FOR TENNIS!
HOW ABOUT SWIMMING? OUR POOL IS CENTAUR-FRIENDLY.
Bible Study Group
I THOUGHT IT'D BE SUPER **BORING** HERE WITH ALL THESE SMART KIDS, BUT I GUESS I WAS WRONG.
LOOKS LIKE FUN!

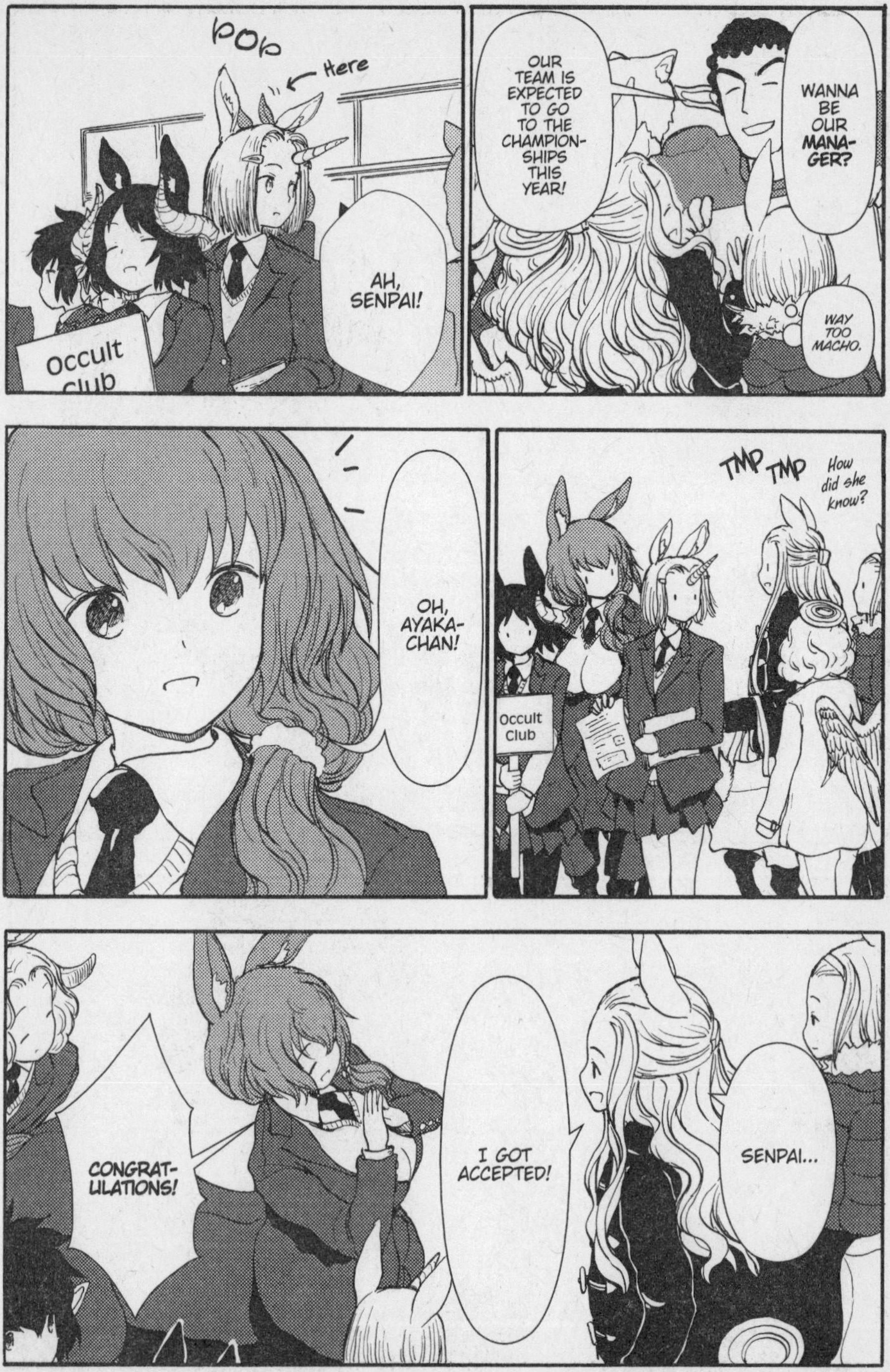

WANNA BE OUR MANA-GER?
OUR TEAM IS EXPECTED TO GO TO THE CHAMPION-SHIPS THIS YEAR!
WAY TOO MACHO.
POP
Here
AH, SENPAI!
Occult Club
TMP TMP
How did she know?
Occult Club
OH, AYAKA-CHAN!
SENPAI...
I GOT ACCEPTED!
CONGRAT-ULATIONS!

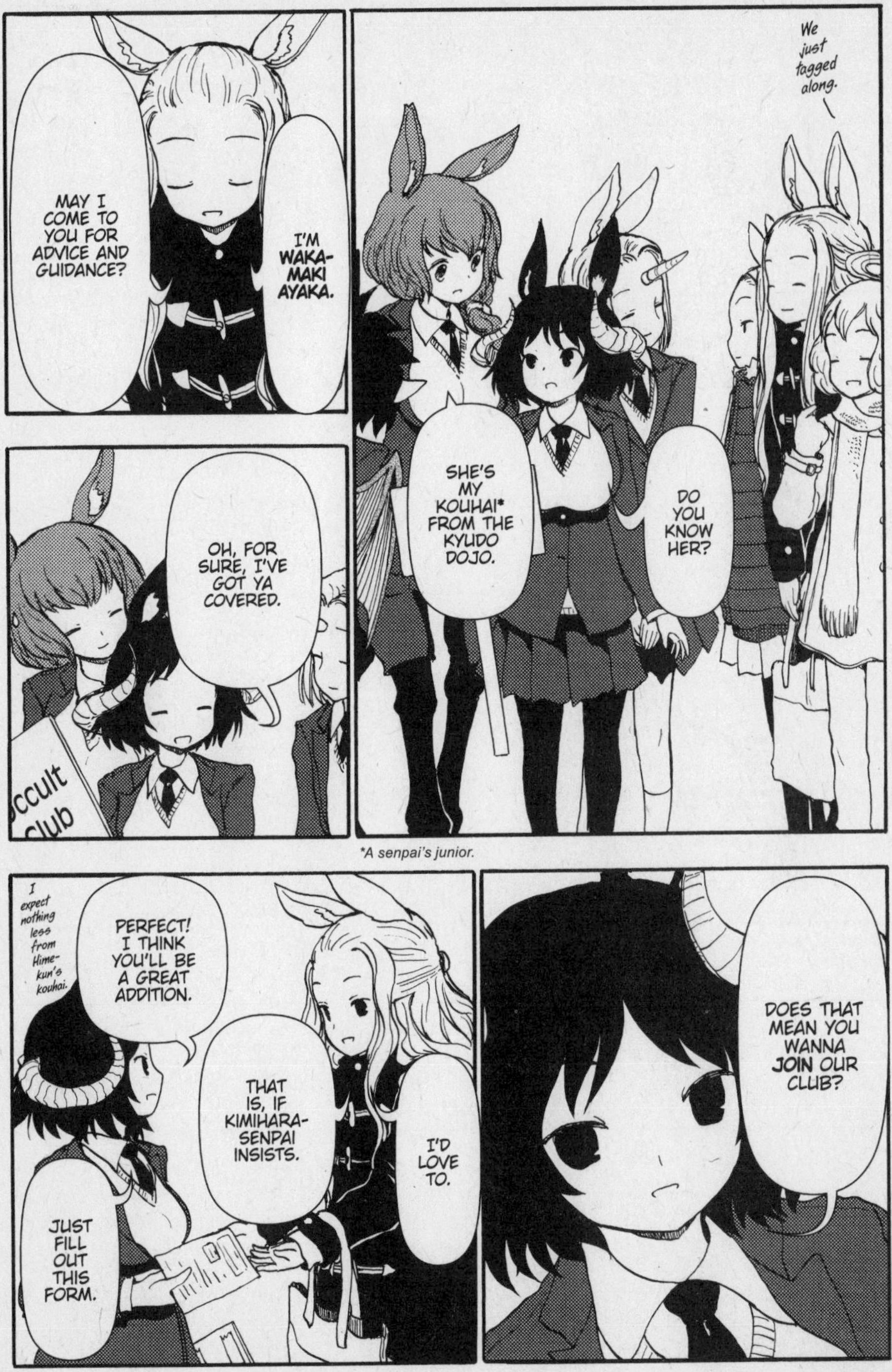
We just tagged along.
DO YOU KNOW HER?
SHE'S MY KOUHAI* FROM THE KYUDO DOJO.
I'M WAKA-MAKI AYAKA.
MAY I COME TO YOU FOR ADVICE AND GUIDANCE?
OH, FOR SURE, I'VE GOT YA COVERED.
ccult club
DOES THAT MEAN YOU WANNA JOIN OUR CLUB?
I'D LOVE TO.
THAT IS, IF KIMIHARA-SENPAI INSISTS.
PERFECT! I THINK YOU'LL BE A GREAT ADDITION.
I expect nothing less from Hime-kun's kouhai.
JUST FILL OUT THIS FORM.
*A senpai's junior.

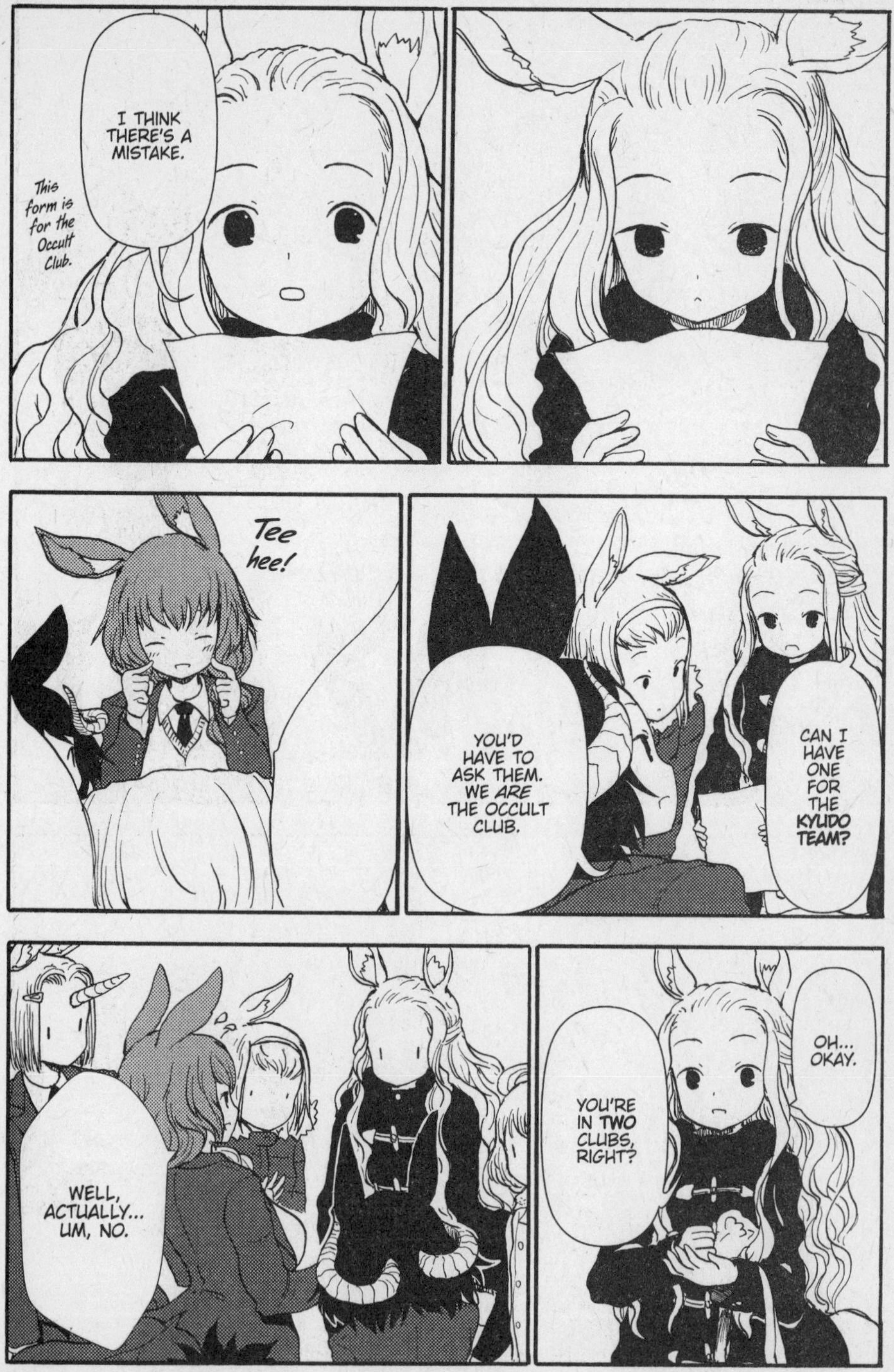
I THINK THERE'S A MISTAKE.
This form is for the Occult Club.
CAN I HAVE ONE FOR THE KYUDO TEAM?
YOU'D HAVE TO ASK THEM. WE *ARE* THE OCCULT CLUB.
Tee hee!
OH... OKAY.
YOU'RE IN TWO CLUBS, RIGHT?
WELL, ACTUALLY... UM, NO.

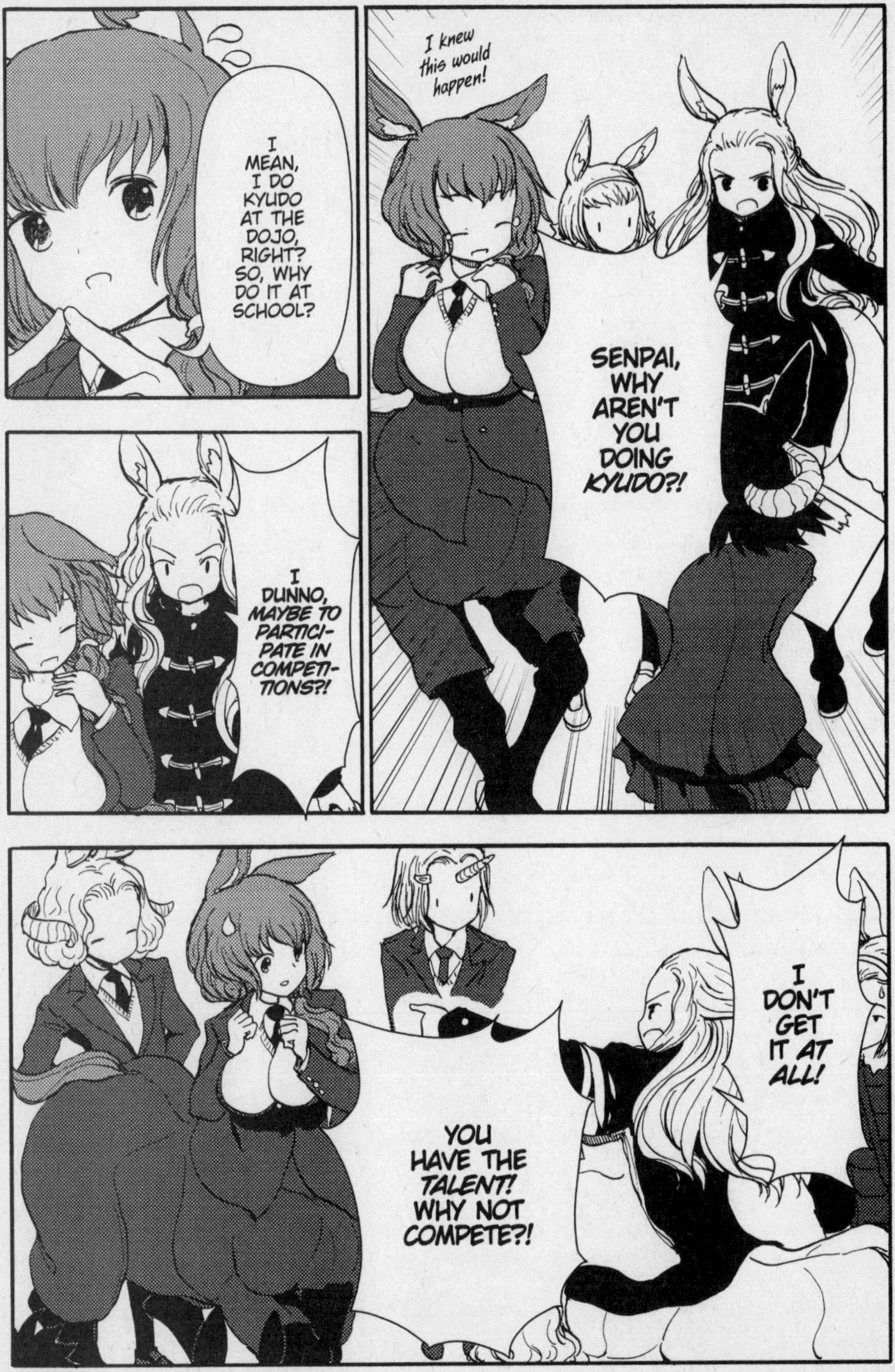
SENPAI, WHY AREN'T YOU DOING *KYUDO*?!
I knew this would happen!
I MEAN, I DO KYUDO AT THE DOJO, RIGHT? SO, WHY DO IT AT SCHOOL?
I DUNNO, *MAYBE TO PARTICIPATE IN COMPETITIONS?!*
I DON'T GET IT AT *ALL!*
YOU HAVE THE *TALENT!* WHY NOT COMPETE?!

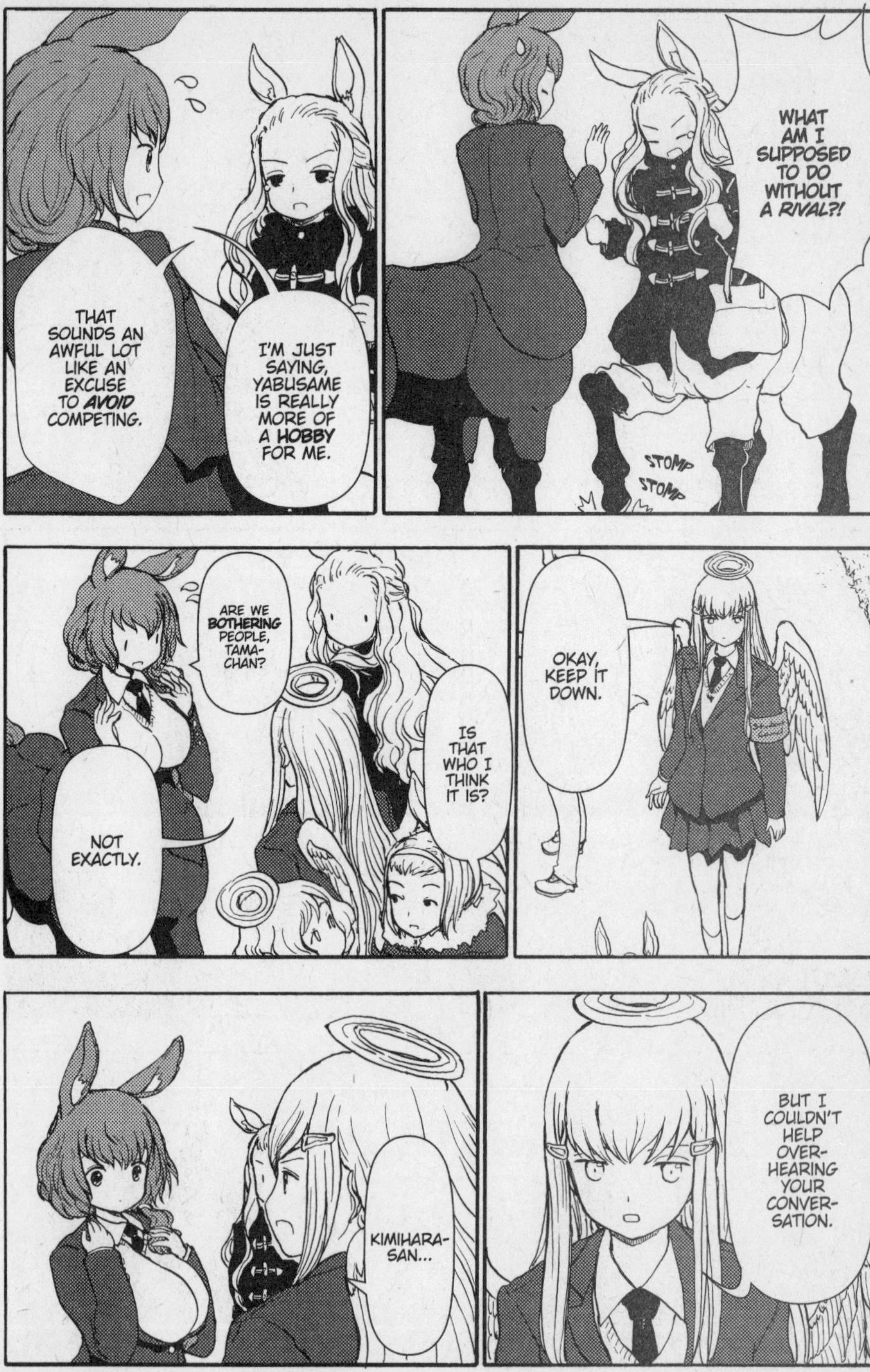
WHAT AM I SUPPOSED TO DO WITHOUT A RIVAL?!
STOMP STOMP
I'M JUST SAYING, YABUSAME IS REALLY MORE OF A HOBBY FOR ME.
THAT SOUNDS AN AWFUL LOT LIKE AN EXCUSE TO AVOID COMPETING.
OKAY, KEEP IT DOWN.
ARE WE BOTHERING PEOPLE, TAMA-CHAN?
IS THAT WHO I THINK IT IS?
NOT EXACTLY.
BUT I COULDN'T HELP OVER-HEARING YOUR CONVER-SATION.
KIMIHARA-SAN...

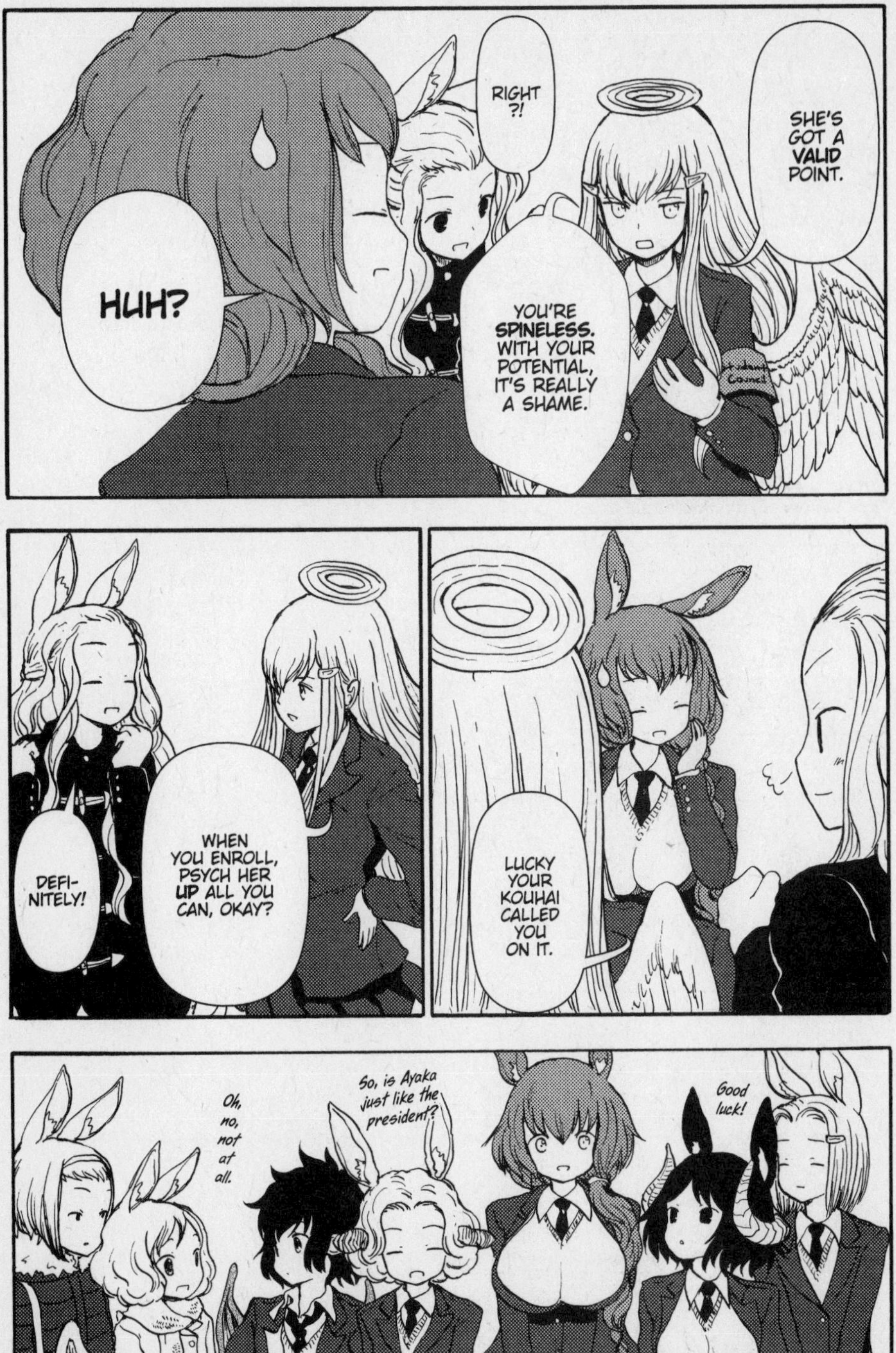
SHE'S GOT A VALID POINT.
RIGHT ?!
YOU'RE SPINELESS. WITH YOUR POTENTIAL, IT'S REALLY A SHAME.
HUH?
LUCKY YOUR KOUHAI CALLED YOU ON IT.
WHEN YOU ENROLL, PSYCH HER UP ALL YOU CAN, OKAY?
DEFI-NITELY!
Good luck!
So, is Ayaka just like the president?
Oh, no, not at all.

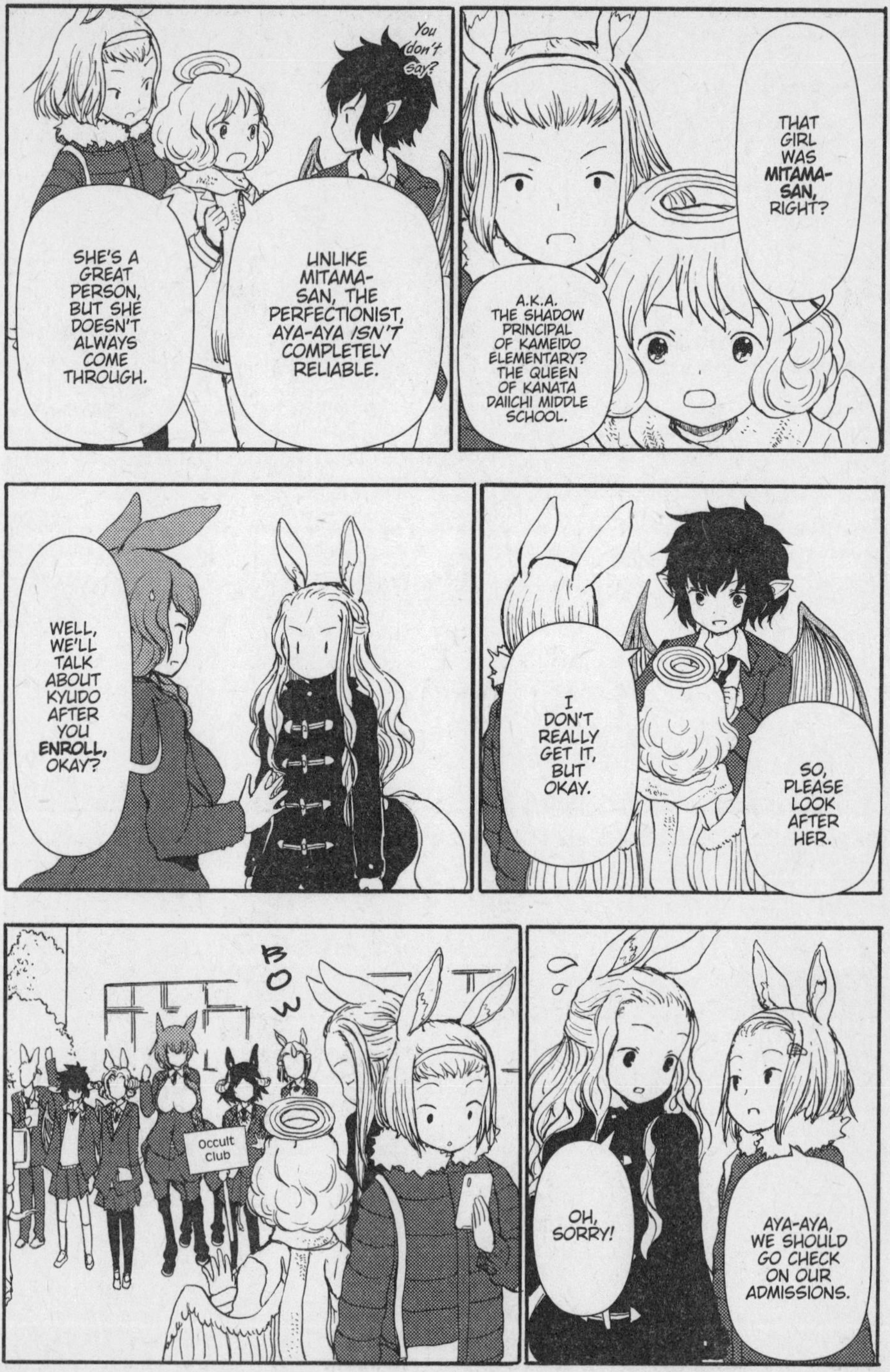
THAT GIRL WAS MITAMA-SAN, RIGHT?
A.K.A. THE SHADOW PRINCIPAL OF KAMEIDO ELEMENTARY? THE QUEEN OF KANATA DAIICHI MIDDLE SCHOOL.
You don't say?
UNLIKE MITAMA-SAN, THE PERFECTIONIST, AYA-AYA *ISN'T* COMPLETELY RELIABLE.
SHE'S A GREAT PERSON, BUT SHE DOESN'T ALWAYS COME THROUGH.
SO, PLEASE LOOK AFTER HER.
I DON'T REALLY GET IT, BUT OKAY.
WELL, WE'LL TALK ABOUT KYUDO AFTER YOU ENROLL, OKAY?
AYA-AYA, WE SHOULD GO CHECK ON OUR ADMISSIONS.
OH, SORRY!
BOW
Occult Club

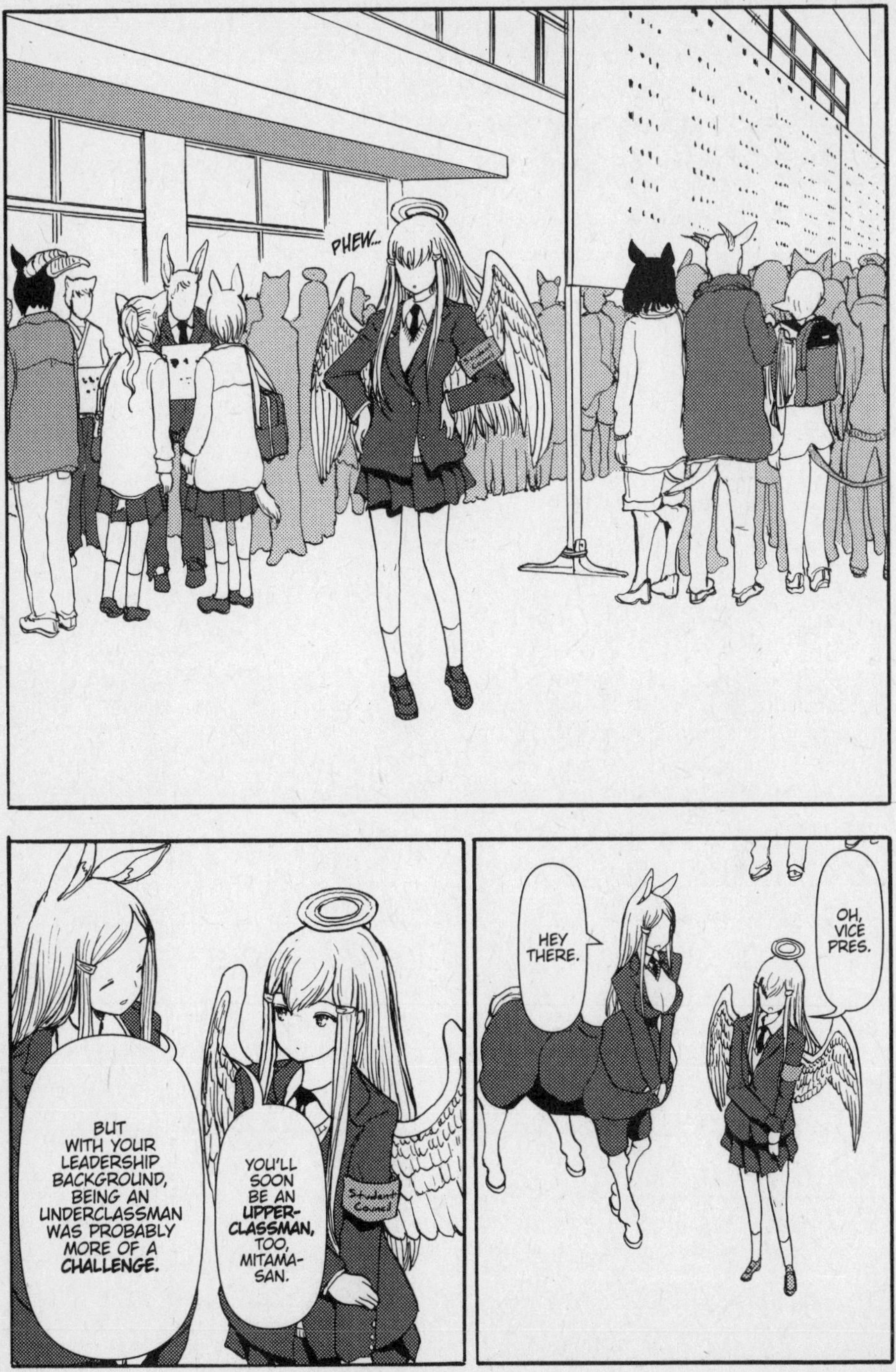
PHEW...
OH, VICE PRES.
HEY THERE.
YOU'LL SOON BE AN UPPER-CLASSMAN, TOO, MITAMA-SAN.
Student Council
BUT WITH YOUR LEADERSHIP BACKGROUND, BEING AN UNDERCLASSMAN WAS PROBABLY MORE OF A CHALLENGE.

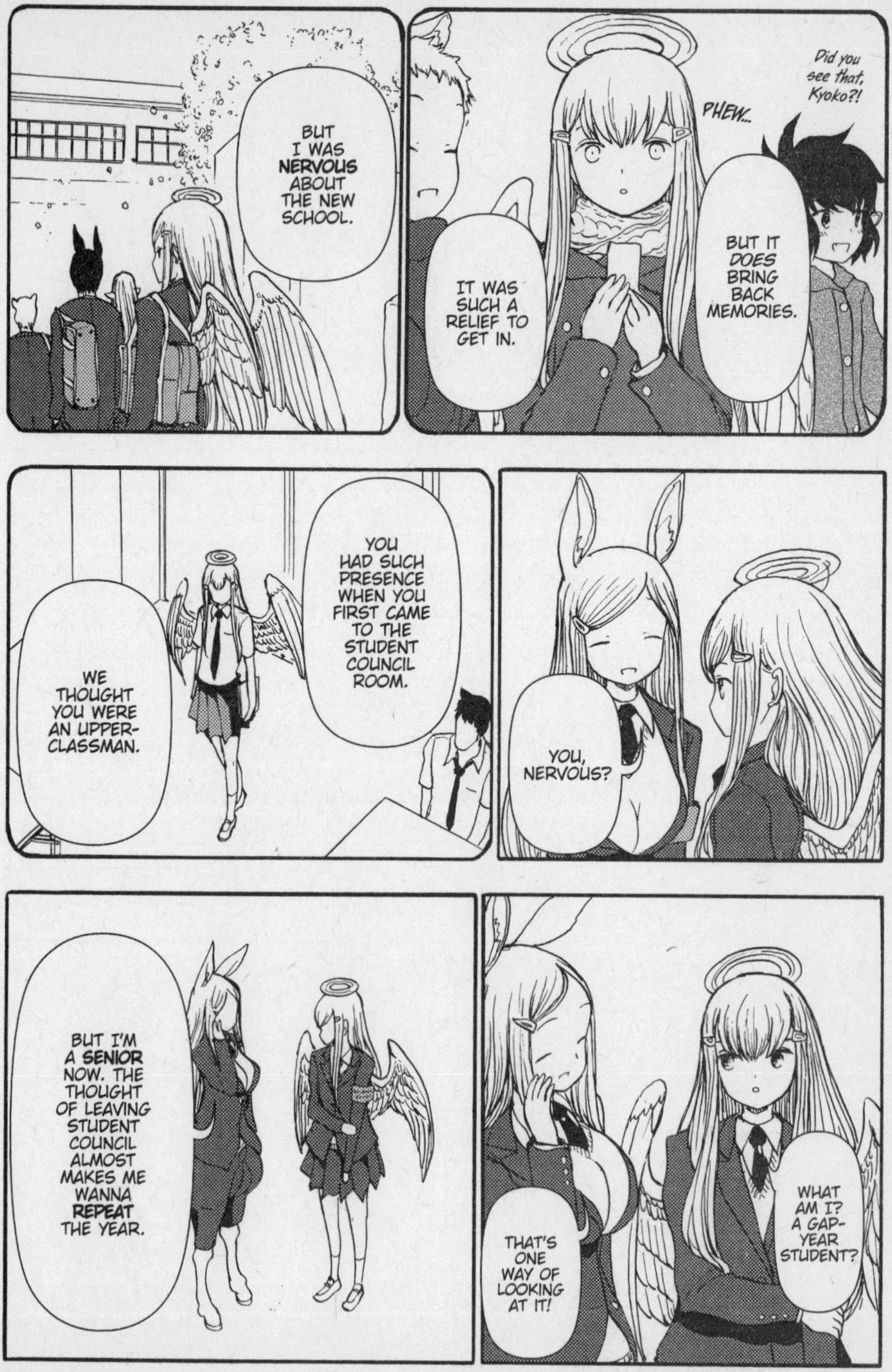
Did you see that, Kyoko?!
PHEW...
BUT IT DOES BRING BACK MEMORIES.
IT WAS SUCH A RELIEF TO GET IN.
BUT I WAS NERVOUS ABOUT THE NEW SCHOOL.
YOU, NERVOUS?
YOU HAD SUCH PRESENCE WHEN YOU FIRST CAME TO THE STUDENT COUNCIL ROOM.
WE THOUGHT YOU WERE AN UPPER-CLASSMAN.
WHAT AM I? A GAP-YEAR STUDENT?
THAT'S ONE WAY OF LOOKING AT IT!
BUT I'M A SENIOR NOW. THE THOUGHT OF LEAVING STUDENT COUNCIL ALMOST MAKES ME WANNA REPEAT THE YEAR.

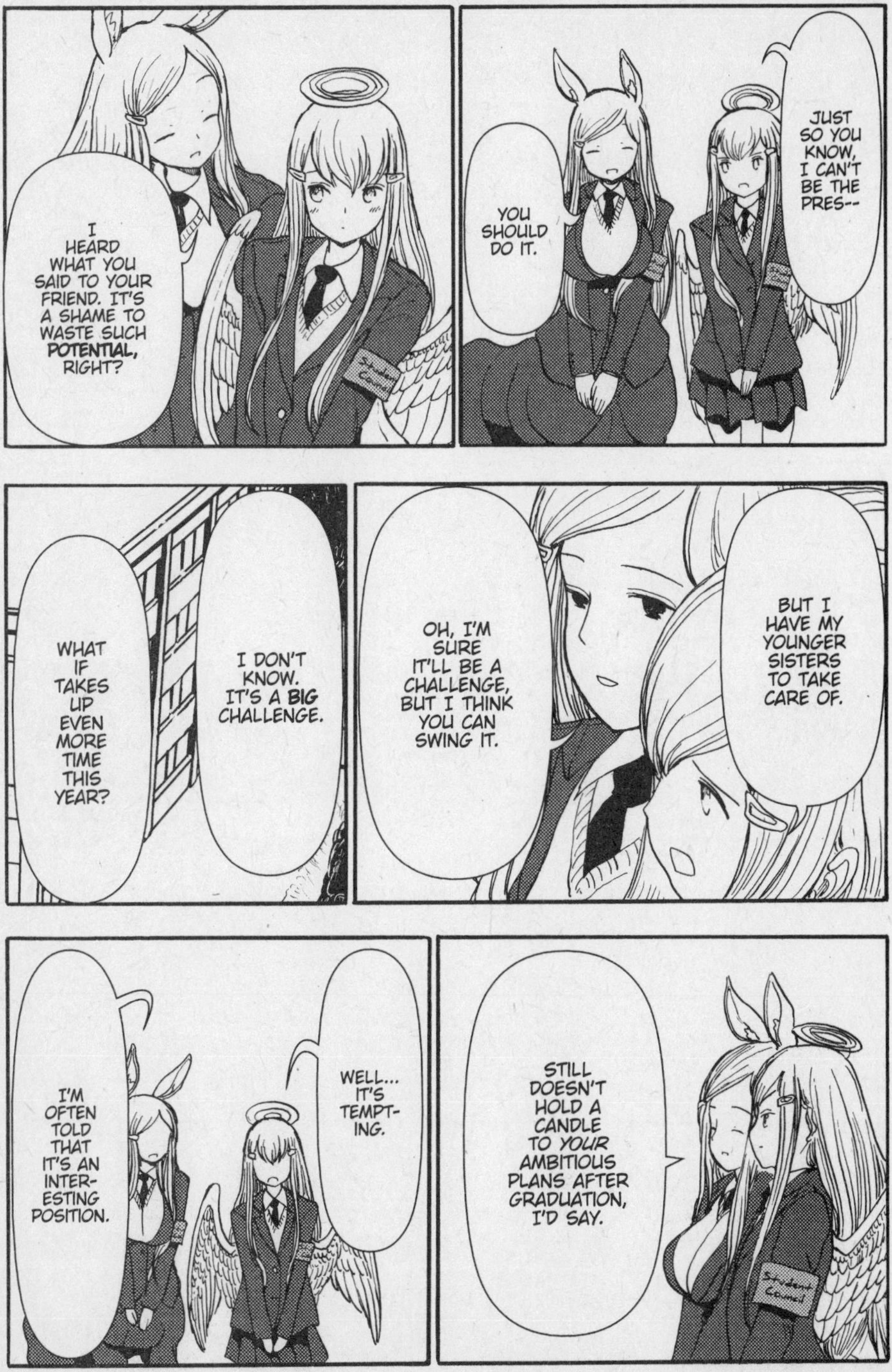
JUST SO YOU KNOW, I CAN'T BE THE PRES--
YOU SHOULD DO IT.
I HEARD WHAT YOU SAID TO YOUR FRIEND. IT'S A SHAME TO WASTE SUCH **POTENTIAL,** RIGHT?
BUT I HAVE MY YOUNGER SISTERS TO TAKE CARE OF.
OH, I'M SURE IT'LL BE A CHALLENGE, BUT I THINK YOU CAN SWING IT.
I DON'T KNOW. IT'S A **BIG** CHALLENGE.
WHAT IF TAKES UP EVEN MORE TIME THIS YEAR?
STILL DOESN'T HOLD A CANDLE TO *YOUR* AMBITIOUS PLANS AFTER GRADUATION, I'D SAY.
WELL... IT'S TEMPT-ING.
I'M OFTEN TOLD THAT IT'S AN INTER-ESTING POSITION.

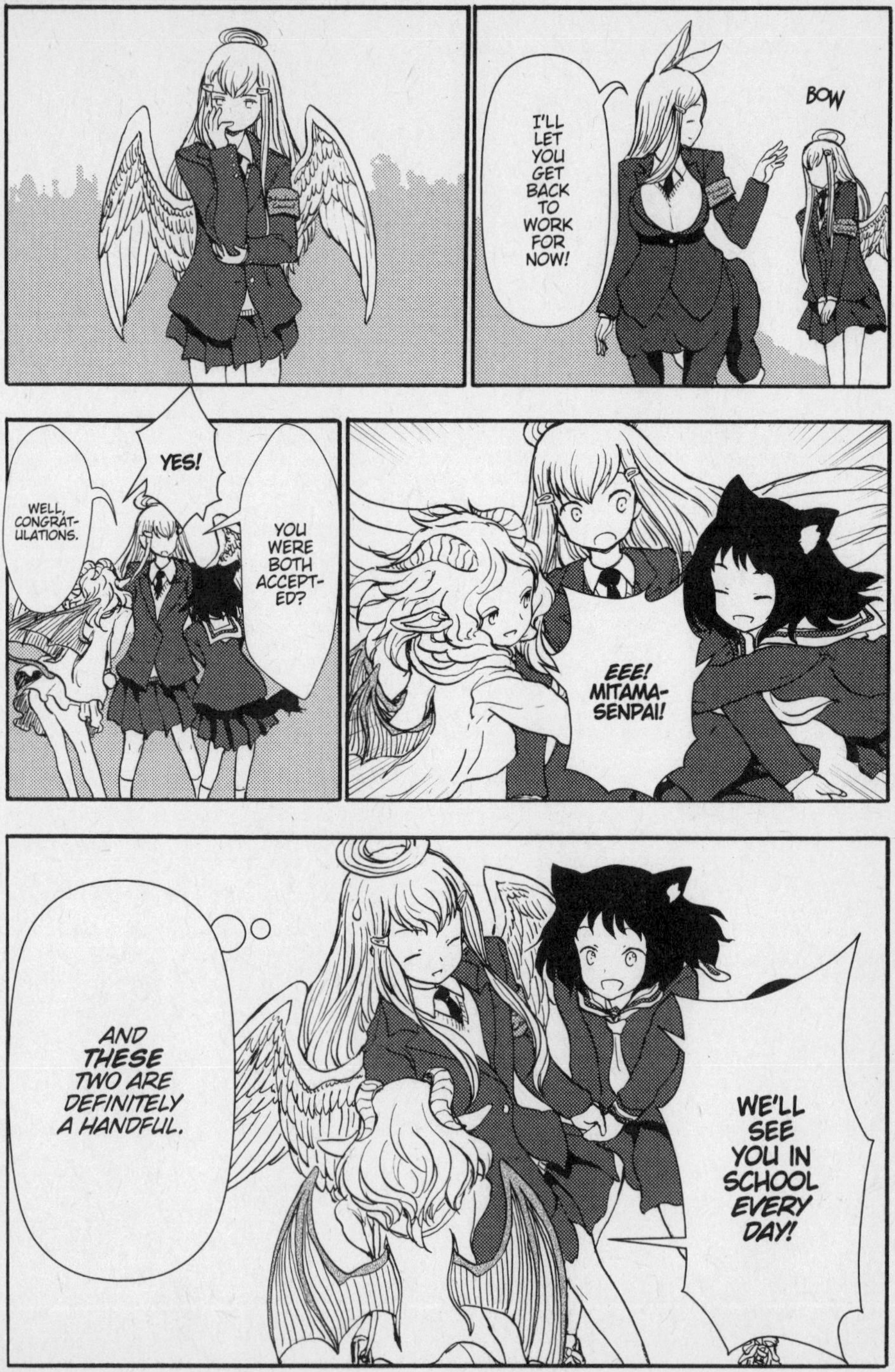
BOW
I'LL LET YOU GET BACK TO WORK FOR NOW!
EEE! MITAMA-SENPAI!
YOU WERE BOTH ACCEPTED?
YES!
WELL, CONGRATULATIONS.
WE'LL SEE YOU IN SCHOOL EVERY DAY!
AND THESE TWO ARE DEFINITELY A HANDFUL.

A Centaur's Life

UNDERSTANDING ANTARCTICANS: PART 1

ANTARCTICANS ARE A NON-MAMMAL RACE THAT SOME BELIEVE FIRST MADE CONTACT WITH MODERN HUMAN CIVILIZATION IN THE MID-TWENTIETH CENTURY, BUT THIS PERSPECTIVE IS CLEARLY BIASED TOWARD THE NORTHERN HEMISPHERE. IN FACT, ANTARCTICANS HAVE INTERACTED WITH PEOPLES IN LATIN AMERICA SINCE ANCIENT TIMES, BUT THE CORRELATION THOSE PEOPLE SAW BETWEEN ANTARCTICANS AND THEIR SERPENT DEITY QUETZALCOATL MAKES IT DIFFICULT TO DETERMINE THE TIMING OF FIRST CONTACT BETWEEN THE RACES. ALTHOUGH MUCH IS UNKNOWN ABOUT THEIR RACE, WE CAN DETERMINE THAT THEIR CIVILIZATION WAS SUFFICIENTLY ADVANCED AT THAT TIME THAT THOSE ANCIENT HUMANS CONSIDERED THEM TO BE DIVINE. THEY ARE SAID TO HAVE AIDED THE AZTEC AND INCA EMPIRES (ALSO KNOWN AS TAWANTINSUYU) IN REPELLING THE ATTEMPTED INVASION BY THE SPANISH CONQUISTADORS, BUT DUE TO THEIR SECRECY, WE ARE UNABLE TO CORROBORATE THIS CLAIM.

DESPITE THEIR LONG RELATIONSHIP, THE PEOPLE OF THE AZTEC AND INCA EMPIRES KNOW VERY LITTLE ABOUT THE ANTARCTICANS, WHO HAVE ALSO REFUSED TO ALLOW ANY MAMMALIAN HUMANS TO ENTER THEIR COUNTRY. THE ONLY INFORMATION WE HAVE ABOUT THIS ENIGMATIC CIVILIZATION COMES FROM THE TESTIMONY OF PEOPLE WHO HAVE HAD CHANCE ENCOUNTERS WITH THEM, AND SOME ANECDOTES OFFERED BY ANTARCTICANS THEMSELVES. AS WE CONTINUE TO PIECE TOGETHER INFORMATION, WE HOPE TO PRESENT MORE KNOWLEDGE IN THE FUTURE. FOR NOW, THIS IS THE MOST CURRENT REPORT WE CAN OFFER.

Note: To our knowledge, all members of both the Warrior and Intellectual subspecies of Antarcticans are female.

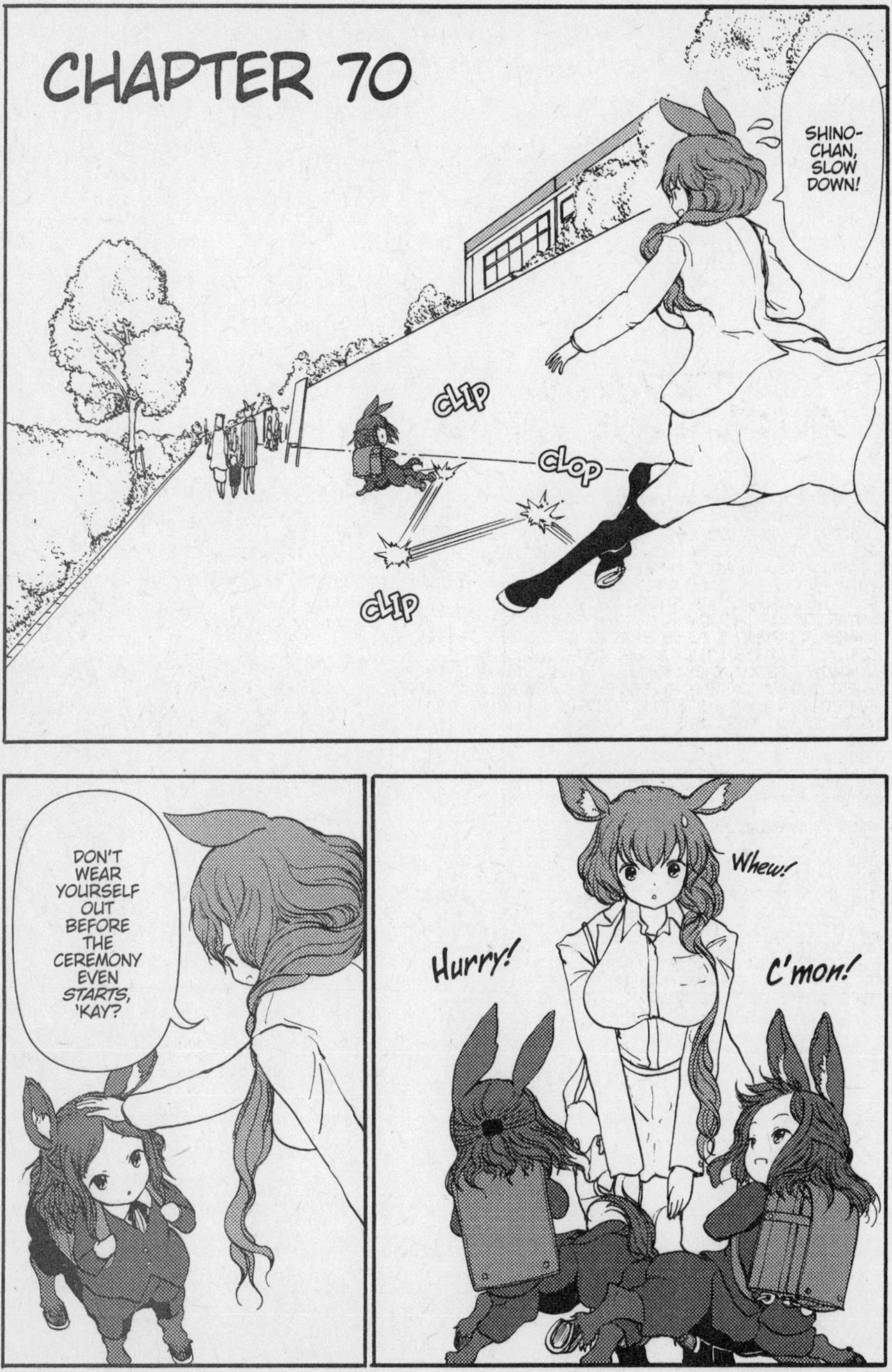
CHAPTER 70
SHINO-CHAN, SLOW DOWN!
CLIP
CLOP
CLIP
Whew!
C'mon!
Hurry!
DON'T WEAR YOURSELF OUT BEFORE THE CEREMONY EVEN *STARTS*, 'KAY?

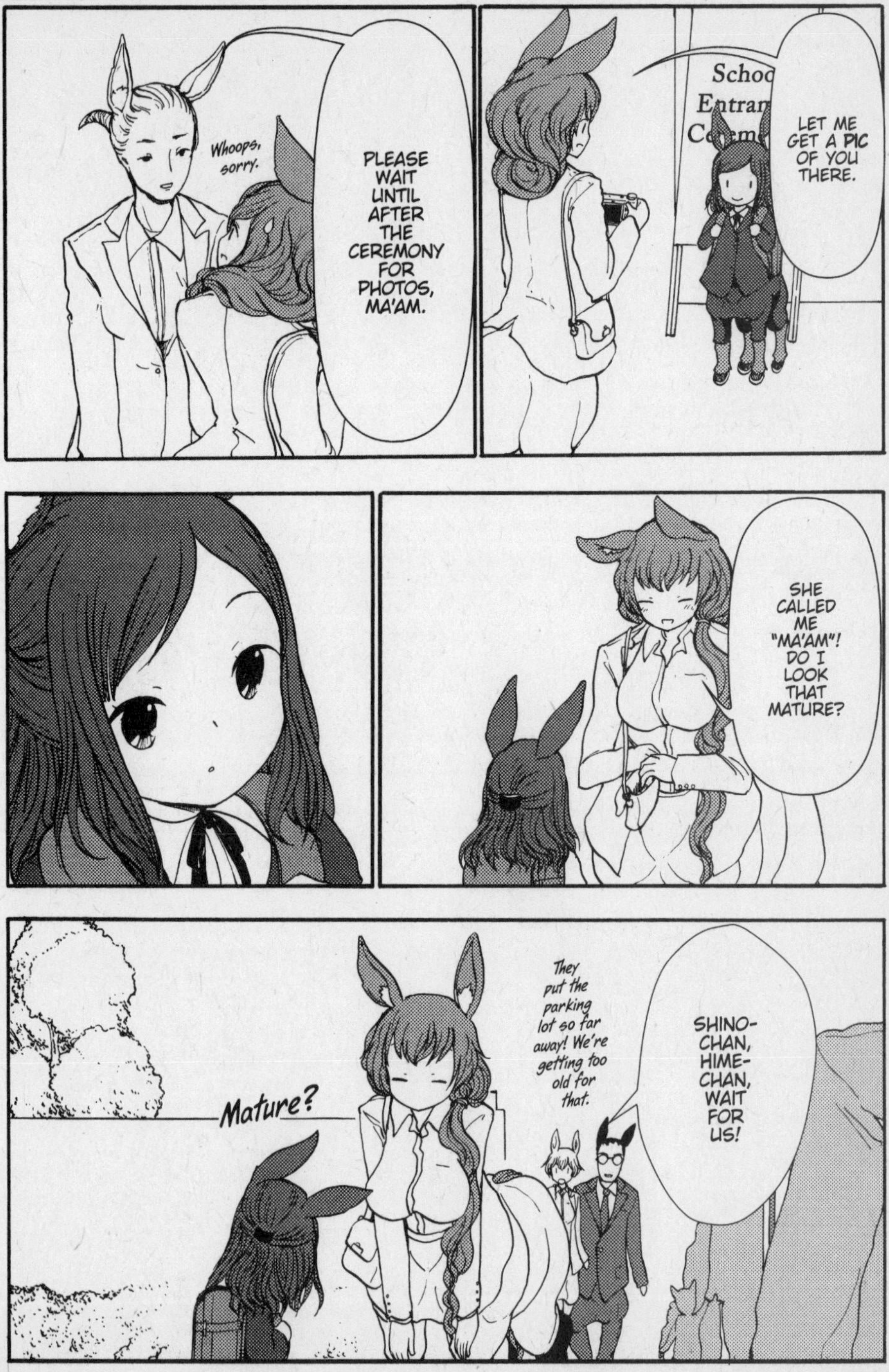
LET ME GET A PIC OF YOU THERE.
PLEASE WAIT UNTIL AFTER THE CEREMONY FOR PHOTOS, MA'AM.
Whoops, sorry.
SHE CALLED ME "MA'AM"! DO I LOOK THAT MATURE?
SHINO-CHAN, HIME-CHAN, WAIT FOR US!
They put the parking lot so far away! We're getting too old for that.
Mature?

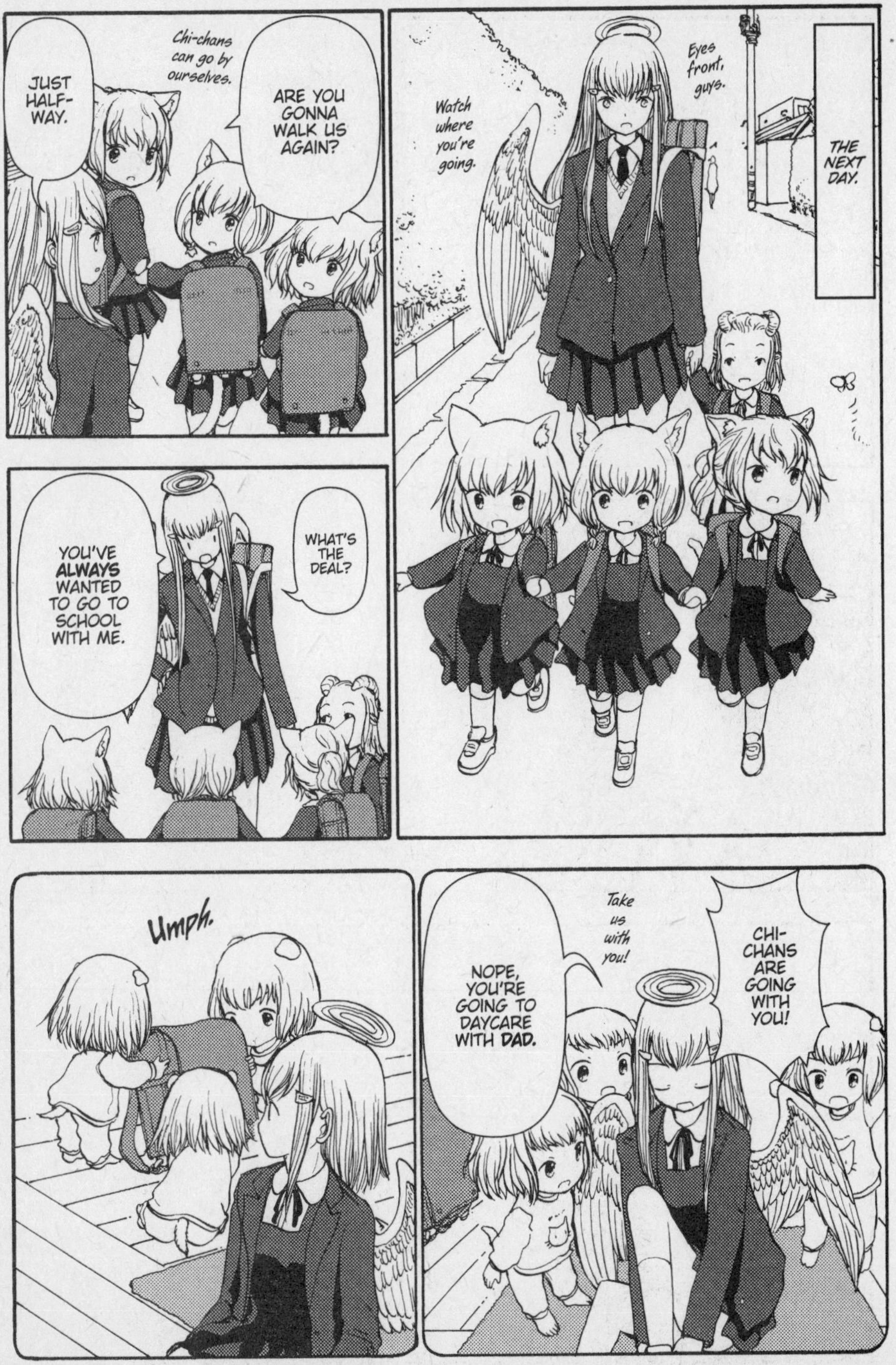
THE NEXT DAY.
Eyes front, guys.
Watch where you're going.
ARE YOU GONNA WALK US AGAIN?
Chi-chans can go by ourselves.
JUST HALF-WAY.
WHAT'S THE DEAL?
YOU'VE ALWAYS WANTED TO GO TO SCHOOL WITH ME.
CHI-CHANS ARE GOING WITH YOU!
Take us with you!
NOPE, YOU'RE GOING TO DAYCARE WITH DAD.
Umph.

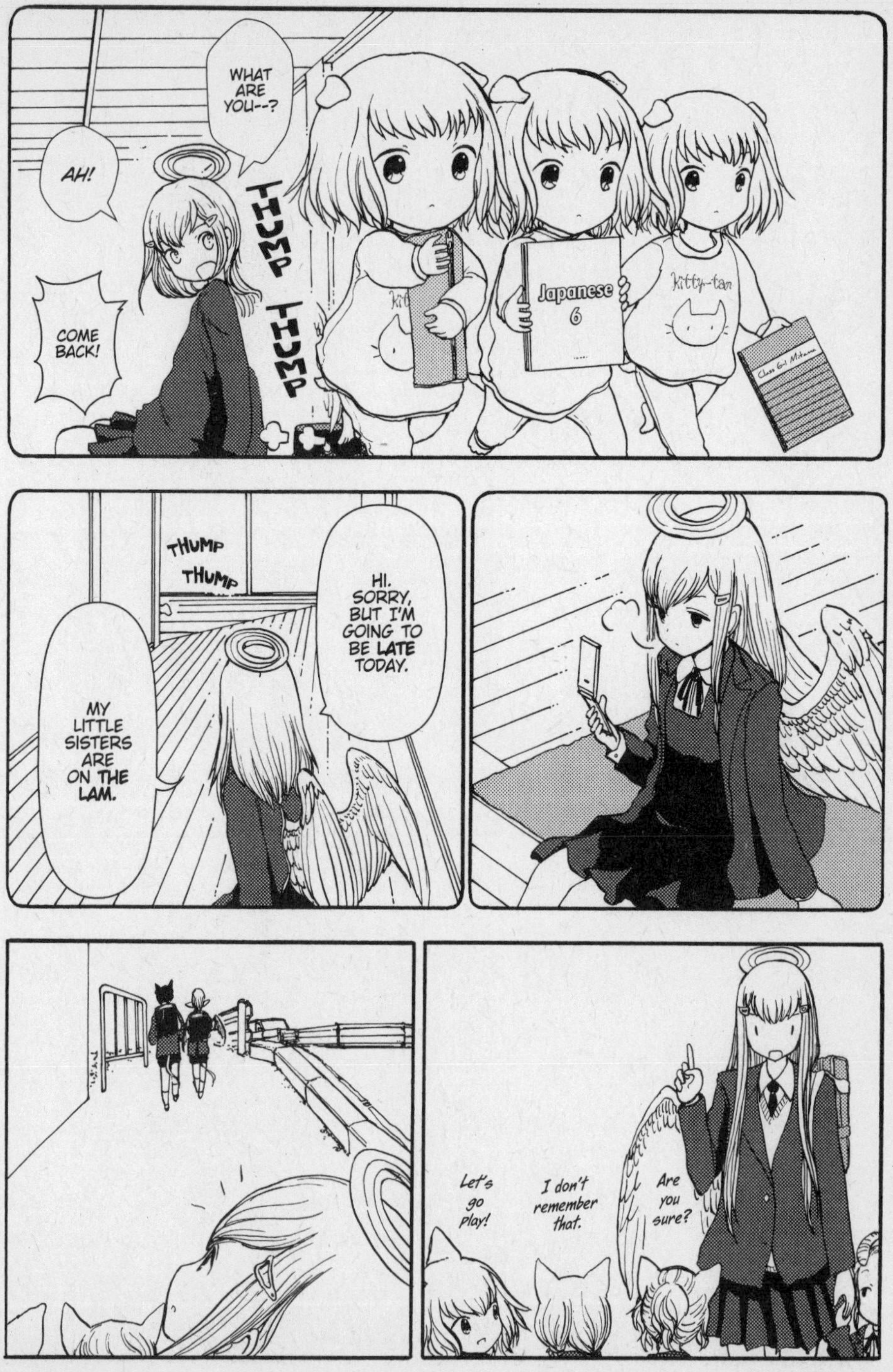

WHAT ARE YOU--?
kitty-tan
Japanese 6
THUMP THUMP THUMP
AH!
COME BACK!
HI. SORRY, BUT I'M GOING TO BE LATE TODAY.
THUMP THUMP
MY LITTLE SISTERS ARE ON THE LAM.
Are you sure?
I don't remember that.
Let's go play!

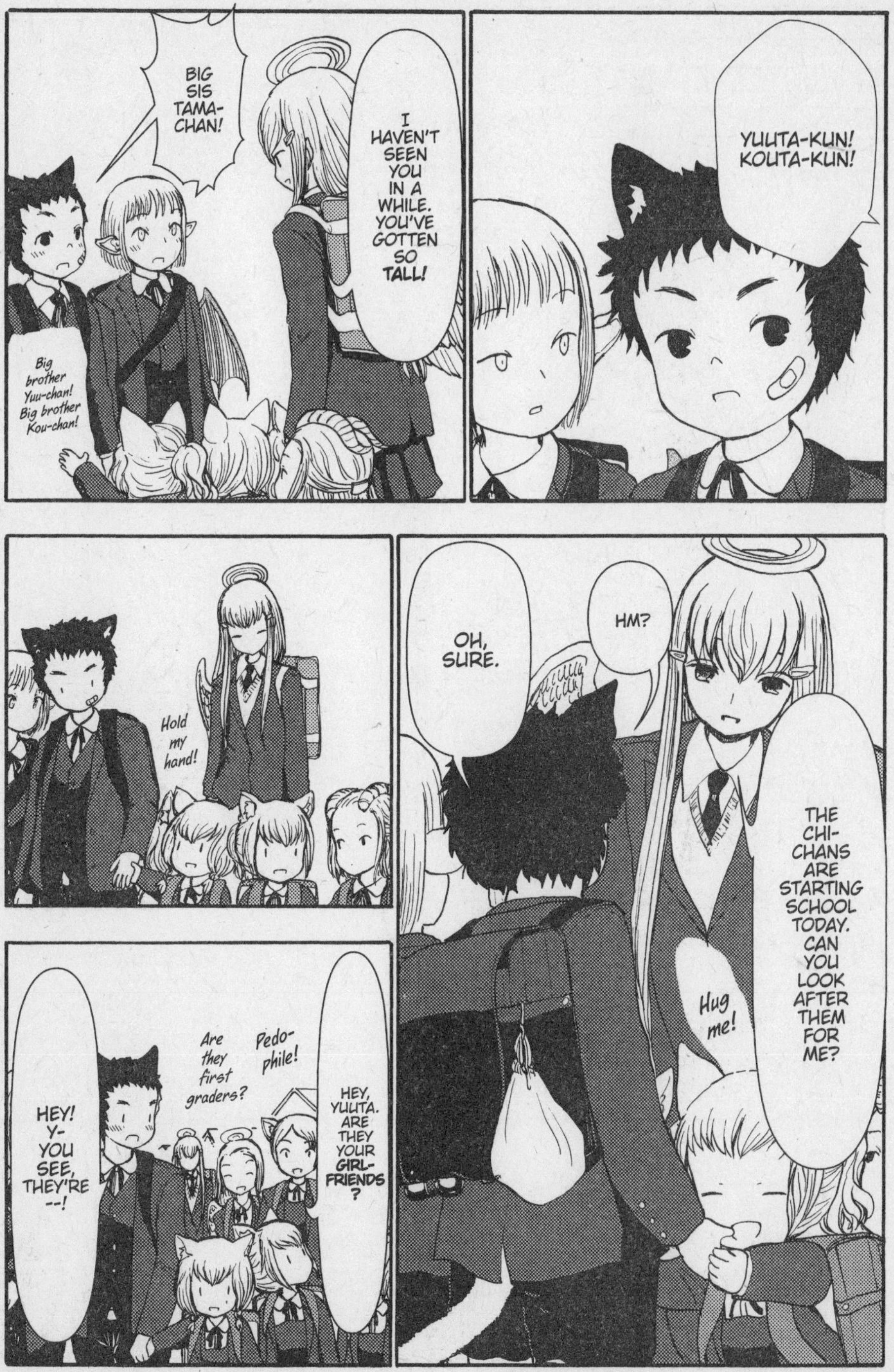
YUUTA-KUN! KOUTA-KUN!
I HAVEN'T SEEN YOU IN A WHILE. YOU'VE GOTTEN SO TALL!
BIG SIS TAMA-CHAN!
Big brother Yuu-chan! Big brother Kou-chan!
HM?
THE CHI-CHANS ARE STARTING SCHOOL TODAY. CAN YOU LOOK AFTER THEM FOR ME?
OH, SURE.
Hug me!
Hold my hand!
HEY, YUUTA. ARE THEY YOUR GIRLFRIENDS?
Pedophile!
Are they first graders?
HEY! Y-YOU SEE, THEY'RE --!

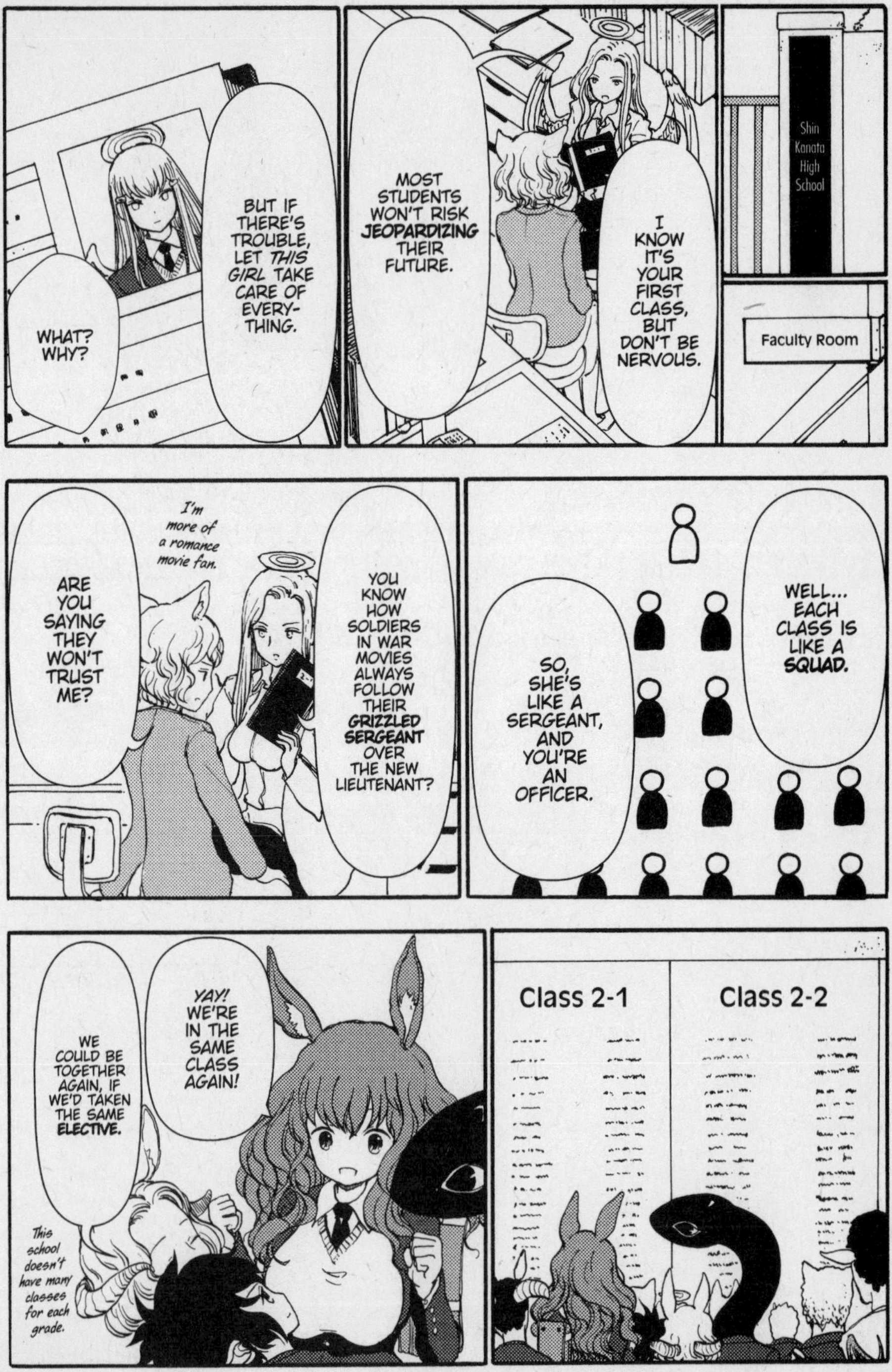
Shin Kanata High School
Faculty Room
I KNOW IT'S YOUR FIRST CLASS, BUT DON'T BE NERVOUS.
MOST STUDENTS WON'T RISK JEOPARDIZING THEIR FUTURE.
BUT IF THERE'S TROUBLE, LET THIS GIRL TAKE CARE OF EVERY-THING.
WHAT? WHY?
WELL... EACH CLASS IS LIKE A SQUAD.
SO, SHE'S LIKE A SERGEANT, AND YOU'RE AN OFFICER.
YOU KNOW HOW SOLDIERS IN WAR MOVIES ALWAYS FOLLOW THEIR GRIZZLED SERGEANT OVER THE NEW LIEUTENANT?
I'm more of a romance movie fan.
ARE YOU SAYING THEY WON'T TRUST ME?
Class 2-1
Class 2-2
YAY! WE'RE IN THE SAME CLASS AGAIN!
WE COULD BE TOGETHER AGAIN, IF WE'D TAKEN THE SAME ELECTIVE.
This school doesn't have many classes for each grade.

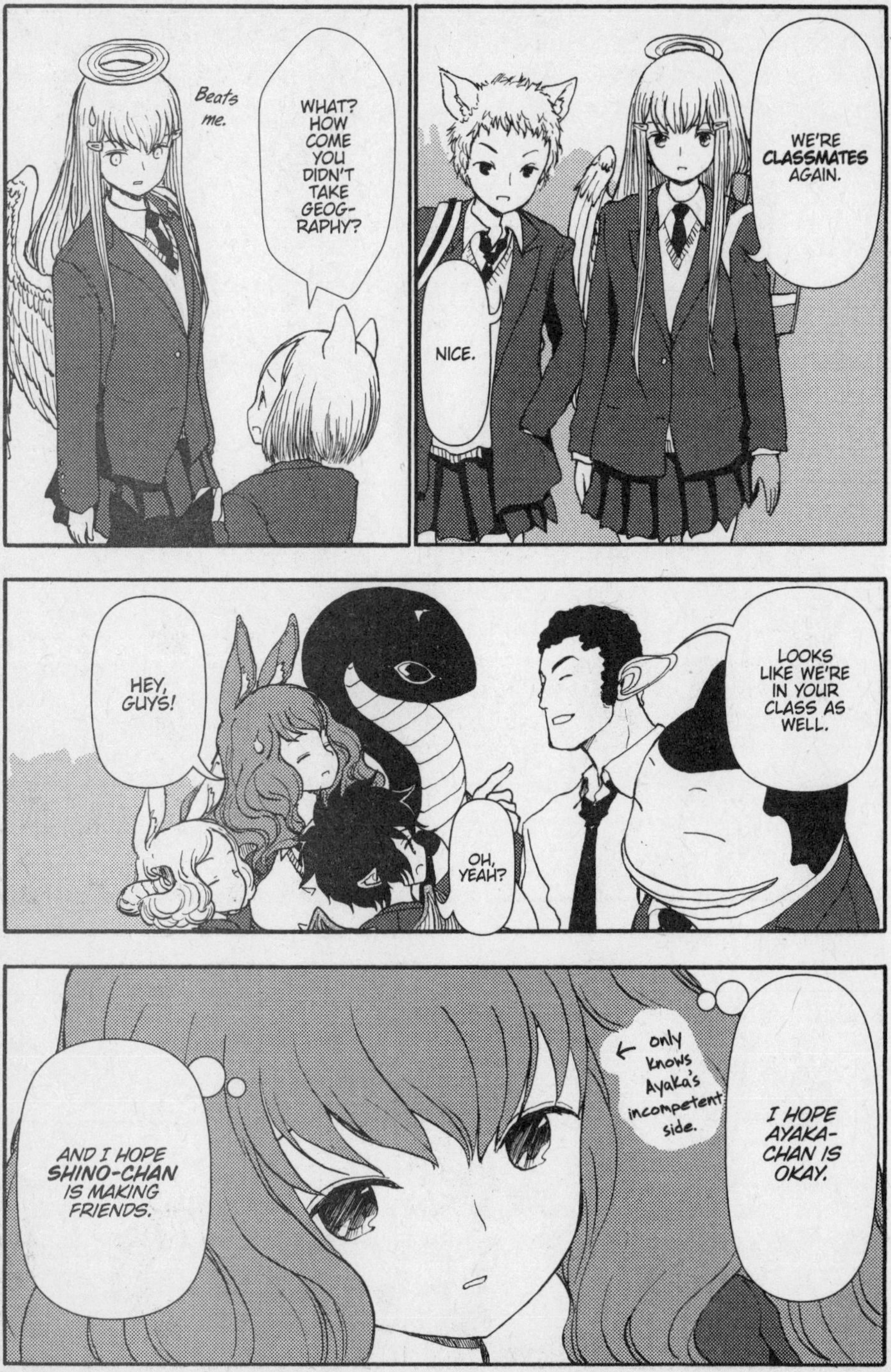
WE'RE CLASSMATES AGAIN.
NICE.
WHAT? HOW COME YOU DIDN'T TAKE GEOG-RAPHY?
Beats me.
LOOKS LIKE WE'RE IN YOUR CLASS AS WELL.
HEY, GUYS!
OH, YEAH?
I HOPE AYAKA-CHAN IS OKAY.
← only knows Ayaka's incompetent side.
AND I HOPE SHINO-CHAN IS MAKING FRIENDS.

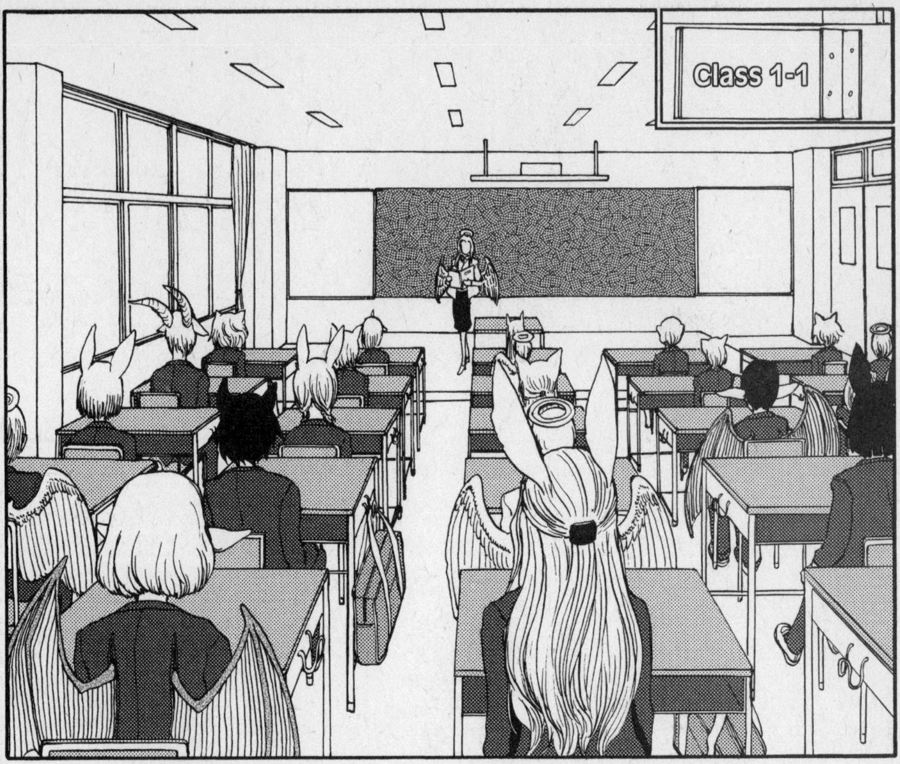
Class 1-1

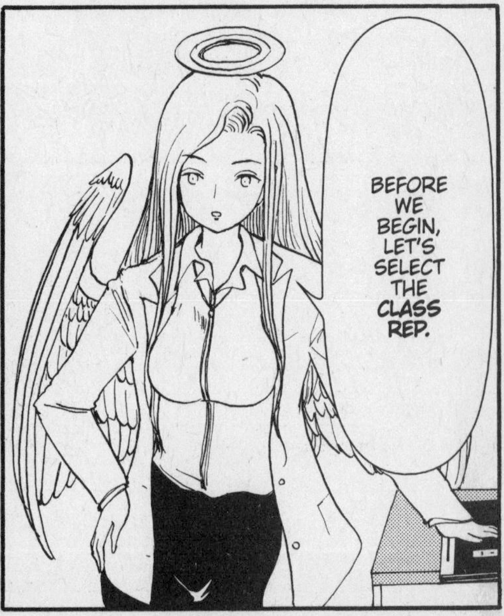
BEFORE WE BEGIN, LET'S SELECT THE **CLASS REP.**

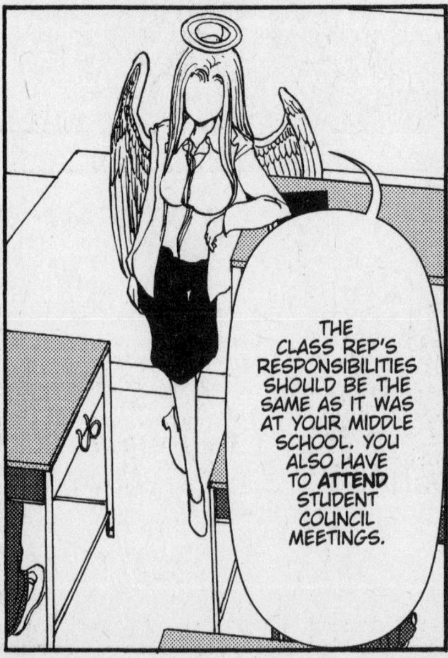
THE CLASS REP'S RESPONSIBILITIES SHOULD BE THE SAME AS IT WAS AT YOUR MIDDLE SCHOOL. YOU ALSO HAVE TO **ATTEND** STUDENT COUNCIL MEETINGS.

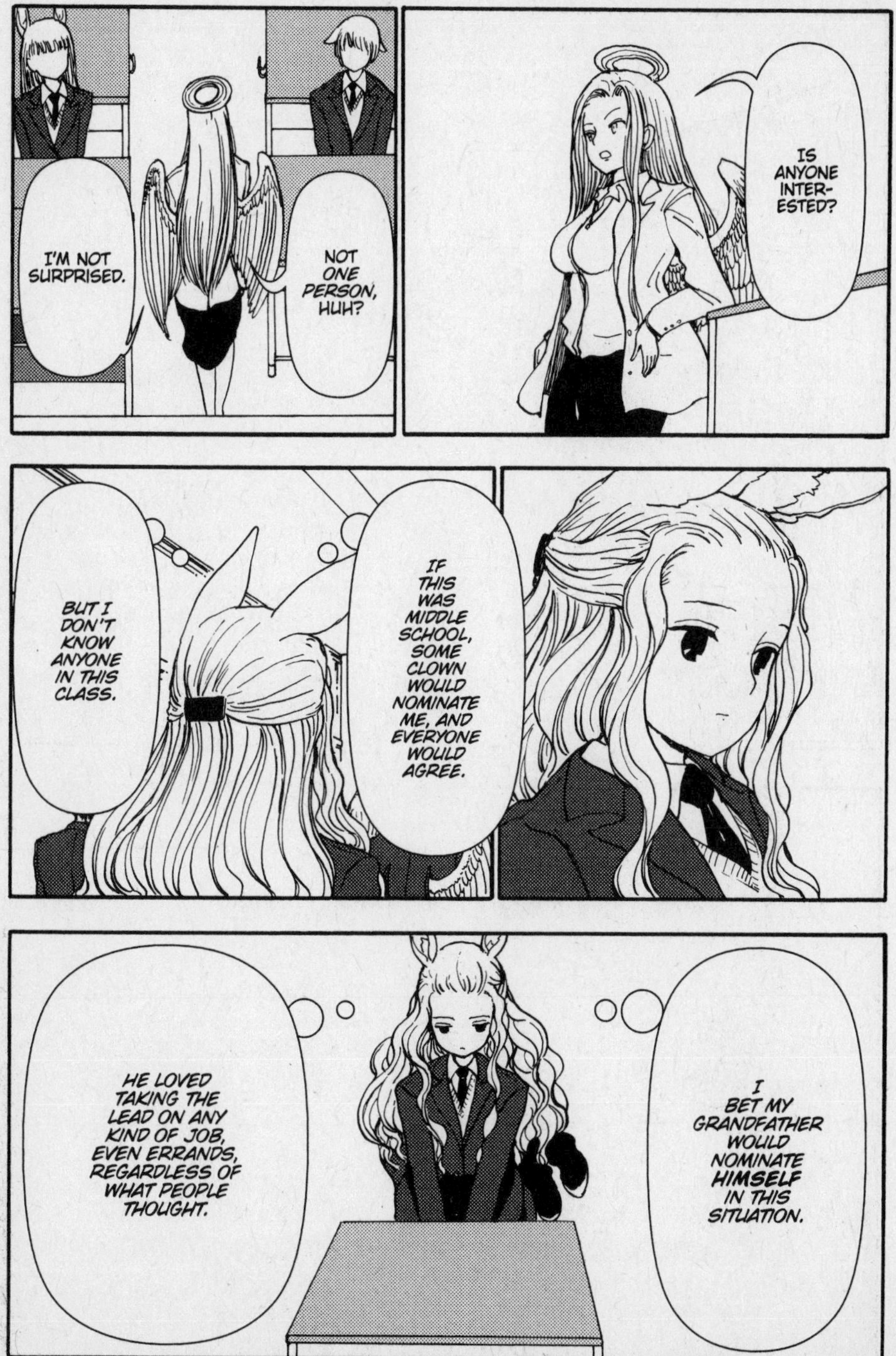
IS ANYONE INTER-ESTED?
NOT ONE PERSON, HUH?
I'M NOT SURPRISED.
IF THIS WAS MIDDLE SCHOOL, SOME CLOWN WOULD NOMINATE ME, AND EVERYONE WOULD AGREE.
BUT I DON'T KNOW ANYONE IN THIS CLASS.
I BET MY GRANDFATHER WOULD NOMINATE **HIMSELF** IN THIS SITUATION.
HE LOVED TAKING THE LEAD ON ANY KIND OF JOB, EVEN ERRANDS, REGARDLESS OF WHAT PEOPLE THOUGHT.

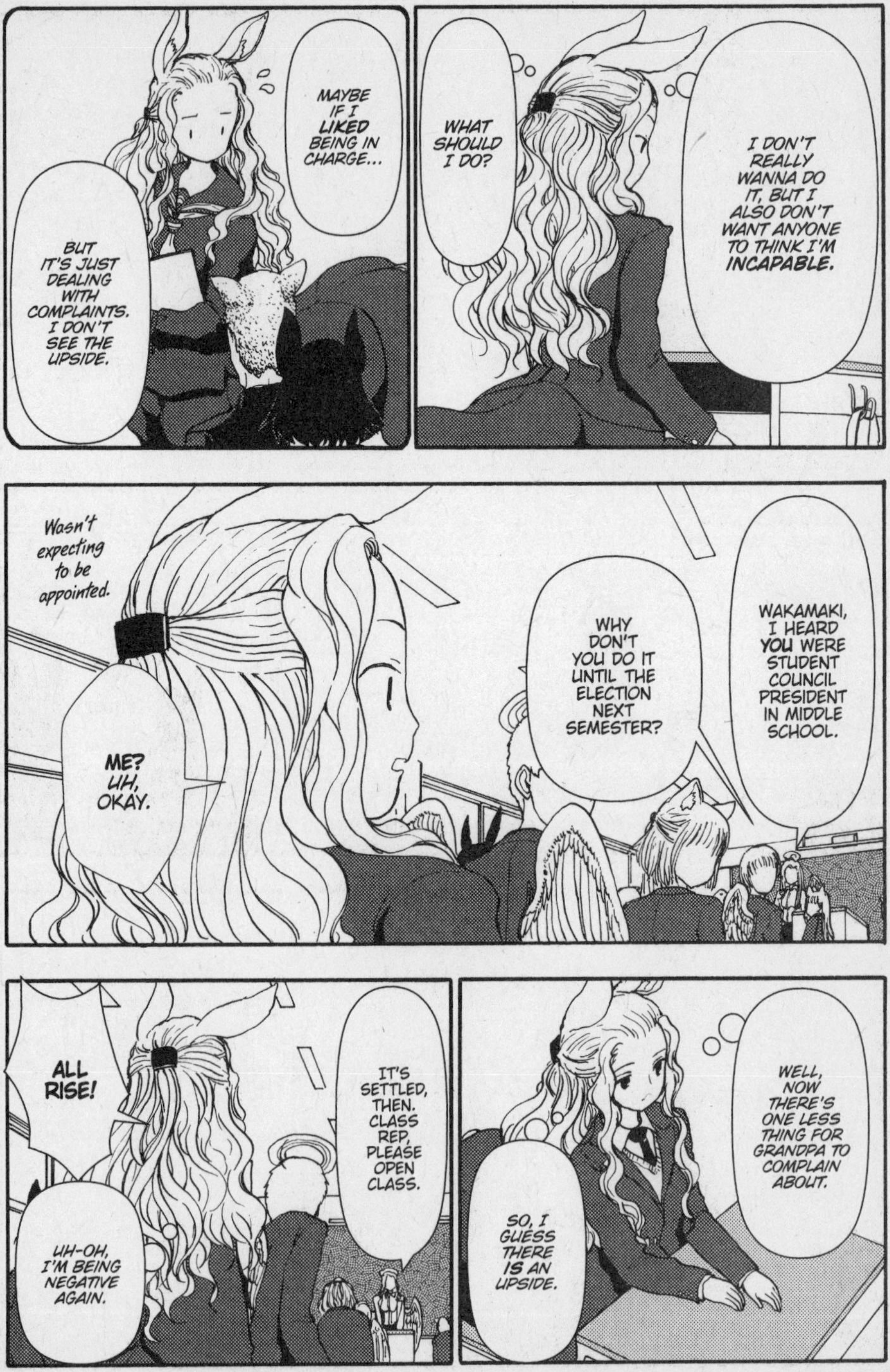
I DON'T REALLY WANNA DO IT, BUT I ALSO DON'T WANT ANYONE TO THINK I'M **INCAPABLE.**
WHAT SHOULD I DO?
MAYBE IF I **LIKED** BEING IN CHARGE...
BUT IT'S JUST DEALING WITH COMPLAINTS. I DON'T SEE THE UPSIDE.
WAKAMAKI, I HEARD **YOU** WERE STUDENT COUNCIL PRESIDENT IN MIDDLE SCHOOL.
WHY DON'T YOU DO IT UNTIL THE ELECTION NEXT SEMESTER?
Wasn't expecting to be appointed.
ME? UH, OKAY.
WELL, NOW THERE'S ONE LESS THING FOR GRANDPA TO COMPLAIN ABOUT.
SO, I GUESS THERE **IS** AN UPSIDE.
IT'S SETTLED, THEN. CLASS REP, PLEASE OPEN CLASS.
ALL RISE!
UH-OH, I'M BEING NEGATIVE AGAIN.

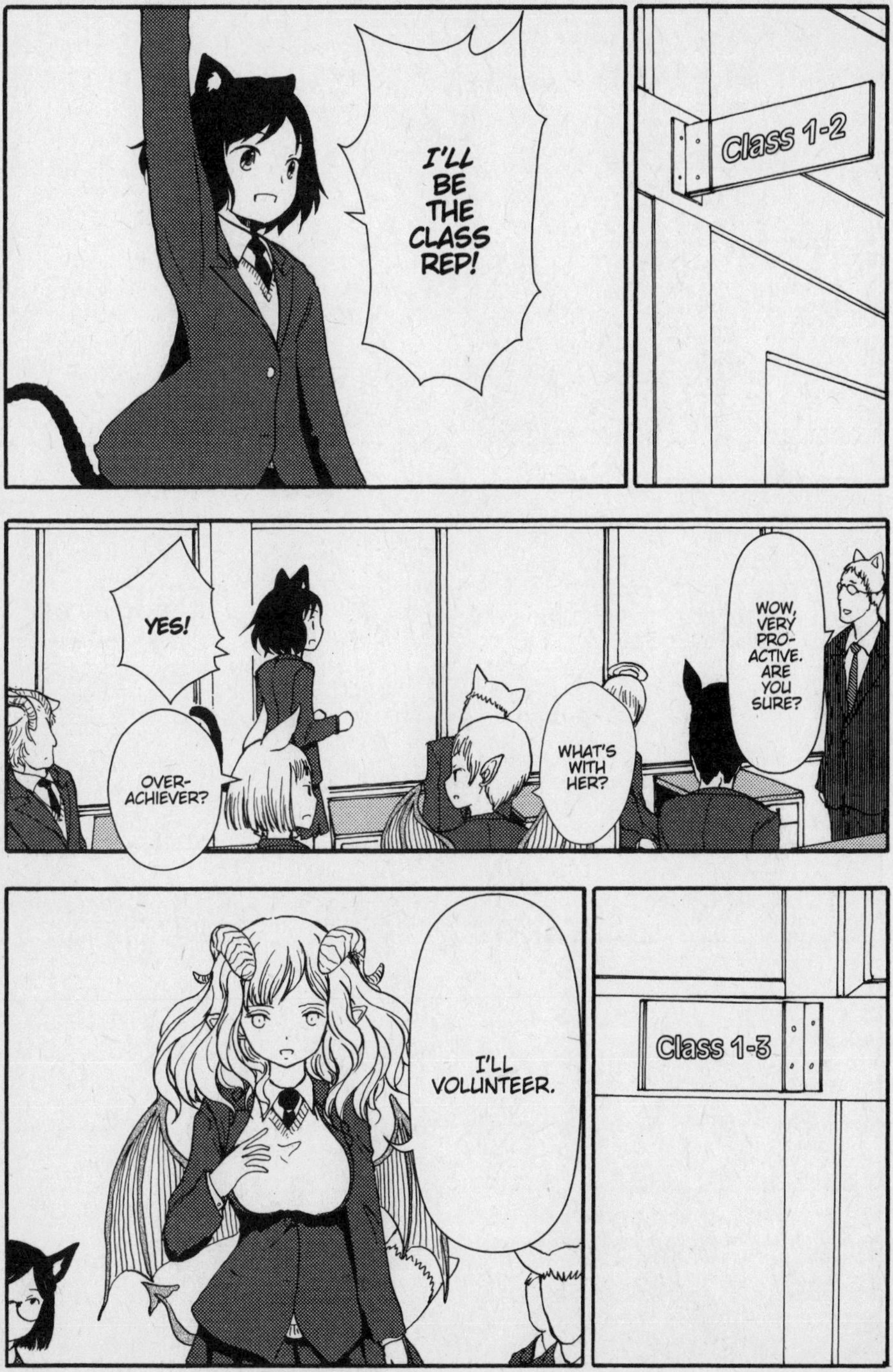
Class 1-2
I'LL BE THE CLASS REP!
WOW, VERY PRO-ACTIVE. ARE YOU SURE?
YES!
WHAT'S WITH HER?
OVER-ACHIEVER?
Class 1-3
I'LL VOLUNTEER.

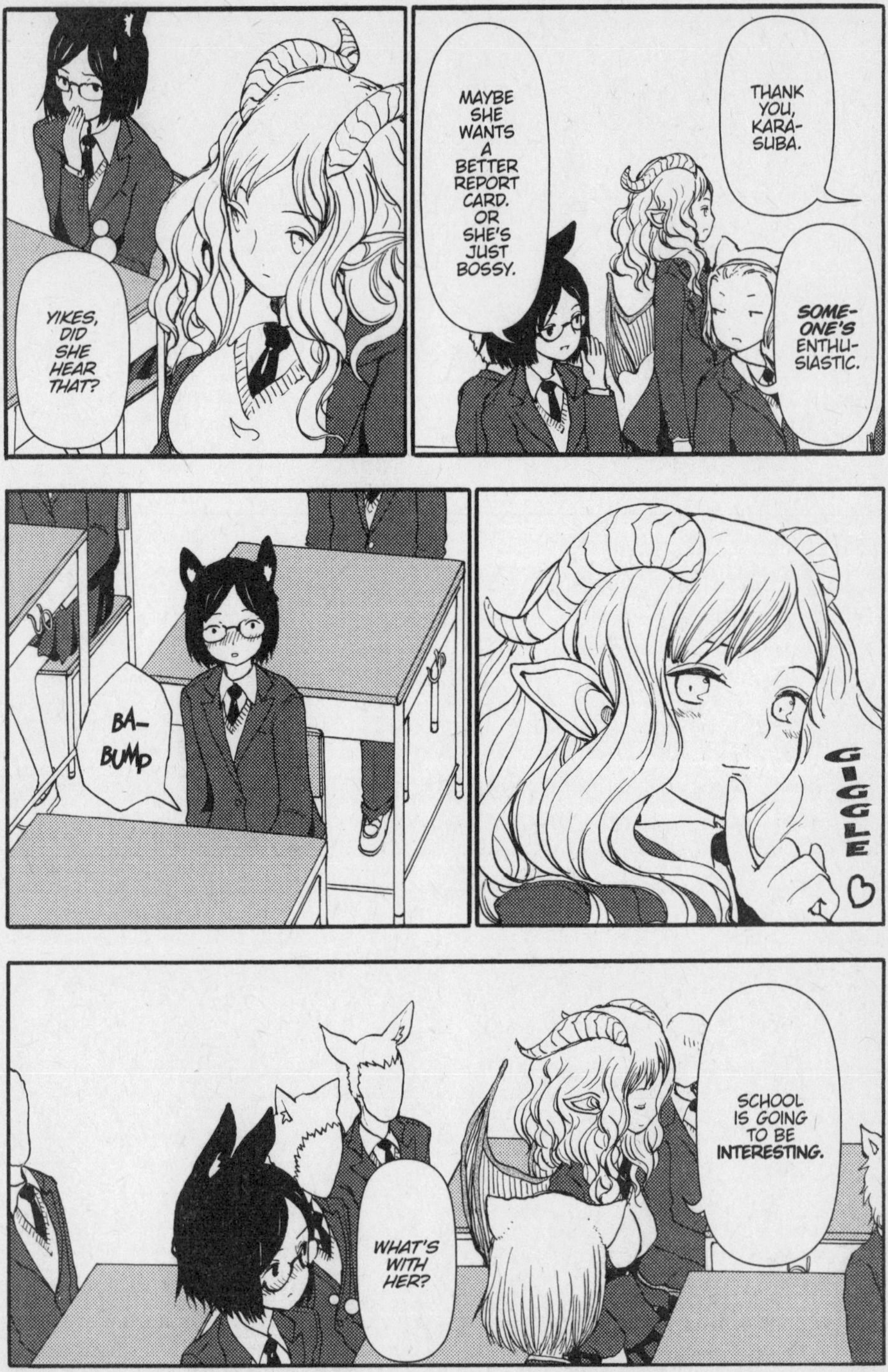
THANK YOU, KARA-SUBA.
SOME-ONE'S ENTHU-SIASTIC.
MAYBE SHE WANTS A BETTER REPORT CARD. OR SHE'S JUST BOSSY.
YIKES, DID SHE HEAR THAT?
GIGGLE
BA-BUMP
SCHOOL IS GOING TO BE INTERESTING.
WHAT'S WITH HER?

A Centaur's Life

UNDERSTANDING ANTARCTICANS: PART 2

WE KNOW FROM AERIAL PHOTOS AND WITNESS TESTIMONY THAT ANTARCTICA IS COVERED BY ICE YEAR-ROUND. MUCH LIKE THE ICE-COVERED ARCTIC, THERE IS NO EVIDENT PLANT LIFE, BUT SOME HARDY LIFE FORMS STILL SEEM TO THRIVE. SOME TRAVELERS REPORT WITNESSING LARGE GROUPS OF AQUATIC, FLIGHTLESS BIRDS THAT STAND UP STRAIGHT AND TOTTER AROUND TO FORM A VAST HUDDLE ACROSS THE ICE. THESE STRANGE BIRDS, WHO SEEM TO HAVE NO FEAR OF HUMANS, ARE NOW KNOWN AS "PENGUINS." CAN WE SURMISE THAT THE ANTARCTICANS HUNTED THEM FOR CLOTHING, FOOD, FUEL, AND TOOLS, IN A LIFESTYLE SIMILAR TO THAT OF SOME ARCTIC PEOPLES? PERHAPS, BUT THAT MAY NOT FIT THE EVIDENCE. ACCORDING TO ANTARCTICANS, THEY PREFER A WARMER CLIMATE, AND HAVE BUILT UNDERGROUND CITIES POWERED BY GEOTHERMAL ENERGY. THERE IS SPECULATION THAT IN ORDER TO SOLVE THE RIDDLE, WE MAY NEED TO CONSIDER A TIME WHEN ANTARCTICA WAS NEITHER COVERED IN ICE NOR ISOLATED FROM THE REST OF THE WORLD.

Note: The Great Auk, which inhabited the Arctic, was once called a penguin. However, that name was later given to another species—the Antarctic Penguin—after the Great Auk became extinct in the 1840s. Antarctic Penguins bear a resemblance to the Great Auk, but they are a separate species.

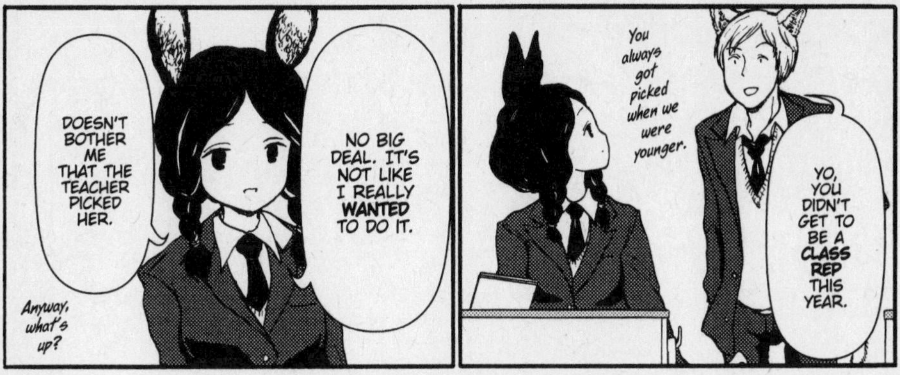
YO, YOU DIDN'T GET TO BE A CLASS REP THIS YEAR.
You always got picked when we were younger.
NO BIG DEAL. IT'S NOT LIKE I REALLY WANTED TO DO IT.
DOESN'T BOTHER ME THAT THE TEACHER PICKED HER.
Anyway, what's up?

CHAPTER 71

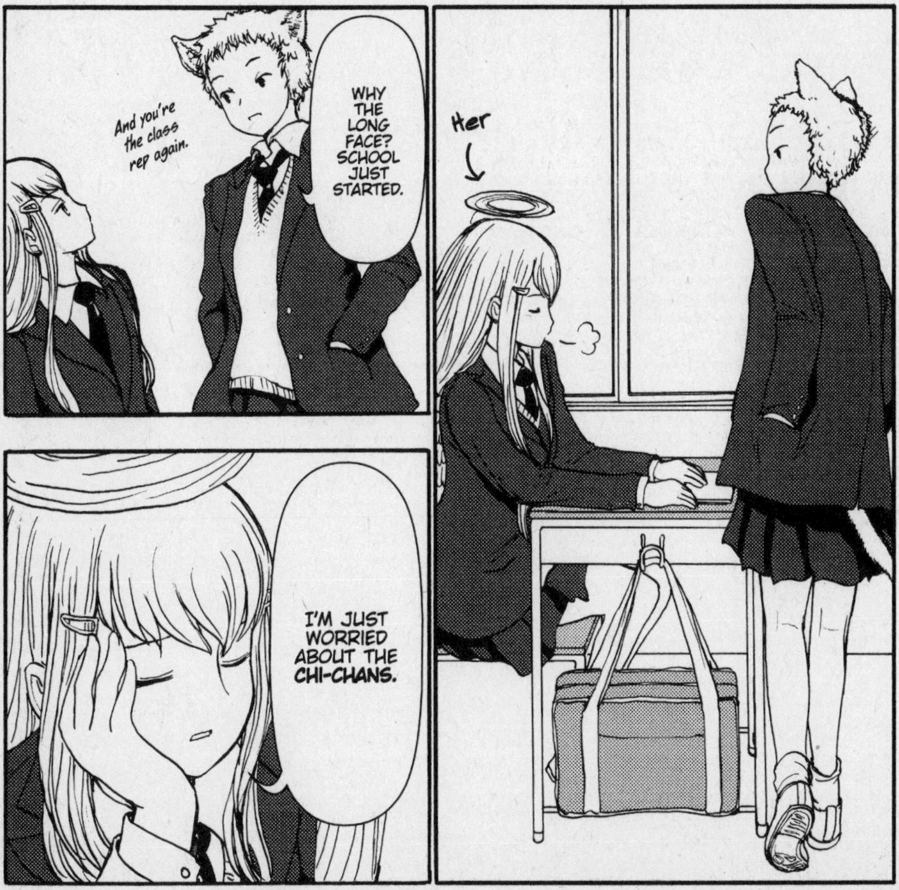
Her
WHY THE LONG FACE? SCHOOL JUST STARTED.
And you're the class rep again.
I'M JUST WORRIED ABOUT THE CHI-CHANS.

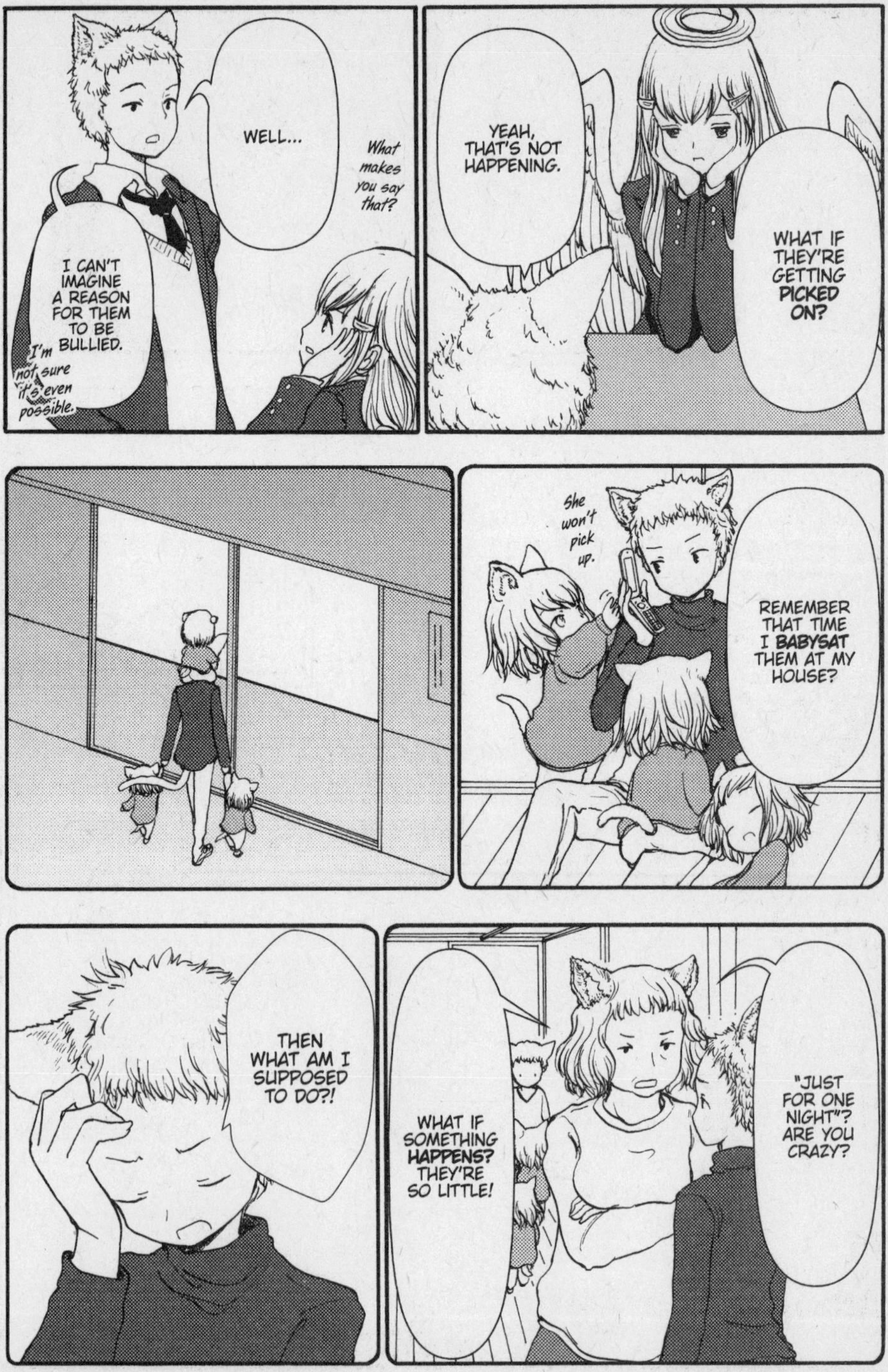
WHAT IF THEY'RE GETTING PICKED ON?
YEAH, THAT'S NOT HAPPENING.
What makes you say that?
WELL...
I CAN'T IMAGINE A REASON FOR THEM TO BE BULLIED.
I'm not sure it's even possible.
REMEMBER THAT TIME I BABYSAT THEM AT MY HOUSE?
She won't pick up.
"JUST FOR ONE NIGHT"? ARE YOU CRAZY?
WHAT IF SOMETHING HAPPENS? THEY'RE SO LITTLE!
THEN WHAT AM I SUPPOSED TO DO?!

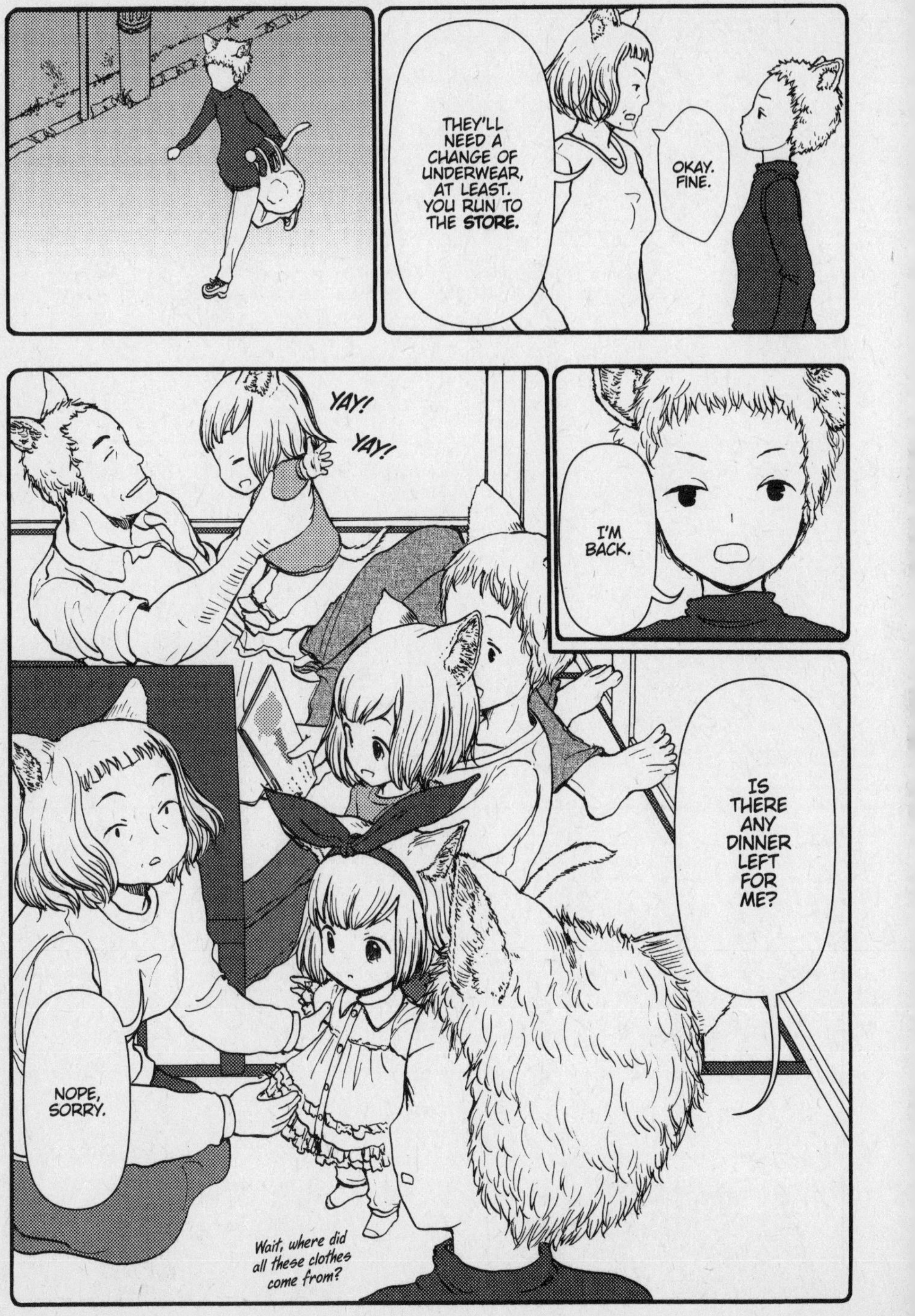
THEY'LL NEED A CHANGE OF UNDERWEAR, AT LEAST. YOU RUN TO THE STORE.
OKAY. FINE.
I'M BACK.
YAY!
YAY!
IS THERE ANY DINNER LEFT FOR ME?
NOPE, SORRY.
Wait, where did all these clothes come from?

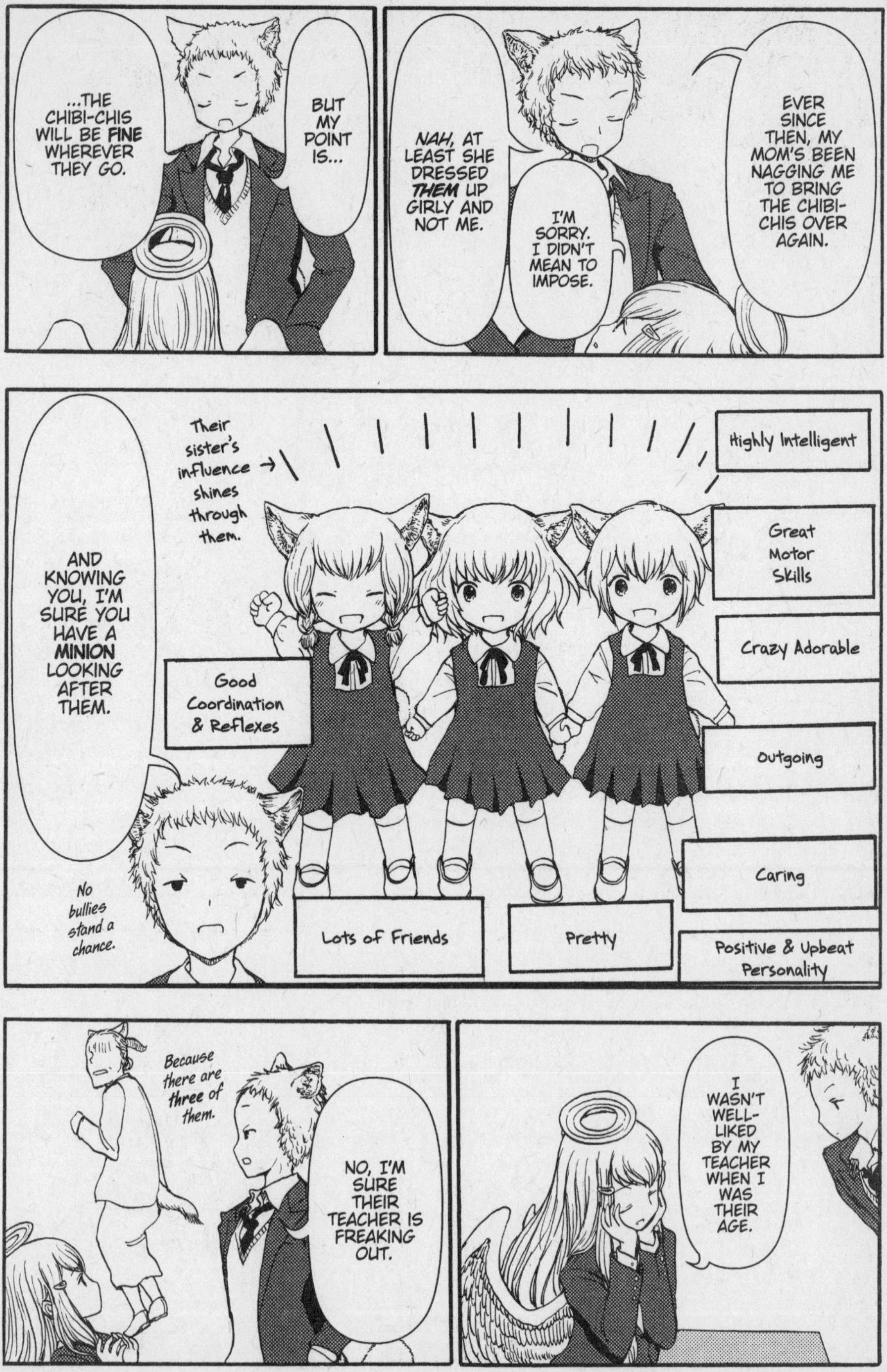
EVER SINCE THEN, MY MOM'S BEEN NAGGING ME TO BRING THE CHIBI-CHIS OVER AGAIN.
I'M SORRY. I DIDN'T MEAN TO IMPOSE.
NAH, AT LEAST SHE DRESSED **THEM** UP GIRLY AND NOT ME.
BUT MY POINT IS...
...THE CHIBI-CHIS WILL BE **FINE** WHEREVER THEY GO.
Highly Intelligent
Great Motor Skills
Crazy Adorable
Outgoing
Caring
Positive & Upbeat Personality
Pretty
Lots of Friends
Good Coordination & Reflexes
Their sister's influence shines through them. →
AND KNOWING YOU, I'M SURE YOU HAVE A **MINION** LOOKING AFTER THEM.
No bullies stand a chance.
I WASN'T WELL-LIKED BY MY TEACHER WHEN I WAS THEIR AGE.
NO, I'M SURE THEIR TEACHER IS FREAKING OUT.
Because there are *three* of them.

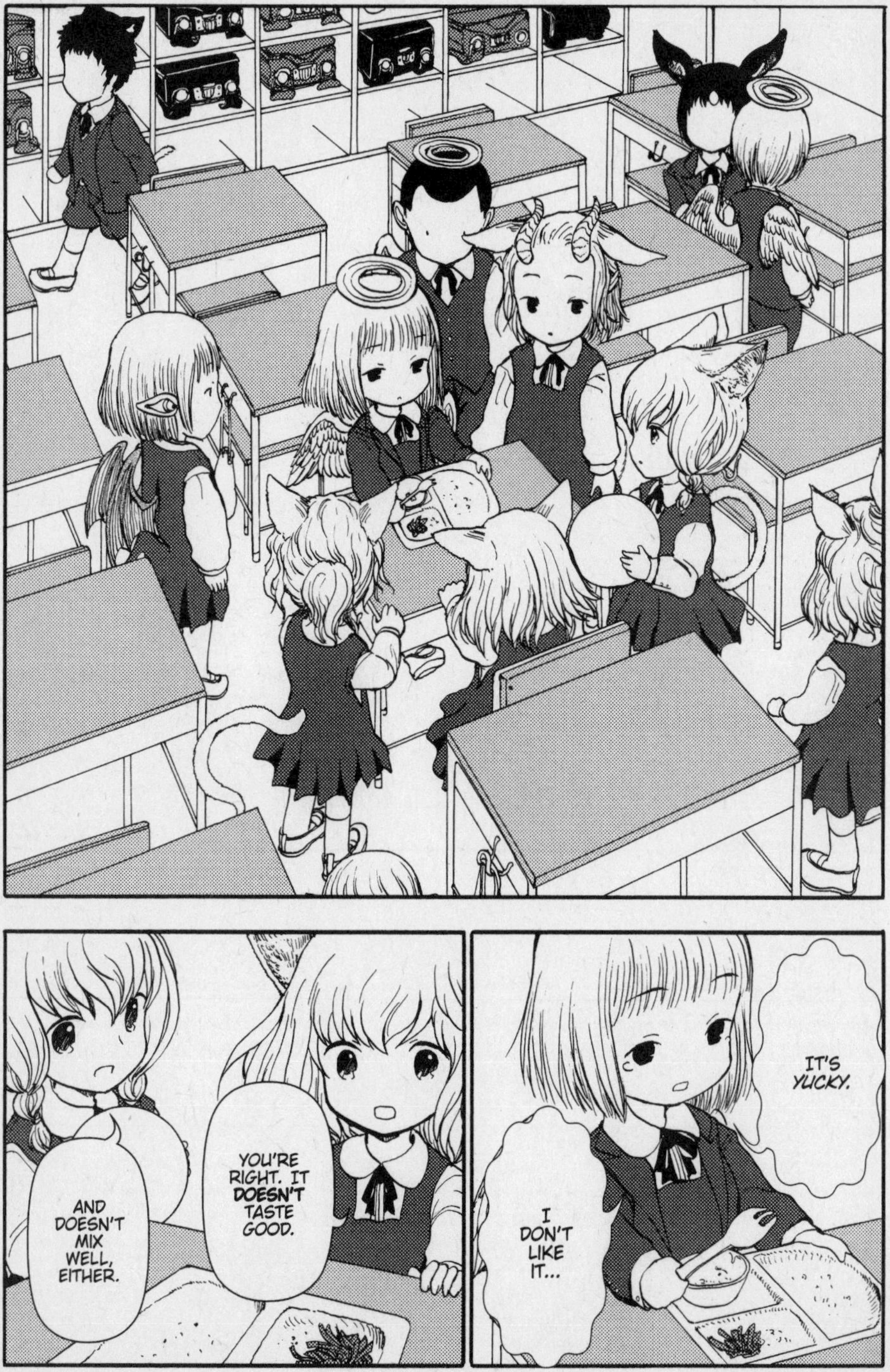
IT'S YUCKY.
I DON'T LIKE IT...
YOU'RE RIGHT. IT DOESN'T TASTE GOOD.
AND DOESN'T MIX WELL, EITHER.

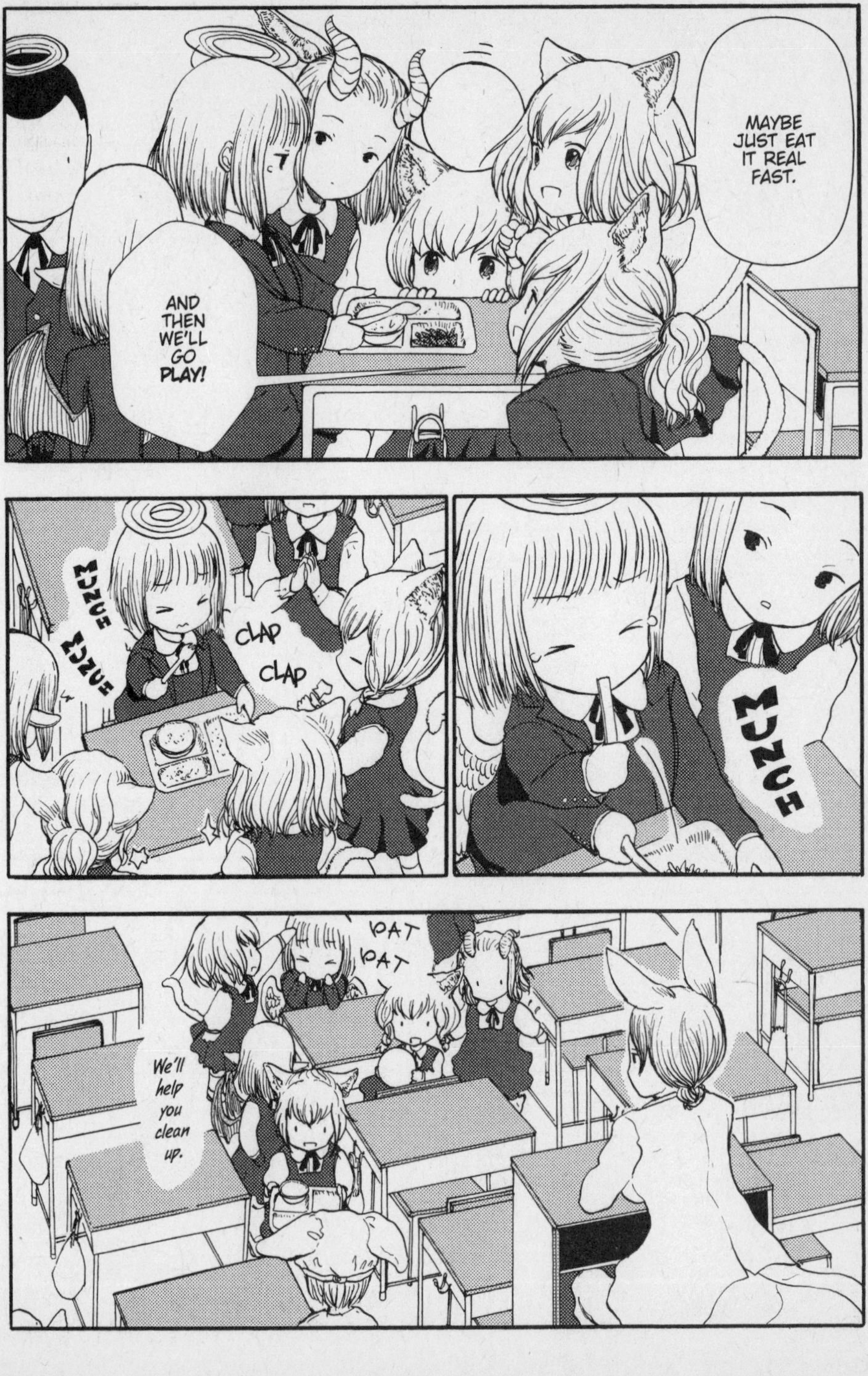
MAYBE JUST EAT IT REAL FAST.
AND THEN WE'LL GO PLAY!
MUNCH
CLAP
CLAP
MUNCH
MUNCH
PAT
PAT
We'll help you clean up.

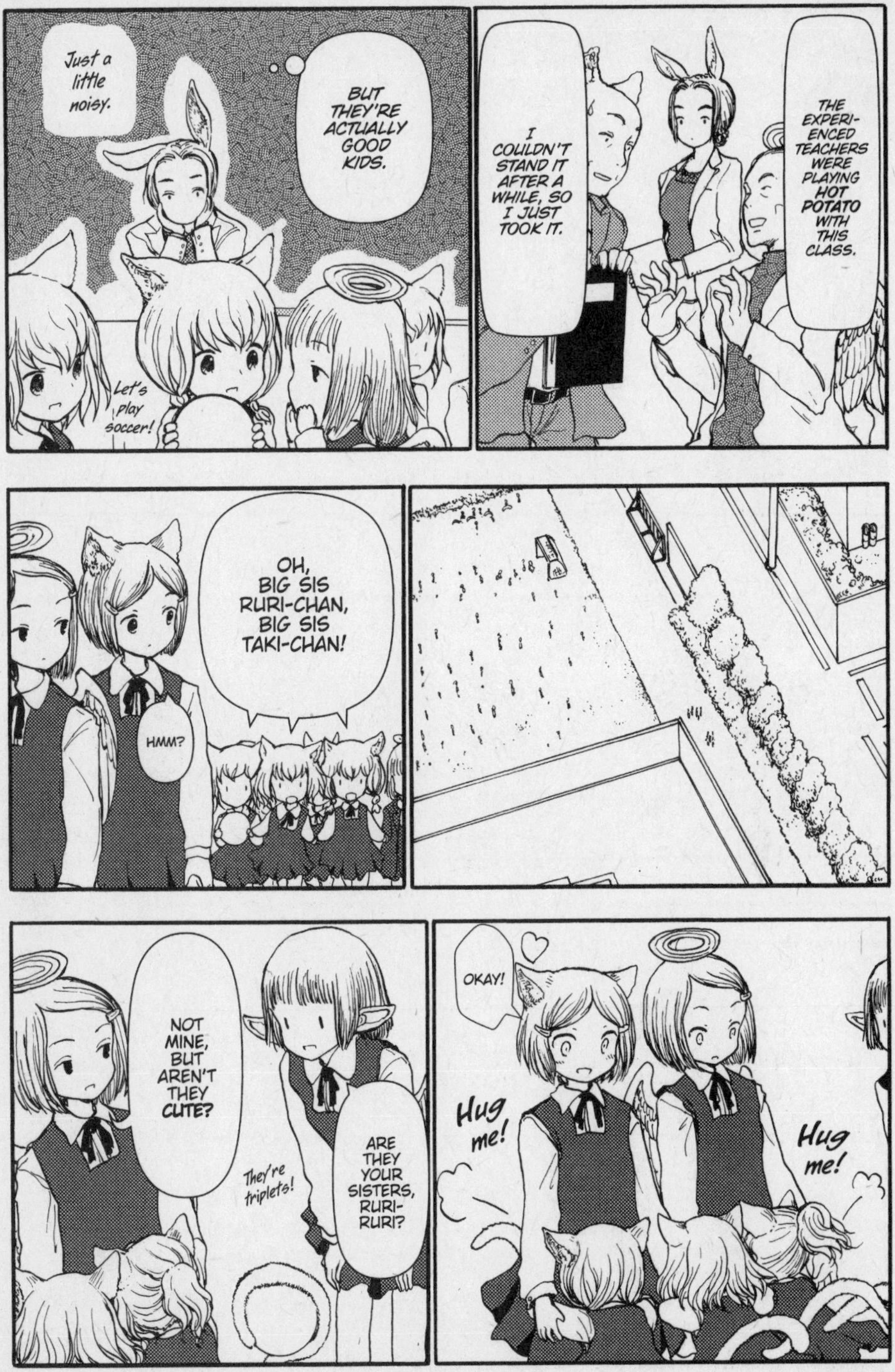
THE EXPERIENCED TEACHERS WERE PLAYING HOT POTATO WITH THIS CLASS.
I COULDN'T STAND IT AFTER A WHILE, SO I JUST TOOK IT.
BUT THEY'RE ACTUALLY GOOD KIDS.
Just a little noisy.
Let's play soccer!
OH, BIG SIS RURI-CHAN, BIG SIS TAKI-CHAN!
HMM?
OKAY!
Hug me!
Hug me!
ARE THEY YOUR SISTERS, RURI-RURI?
NOT MINE, BUT AREN'T THEY CUTE?
They're triplets!

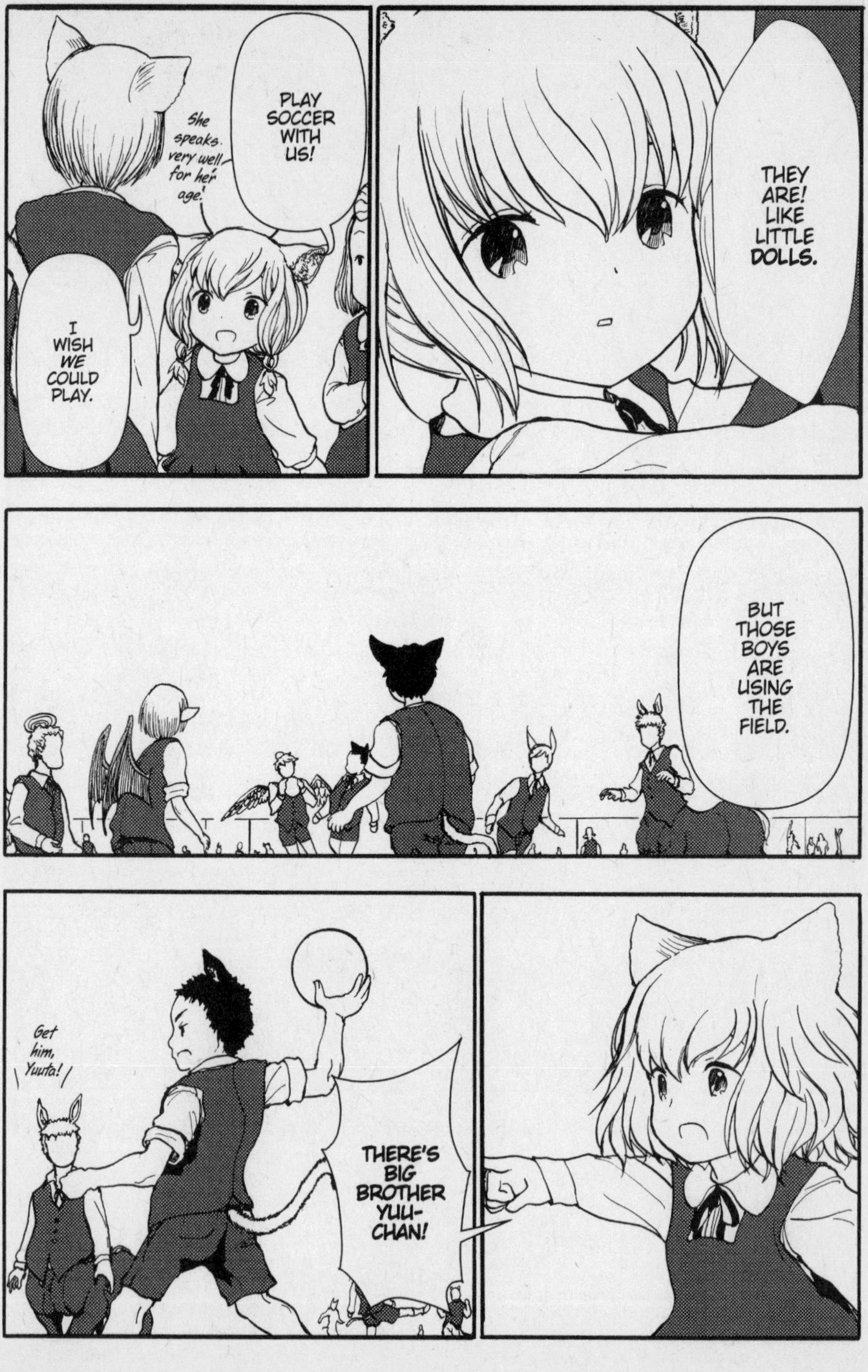
THEY ARE! LIKE LITTLE DOLLS.
PLAY SOCCER WITH US!
She speaks very well for her age.
I WISH WE COULD PLAY.
BUT THOSE BOYS ARE USING THE FIELD.
THERE'S BIG BROTHER YUU-CHAN!
Get him, Yuuta!

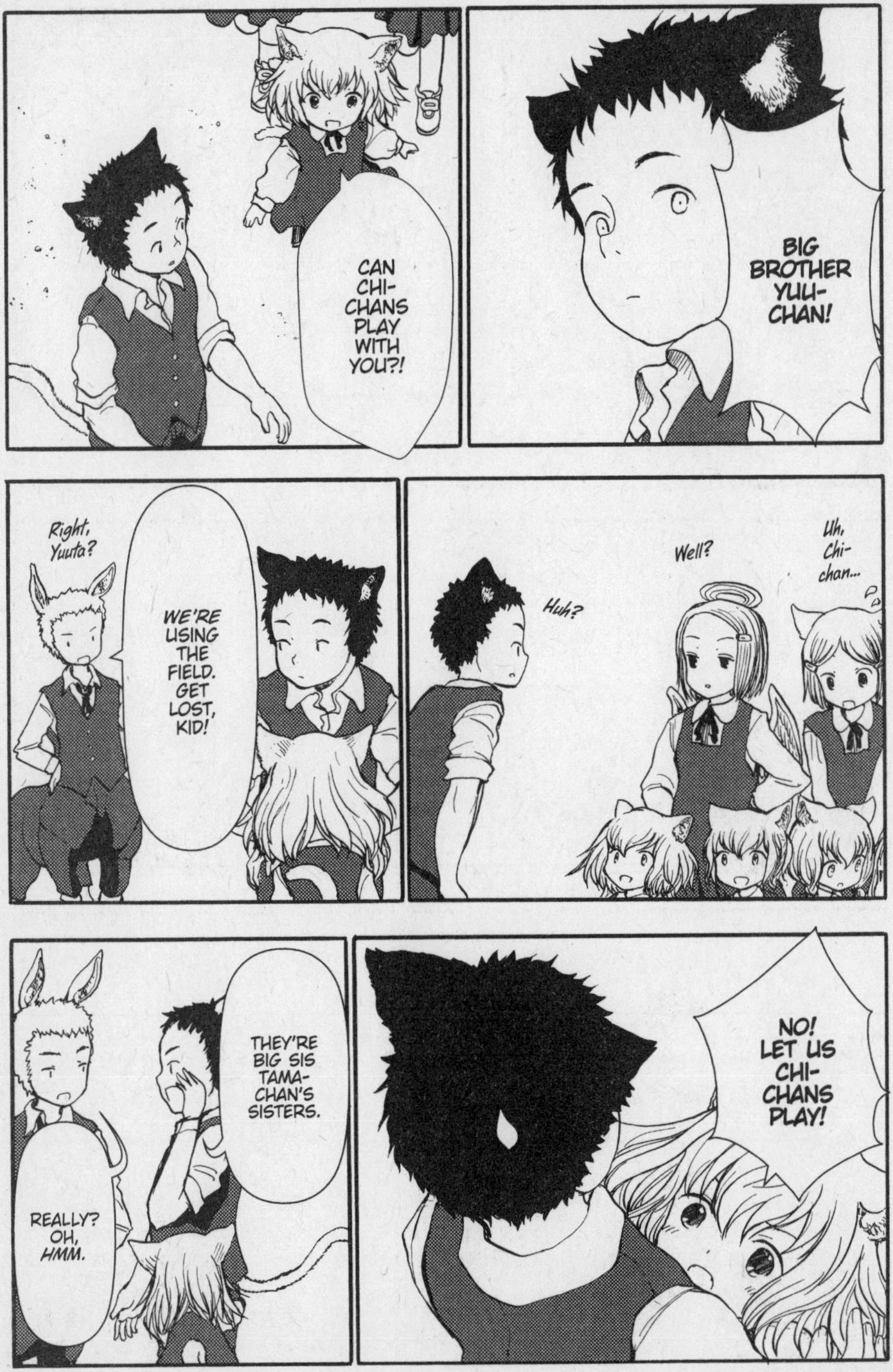
BIG BROTHER YUU-CHAN!
CAN CHI-CHANS PLAY WITH YOU?!
Uh, Chi-chan...
Well?
Huh?
WE'RE USING THE FIELD. GET LOST, KID!
Right, Yuuta?
NO! LET US CHI-CHANS PLAY!
THEY'RE BIG SIS TAMA-CHAN'S SISTERS.
REALLY? OH, HMM.

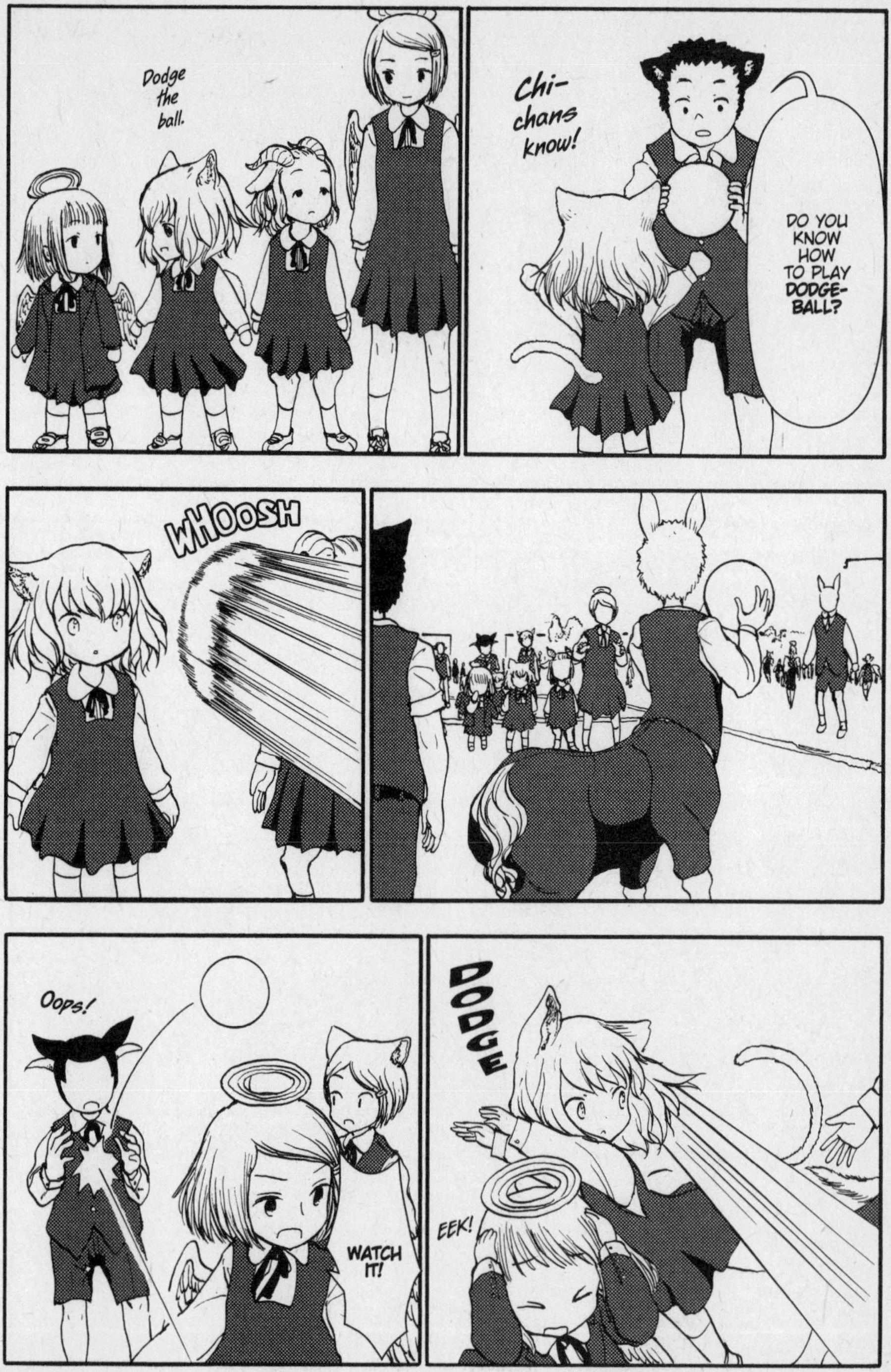
DO YOU KNOW HOW TO PLAY DODGE-BALL?
Chi-chans know!
Dodge the ball.
WHOOSH
DODGE
EEK!
WATCH IT!
Oops!

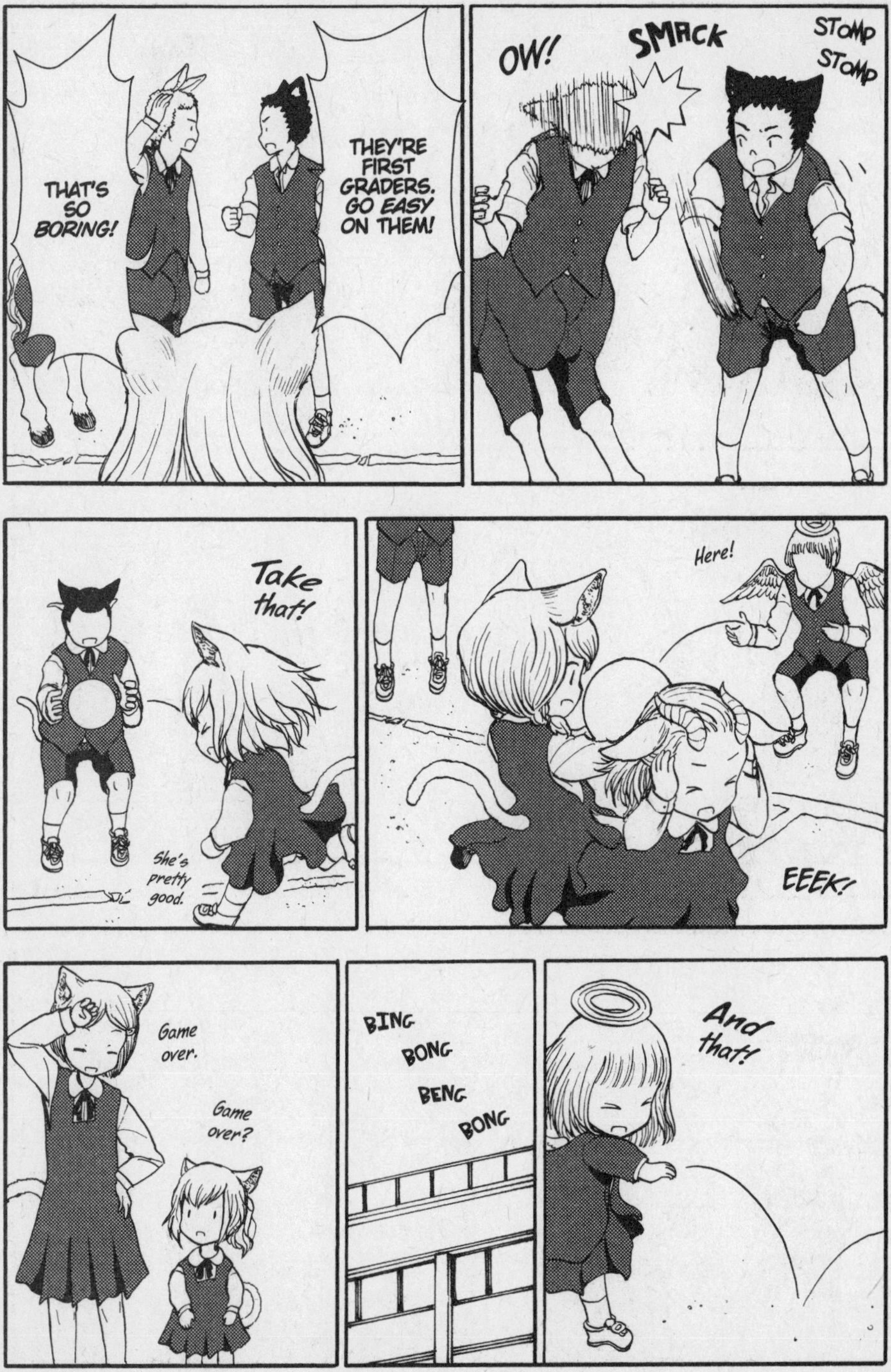
STOMP STOMP
SMACK
OW!
THEY'RE FIRST GRADERS. GO EASY ON THEM!
THAT'S SO BORING!
Here!
EEEK!
Take that!
She's pretty good.
And that!
BING BONG BENG BONG
Game over.
Game over?

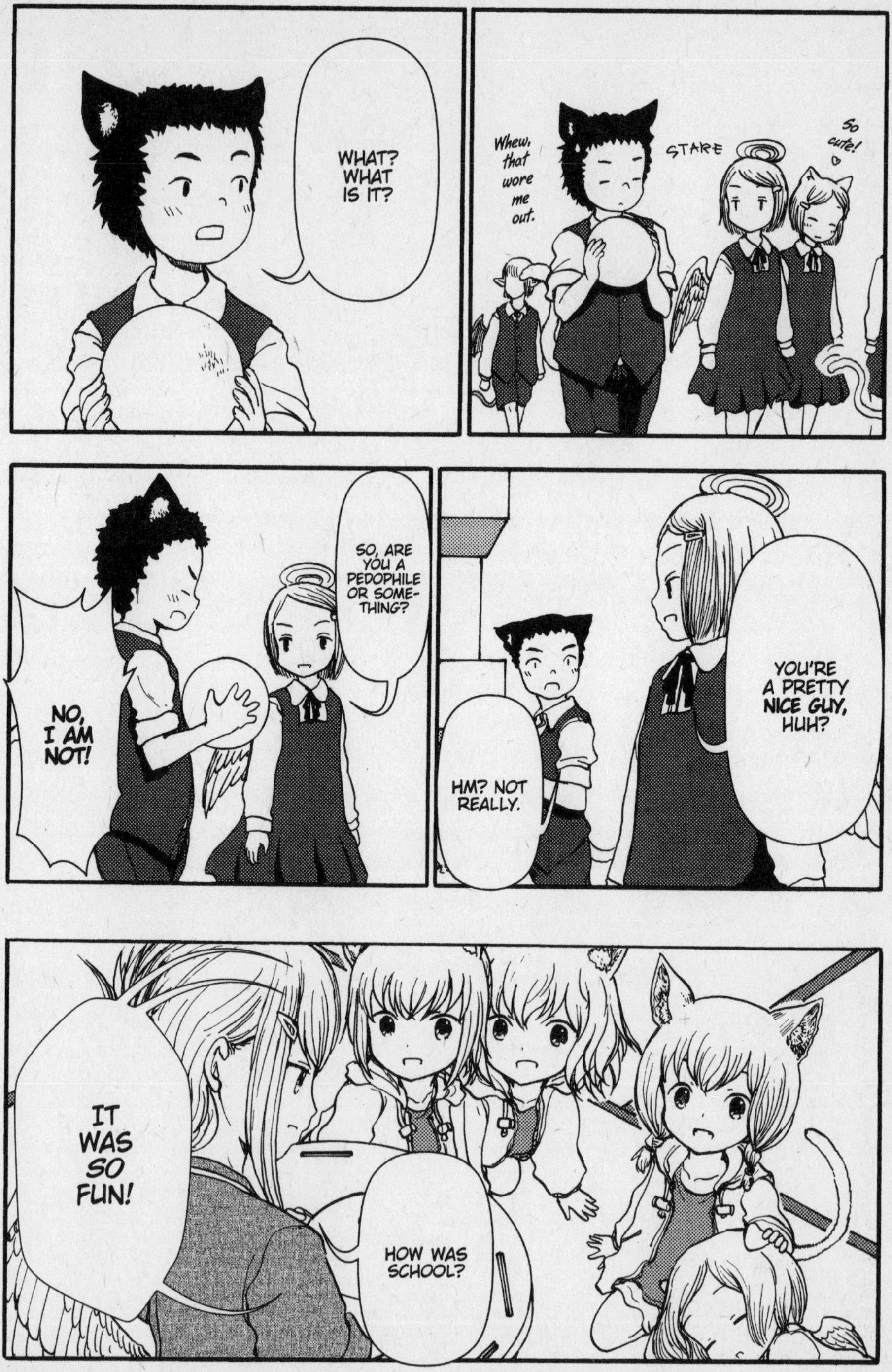
So cute!
STARE
Whew, that wore me out.
WHAT? WHAT IS IT?
YOU'RE A PRETTY NICE GUY, HUH?
HM? NOT REALLY.
SO, ARE YOU A PEDOPHILE OR SOME-THING?
NO, I AM NOT!
HOW WAS SCHOOL?
IT WAS SO FUN!

A Centaur's Life

UNDERSTANDING ANTARCTICANS: PART 3

DUE TO THE CONSTANT SLOW MOVEMENT OF TECTONIC PLATES, THE CONTINENT WE CALL ANTARCTICA HAS BEEN JOINING WITH AND SEPARATING FROM VARIOUS LARGER LANDMASSES FOR HUNDREDS OF MILLIONS OF YEARS. AROUND 250 MILLION YEARS AGO, ALL THE CONTINENTS ON EARTH WERE JOINED AS ONE SINGLE SUPERCONTINENT KNOWN AS PANGAEA. AT THE TIME, MANY PLANTS AND ANIMALS SUCH AS LYSTROSAURUS (A MAMMAL-LIKE REPTILE) AND GLOSSOPTERIS (A GYMNOSPERM) THRIVED ACROSS PANGAEA, INCLUDING THE PART THAT WOULD LATER BECOME ANTARCTICA. FOSSIL REMAINS OF THESE LIFEFORMS LATER BECAME EVIDENCE FOR THE THEORY OF CONTINENTAL DRIFT. EVENTUALLY, THE SUPERCONTINENT BROKE APART INTO SMALLER LANDMASSES. THE ONE KNOWN AS GONDWANA WAS MADE UP OF MOST OF THE LAND IN THE PRESENT SOUTHERN HEMISPHERE, AGAIN INCLUDING WHAT WOULD LATER BECOME ANTARCTICA, AND WAS FORESTED THROUGHOUT WITH A TROPICAL OR SUBTROPICAL CLIMATE. OVER TIME, THIS LANDMASS BROKE APART AS WELL, WITH AUSTRALIA AND THEN SOUTH AMERICA FINALLY PULLING AWAY TO COMPLETE ANTARCTICA'S ISOLATION, LONG AFTER THE DINOSAURS HAD GONE EXTINCT AND THE AGE OF MAMMALS HAD BEGUN. THE SEPARATION OF SOUTH AMERICA ALLOWED FOR THE ANTARCTIC CIRCUMPOLAR CURRENT TO FORM, AND THE FORESTS SPANNING THE CONTINENT SLOWLY GAVE WAY TO ICE. ONCE A LUSH TROPICAL LAND, ANTARCTICA HAS NOW BEEN LOCKED IN DEEP FREEZE FOR ABOUT 20 MILLION YEARS.

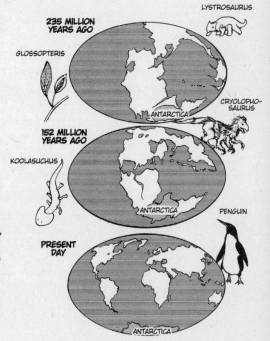

235 MILLION YEARS AGO

GLOSSOPTERIS

LYSTROSAURUS

ANTARCTICA

CRYOLOPHO-SAURUS

152 MILLION YEARS AGO

KOOLASUCHUS

ANTARCTICA

PENGUIN

PRESENT DAY

ANTARCTICA

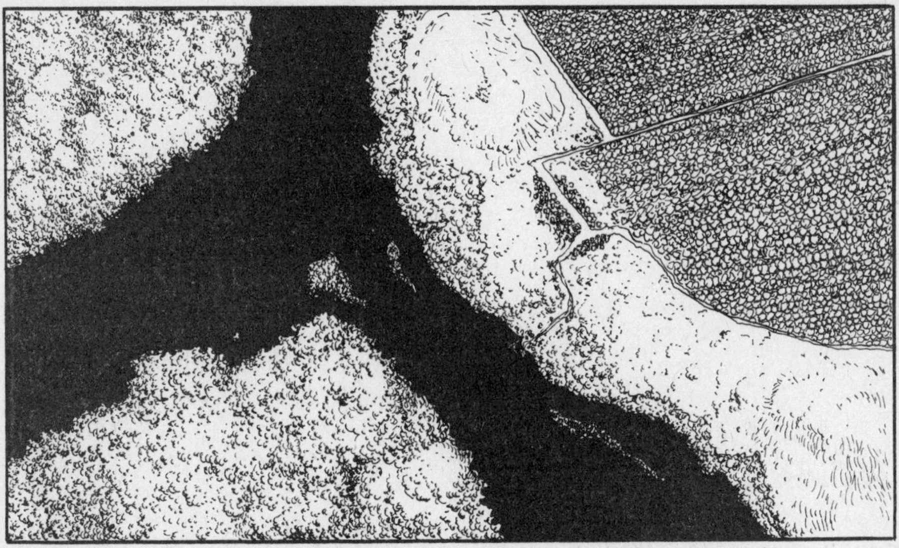

CHAPTER 72

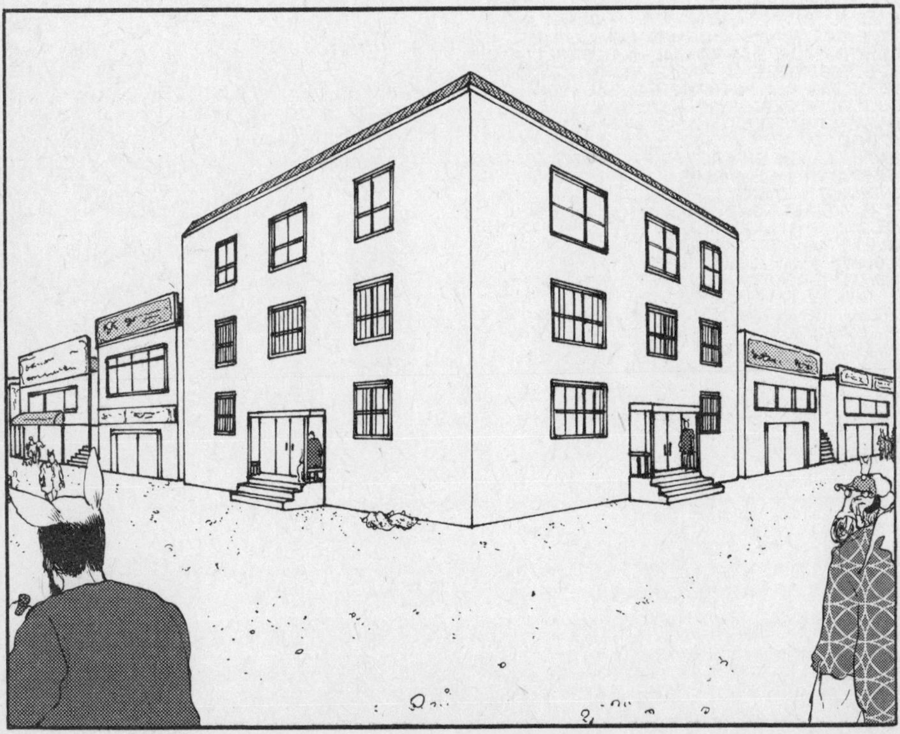

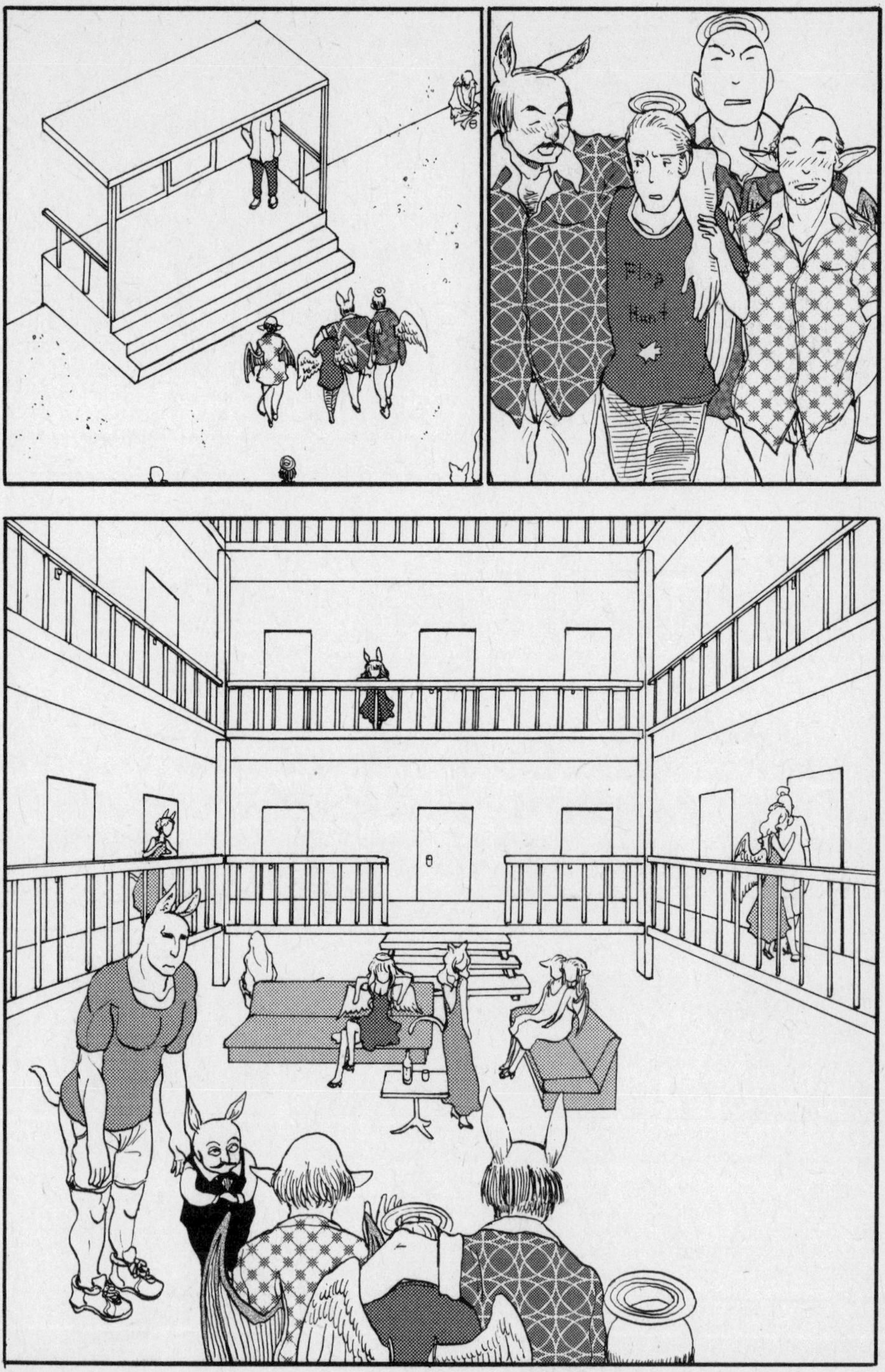
Flog
Hunt

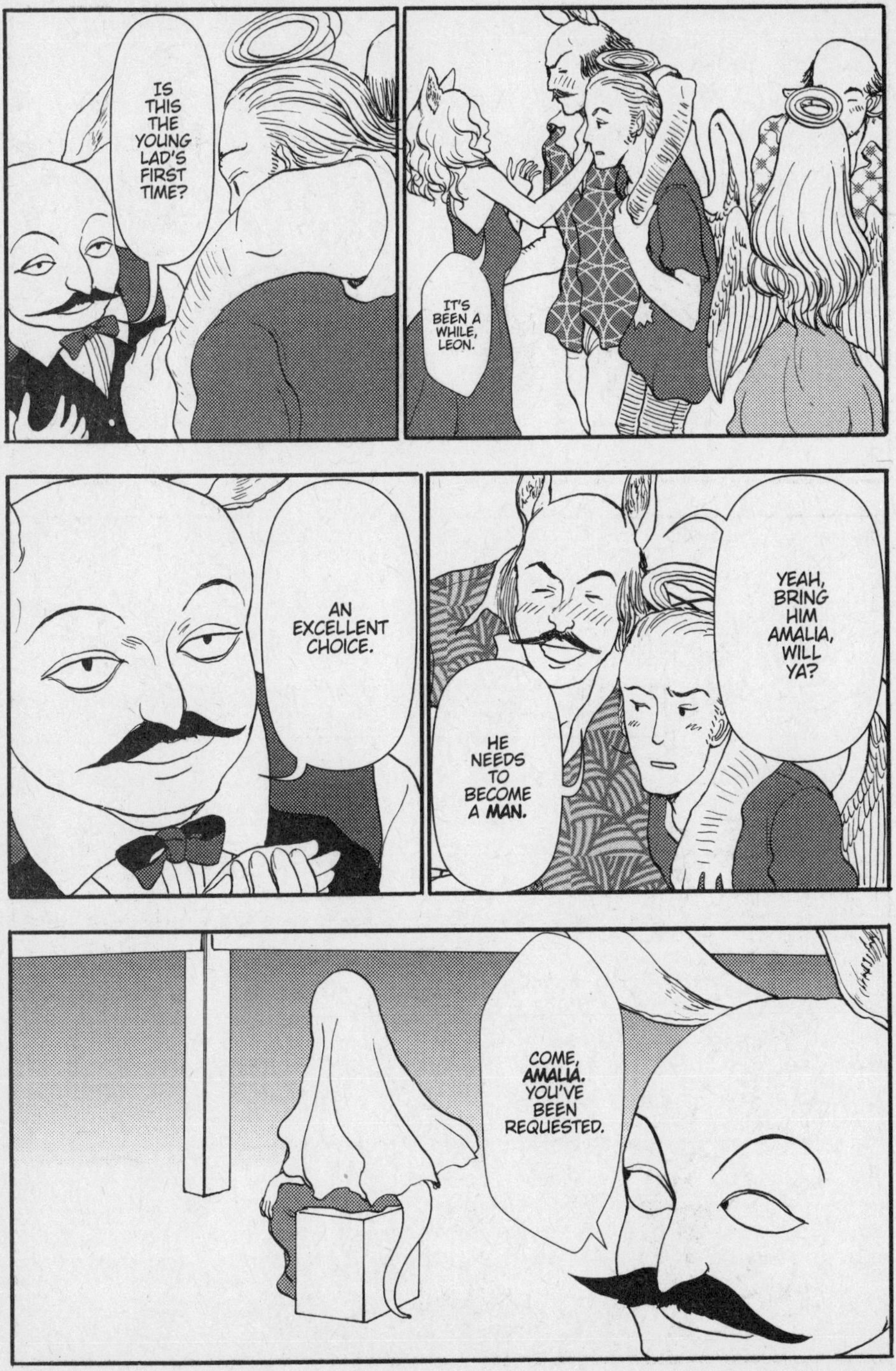
IT'S BEEN A WHILE, LEON.
IS THIS THE YOUNG LAD'S FIRST TIME?
YEAH, BRING HIM AMALIA, WILL YA?
HE NEEDS TO BECOME A **MAN.**
AN EXCELLENT CHOICE.
COME, **AMALIA.** YOU'VE BEEN REQUESTED.

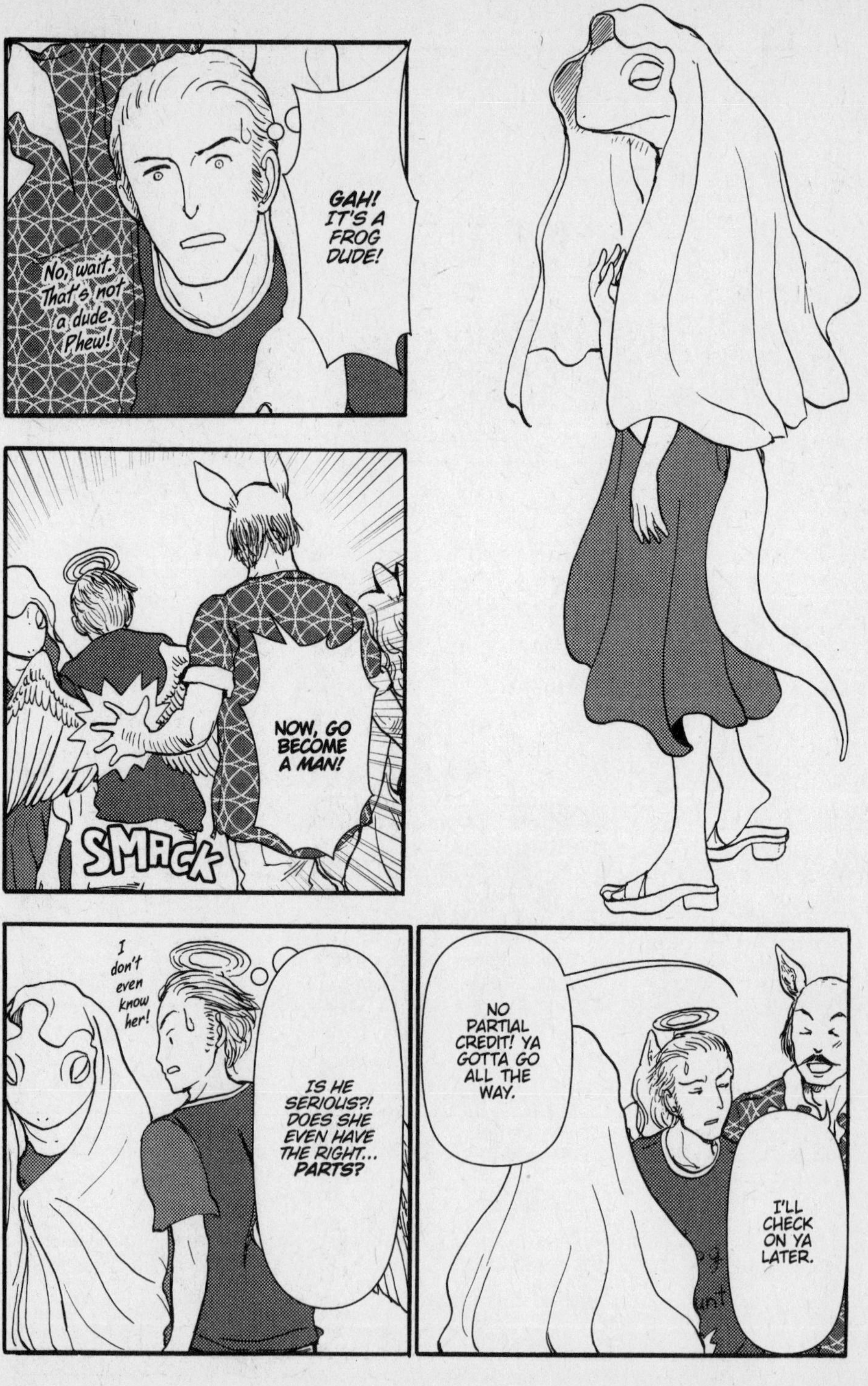
GAH! IT'S A FROG DUDE!
No, wait. That's not a dude. Phew!
NOW, GO BECOME A MAN!
SMACK
NO PARTIAL CREDIT! YA GOTTA GO ALL THE WAY.
I'LL CHECK ON YA LATER.
IS HE SERIOUS?! DOES SHE EVEN HAVE THE RIGHT... PARTS?
I don't even know her!

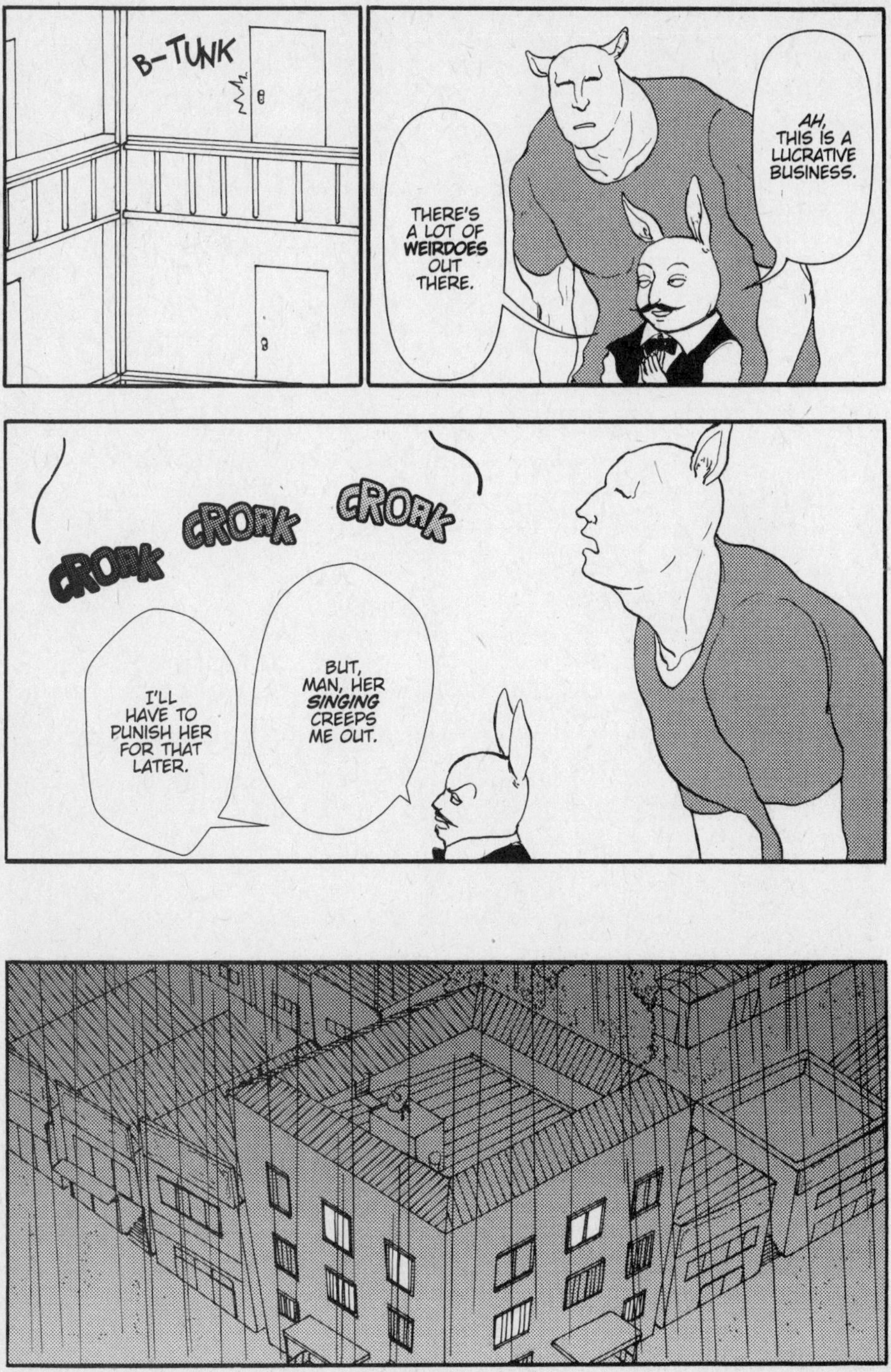
AH, THIS IS A LUCRATIVE BUSINESS.
THERE'S A LOT OF WEIRDOES OUT THERE.
B-TUNK
CROAK
CROAK
CROAK
BUT, MAN, HER SINGING CREEPS ME OUT.
I'LL HAVE TO PUNISH HER FOR THAT LATER.

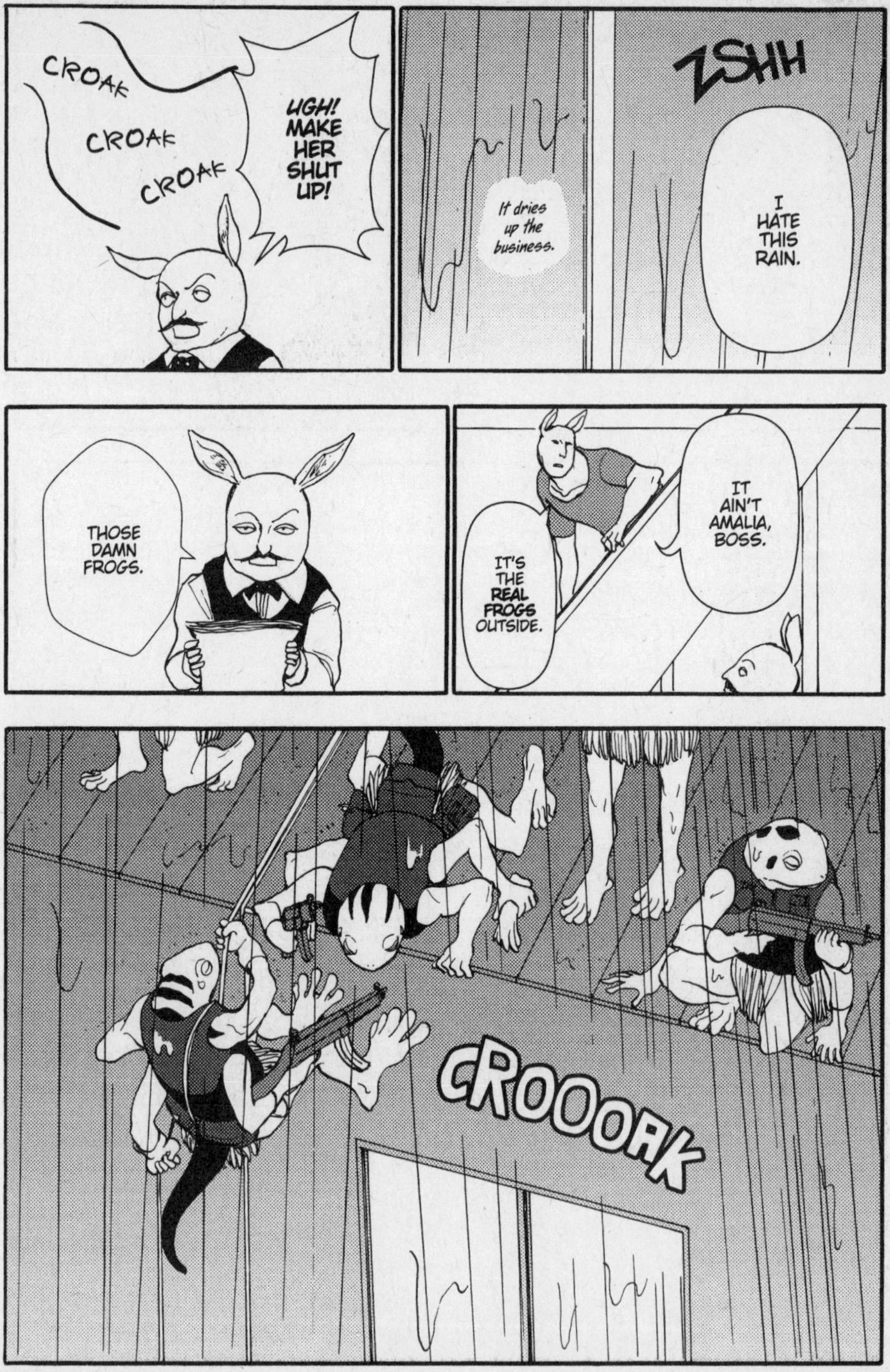
ZSHH
I HATE THIS RAIN.
It dries up the business.
CROAK CROAK CROAK
UGH! MAKE HER SHUT UP!
IT AIN'T AMALIA, BOSS.
IT'S THE REAL FROGS OUTSIDE.
THOSE DAMN FROGS.
CROOOAK

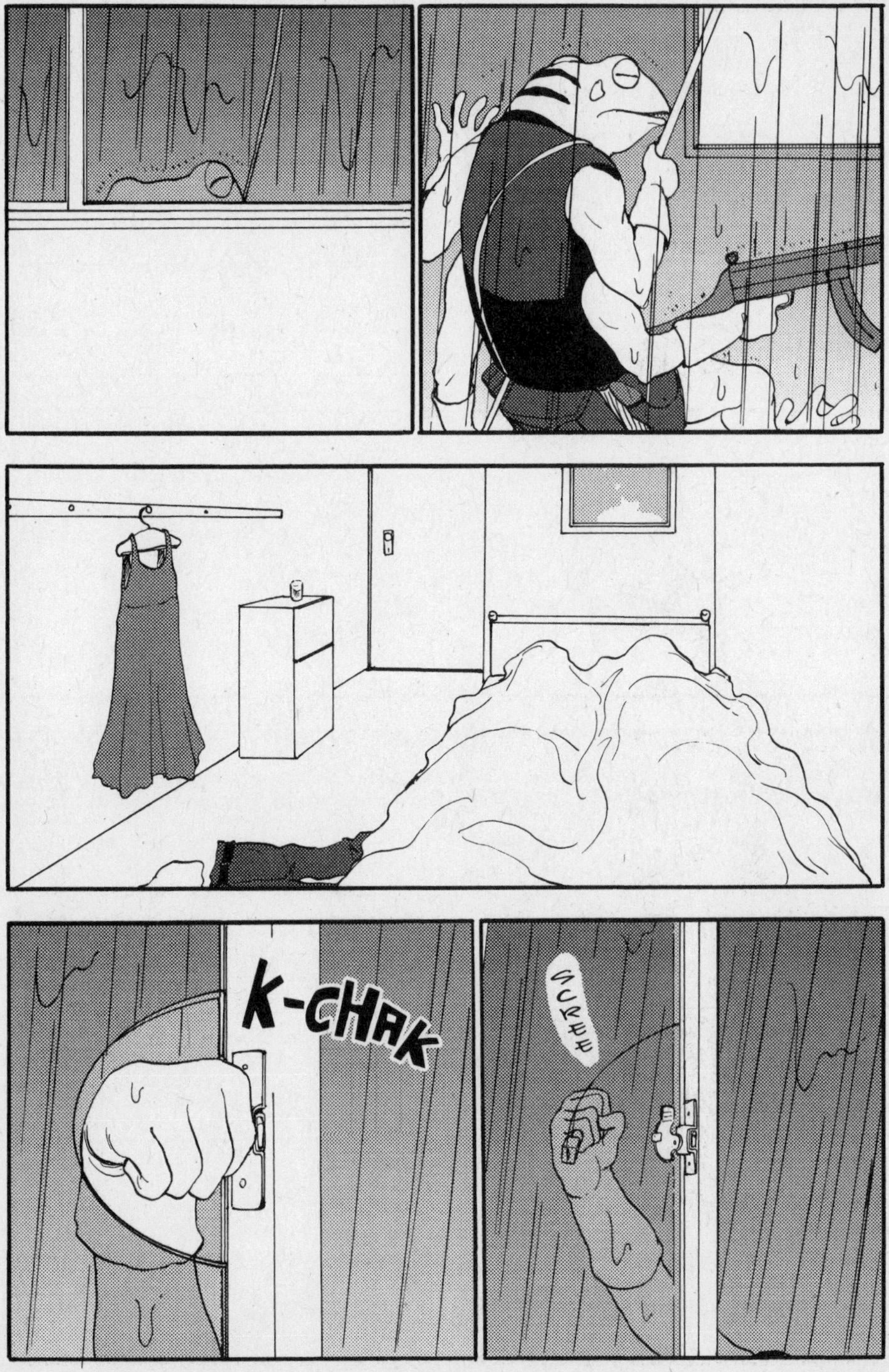
SCREE
K-CHAK

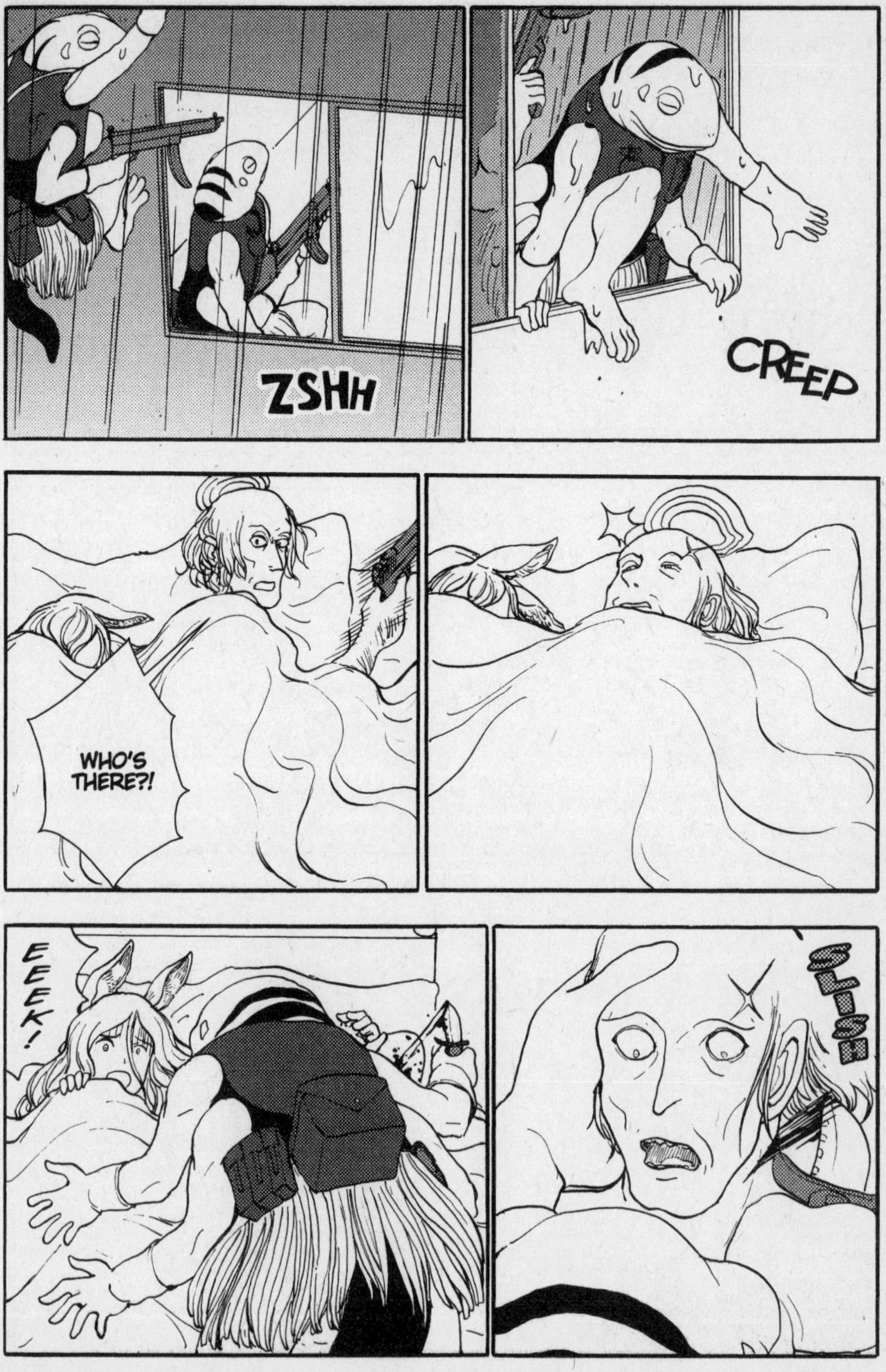
CREEP
ZSHH
WHO'S THERE?!
SLISH
EEEK!

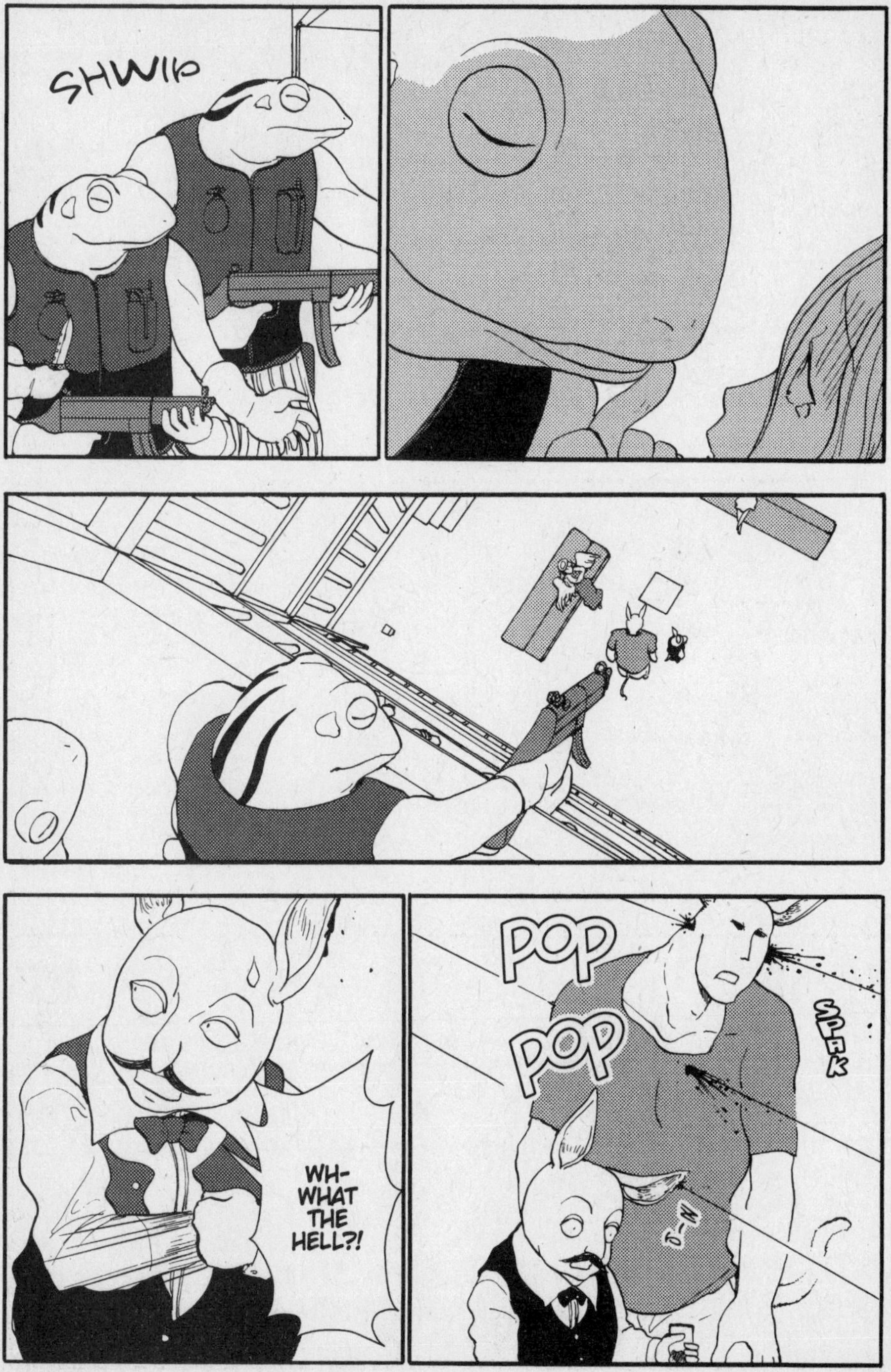
SHWIP
POP
POP
SPAK
WH- WHAT THE HELL?!

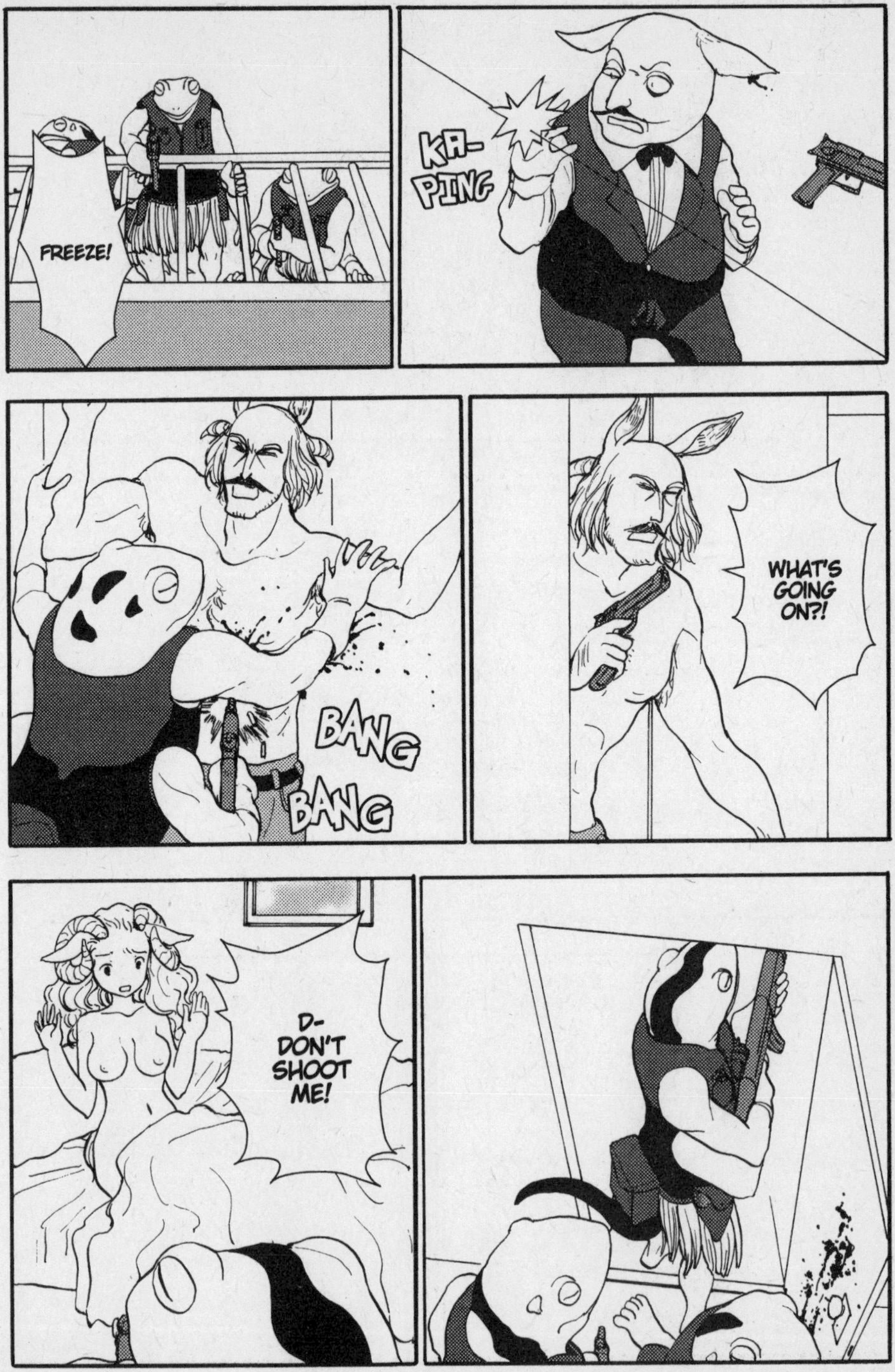
KA-PING
FREEZE!
WHAT'S GOING ON?!
BANG
BANG
D-DON'T SHOOT ME!

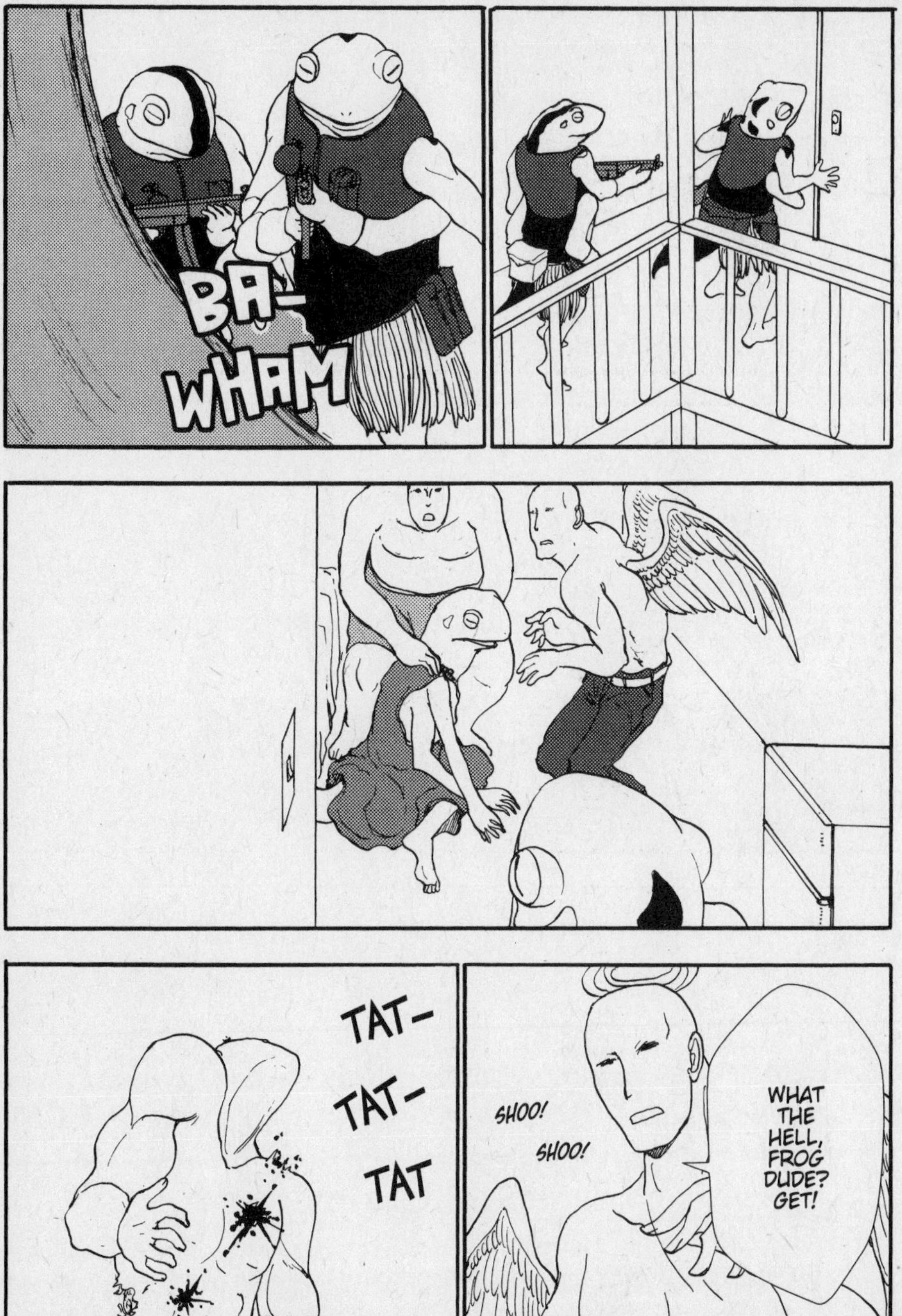
BA-WHAM
WHAT THE HELL, FROG DUDE? GET!
SHOO!
SHOO!
TAT-TAT-TAT

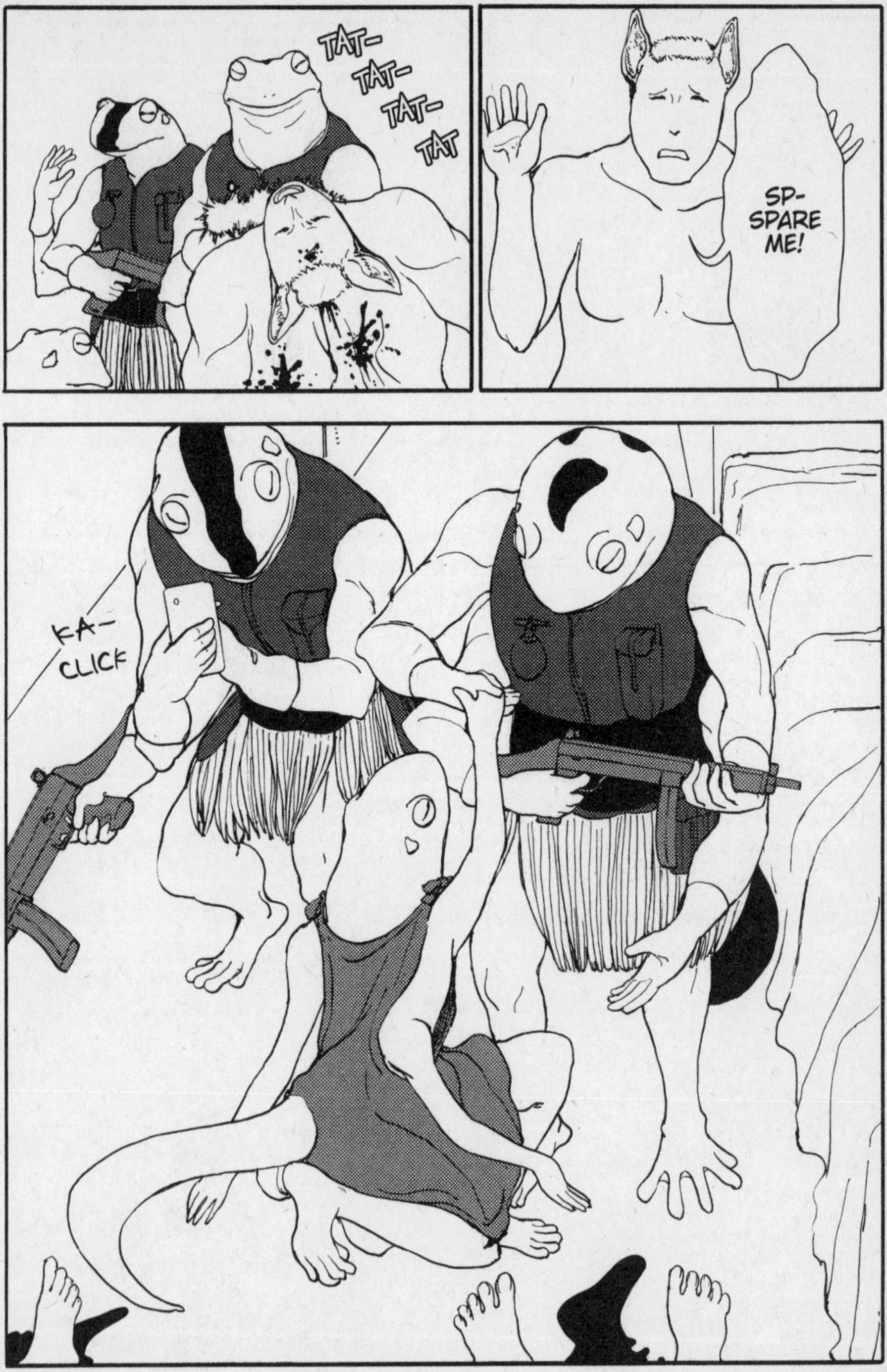
SP- SPARE ME!
TAT- TAT- TAT- TAT
KA- CLICK

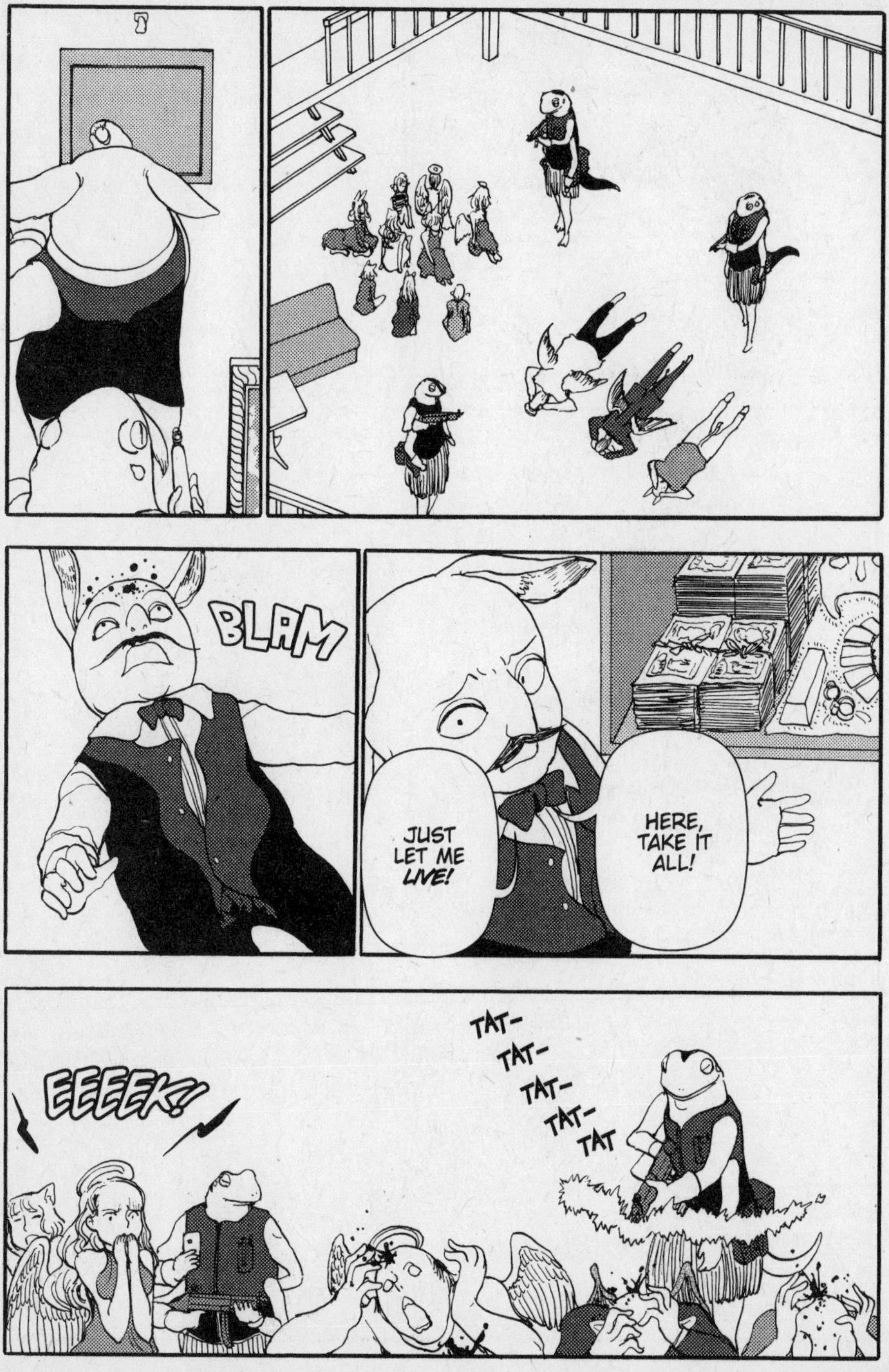
HERE, TAKE IT ALL!
JUST LET ME *LIVE!*
BLAM
TAT- TAT- TAT- TAT- TAT
EEEEK!

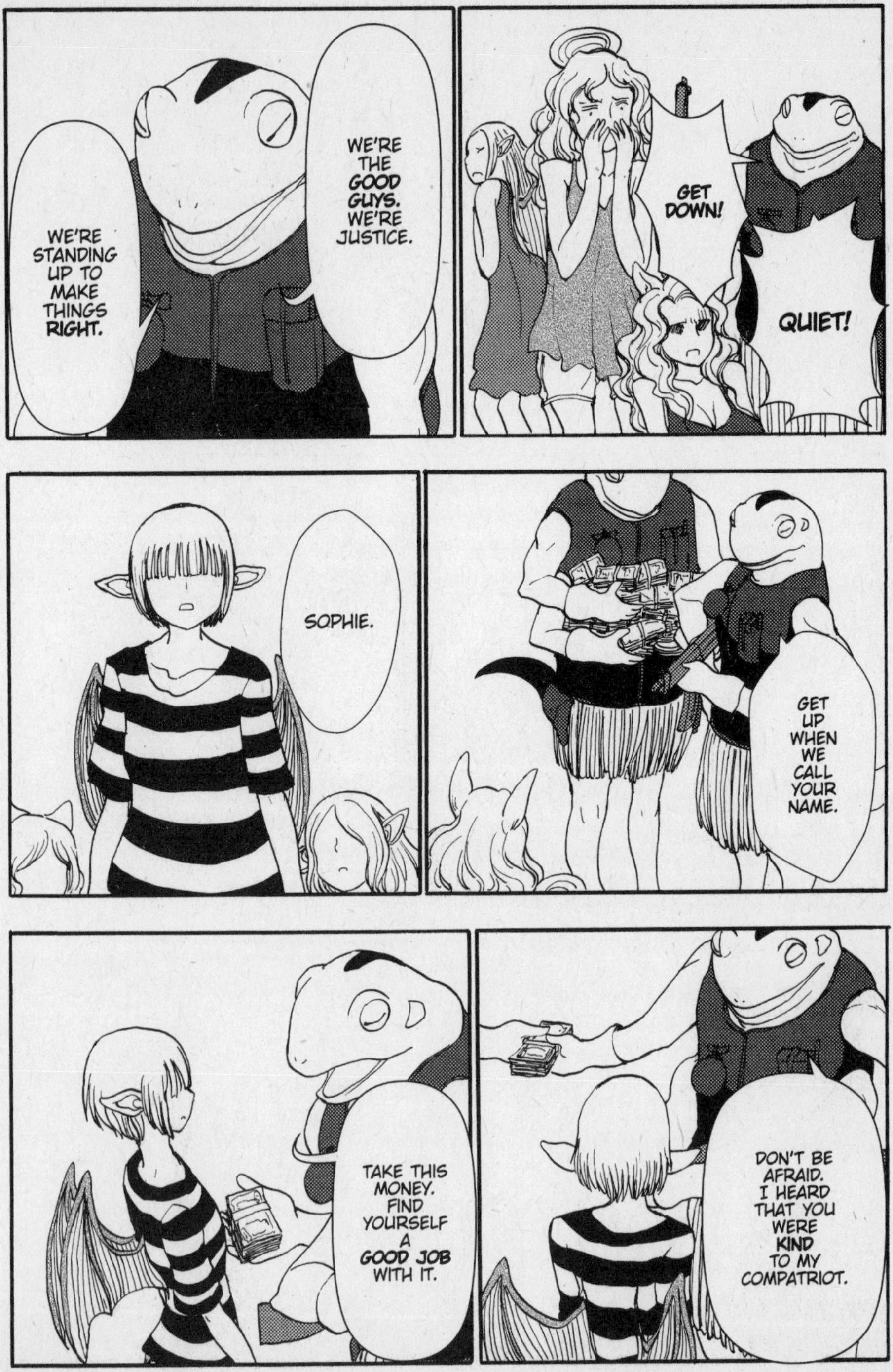

GET DOWN!
QUIET!
WE'RE THE **GOOD GUYS.** WE'RE JUSTICE.
WE'RE STANDING UP TO MAKE THINGS **RIGHT.**
GET UP WHEN WE CALL YOUR NAME.
SOPHIE.
DON'T BE AFRAID. I HEARD THAT YOU WERE **KIND** TO MY COMPATRIOT.
TAKE THIS MONEY. FIND YOURSELF A **GOOD JOB** WITH IT.

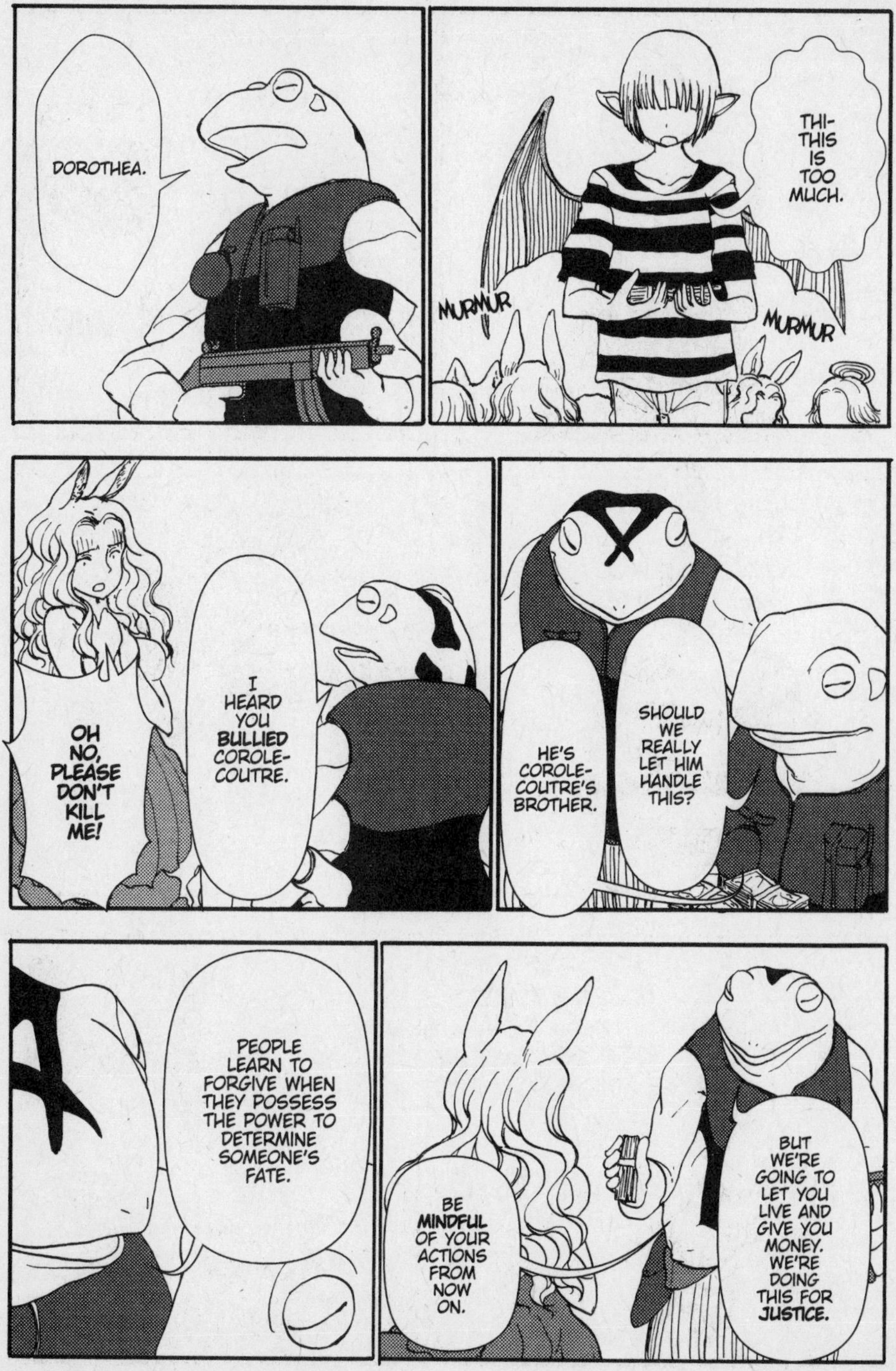
THI-THIS IS TOO MUCH.
MURMUR
MURMUR
DOROTHEA.
SHOULD WE REALLY LET HIM HANDLE THIS?
HE'S COROLE-COUTRE'S BROTHER.
I HEARD YOU BULLIED COROLE-COUTRE.
OH NO, PLEASE DON'T KILL ME!
BUT WE'RE GOING TO LET YOU LIVE AND GIVE YOU MONEY. WE'RE DOING THIS FOR JUSTICE.
BE MINDFUL OF YOUR ACTIONS FROM NOW ON.
PEOPLE LEARN TO FORGIVE WHEN THEY POSSESS THE POWER TO DETERMINE SOMEONE'S FATE.

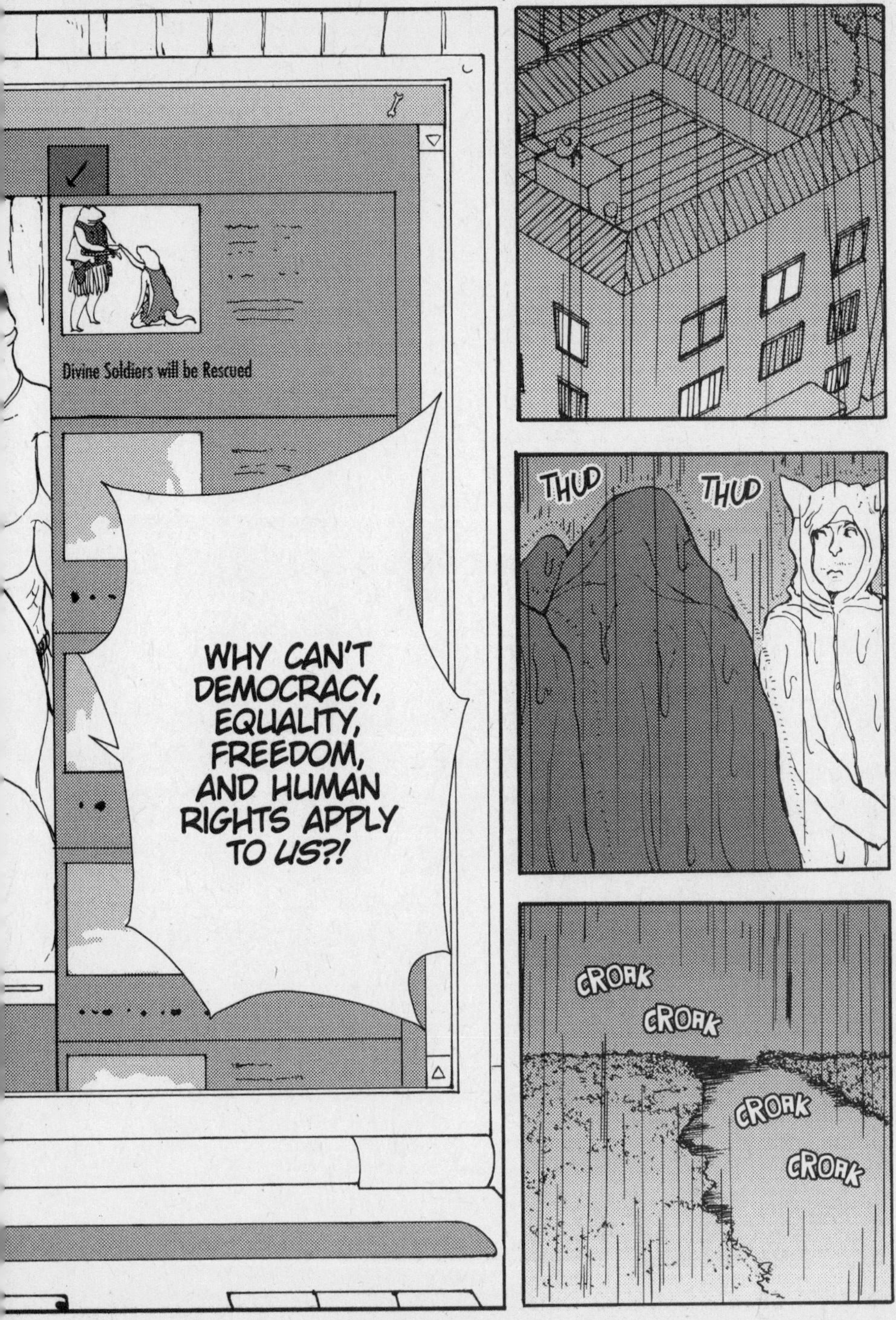
THUD
THUD
CROAK
CROAK
CROAK
CROAK
Divine Soldiers will be Rescued
WHY CAN'T DEMOCRACY, EQUALITY, FREEDOM, AND HUMAN RIGHTS APPLY TO US?!

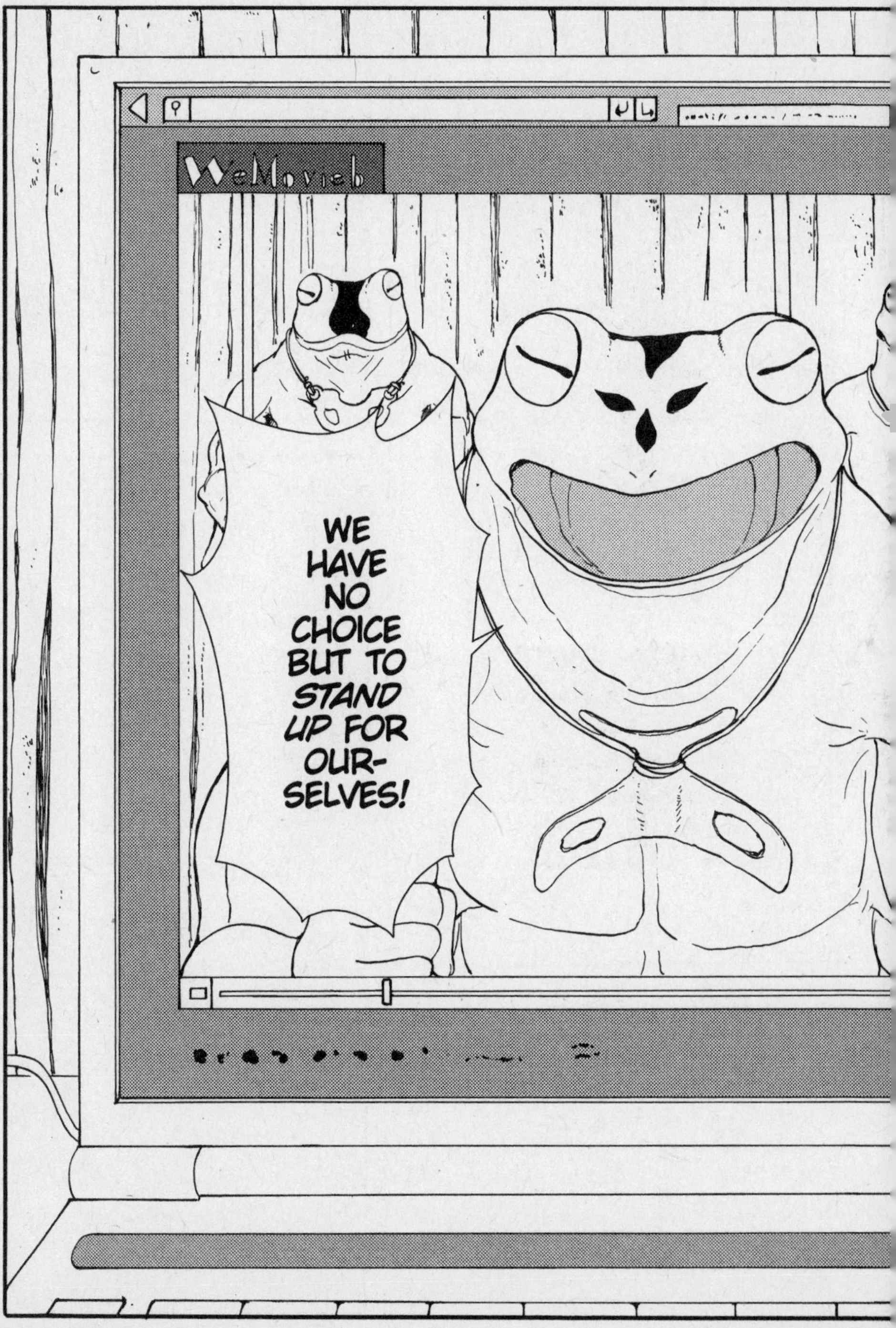
WE HAVE NO CHOICE BUT TO STAND UP FOR OUR-SELVES!

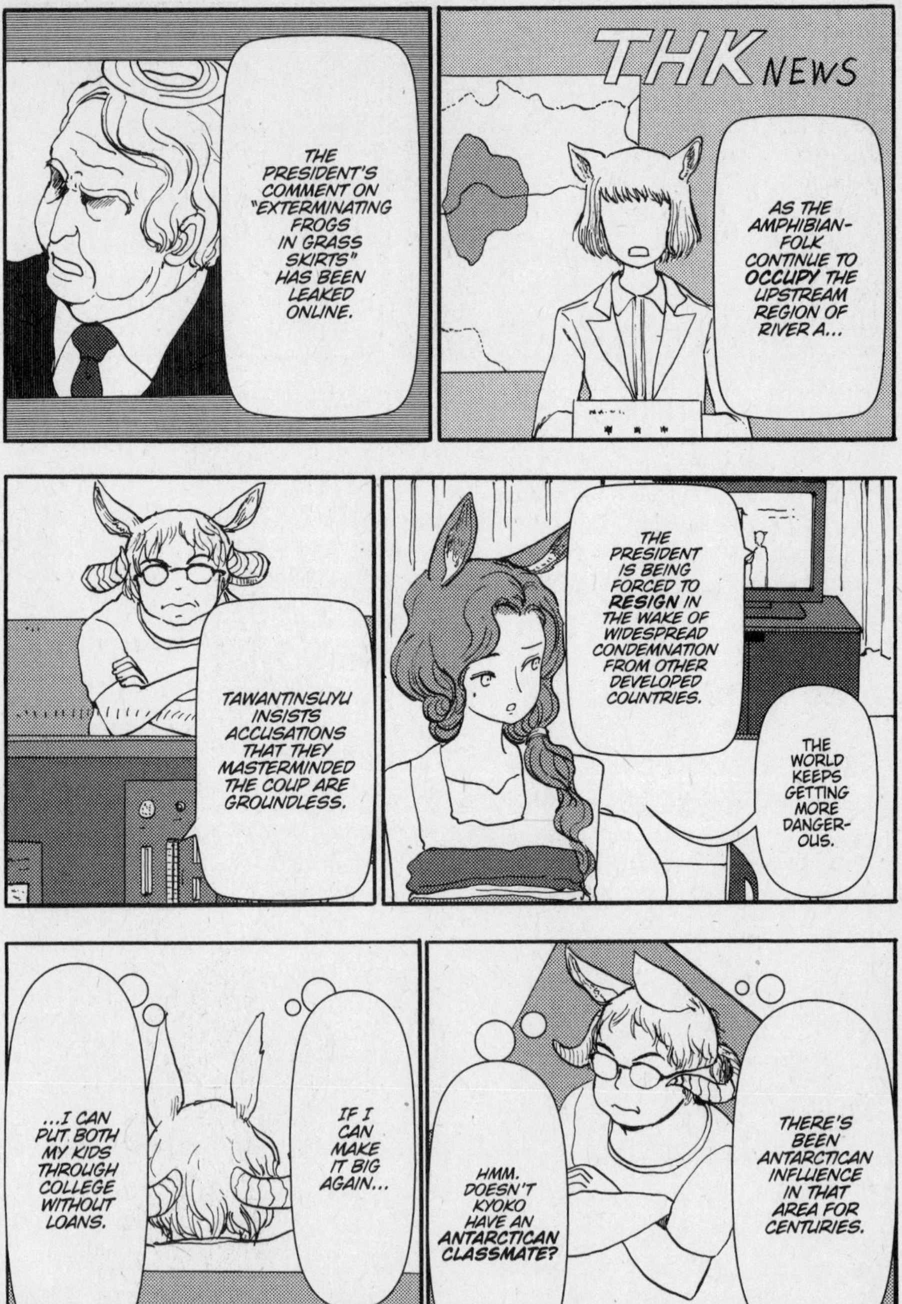
THK NEWS
AS THE AMPHIBIAN-FOLK CONTINUE TO OCCUPY THE UPSTREAM REGION OF RIVER A...
THE PRESIDENT'S COMMENT ON "EXTERMINATING FROGS IN GRASS SKIRTS" HAS BEEN LEAKED ONLINE.
THE PRESIDENT IS BEING FORCED TO RESIGN IN THE WAKE OF WIDESPREAD CONDEMNATION FROM OTHER DEVELOPED COUNTRIES.
THE WORLD KEEPS GETTING MORE DANGER-OUS.
TAWANTINSUYU INSISTS ACCUSATIONS THAT THEY MASTERMINDED THE COUP ARE GROUNDLESS.
THERE'S BEEN ANTARCTICAN INFLUENCE IN THAT AREA FOR CENTURIES.
HMM. DOESN'T KYOKO HAVE AN ANTARCTICAN CLASSMATE?
IF I CAN MAKE IT BIG AGAIN...
...I CAN PUT BOTH MY KIDS THROUGH COLLEGE WITHOUT LOANS.

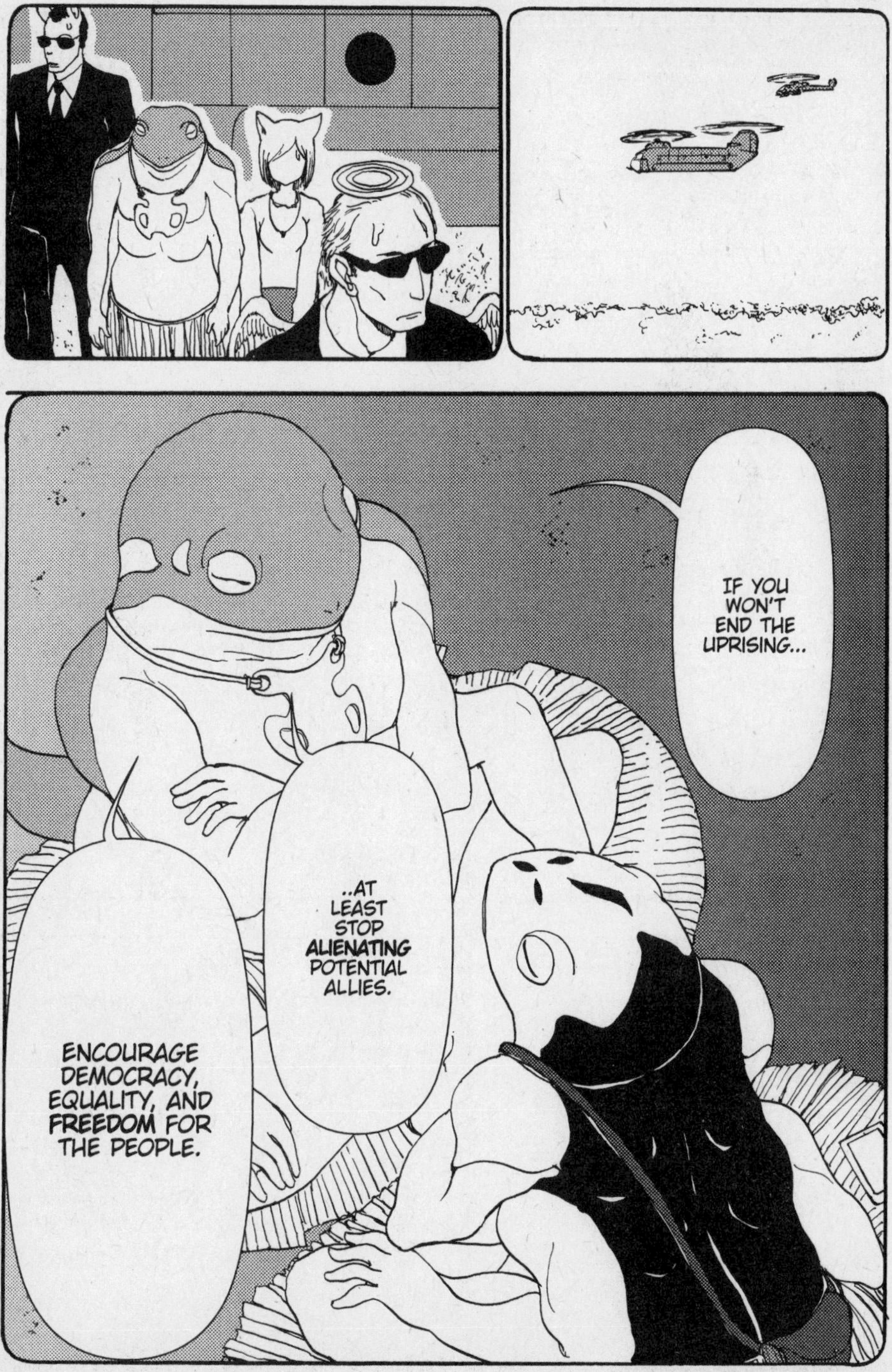
IF YOU WON'T END THE UPRISING...
..AT LEAST STOP ALIENATING POTENTIAL ALLIES.
ENCOURAGE DEMOCRACY, EQUALITY, AND FREEDOM FOR THE PEOPLE.

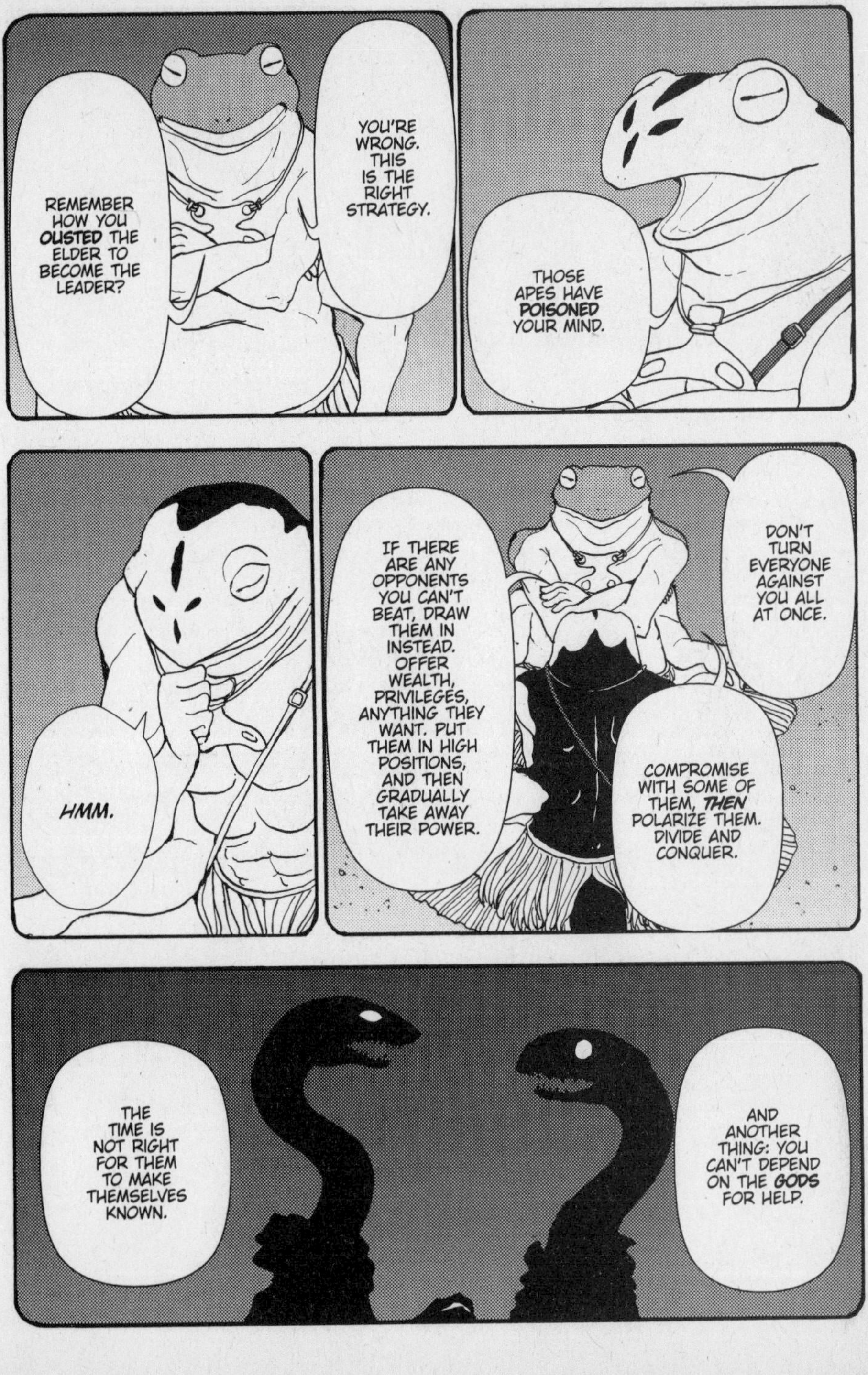
THOSE APES HAVE **POISONED** YOUR MIND.
YOU'RE WRONG. THIS IS THE RIGHT STRATEGY.
REMEMBER HOW YOU **OUSTED** THE ELDER TO BECOME THE LEADER?
DON'T TURN EVERYONE AGAINST YOU ALL AT ONCE.
IF THERE ARE ANY OPPONENTS YOU CAN'T BEAT, DRAW THEM IN INSTEAD. OFFER WEALTH, PRIVILEGES, ANYTHING THEY WANT. PUT THEM IN HIGH POSITIONS, AND THEN GRADUALLY TAKE AWAY THEIR POWER.
COMPROMISE WITH SOME OF THEM, ***THEN*** POLARIZE THEM. DIVIDE AND CONQUER.
HMM.
AND ANOTHER THING: YOU CAN'T DEPEND ON THE **GODS** FOR HELP.
THE TIME IS NOT RIGHT FOR THEM TO MAKE THEMSELVES KNOWN.

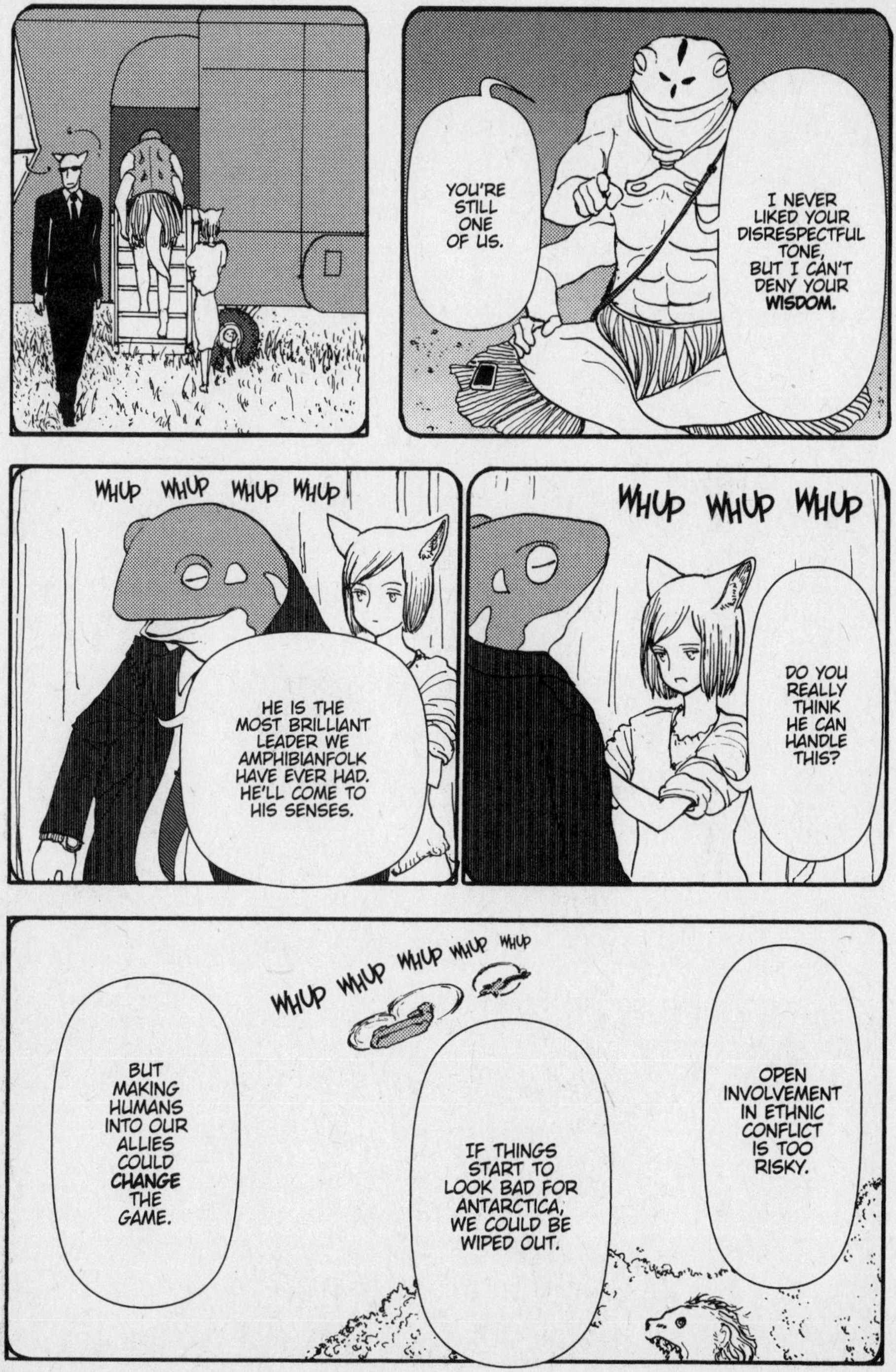
I NEVER LIKED YOUR DISRESPECTFUL TONE, BUT I CAN'T DENY YOUR **WISDOM.**
YOU'RE STILL ONE OF US.
WHUP WHUP WHUP
DO YOU REALLY THINK HE CAN HANDLE THIS?
WHUP WHUP WHUP WHUP
HE IS THE MOST BRILLIANT LEADER WE AMPHIBIANFOLK HAVE EVER HAD. HE'LL COME TO HIS SENSES.
WHUP WHUP WHUP WHUP WHUP
OPEN INVOLVEMENT IN ETHNIC CONFLICT IS TOO RISKY.
IF THINGS START TO LOOK BAD FOR ANTARCTICA, WE COULD BE WIPED OUT.
BUT MAKING HUMANS INTO OUR ALLIES COULD **CHANGE** THE GAME.

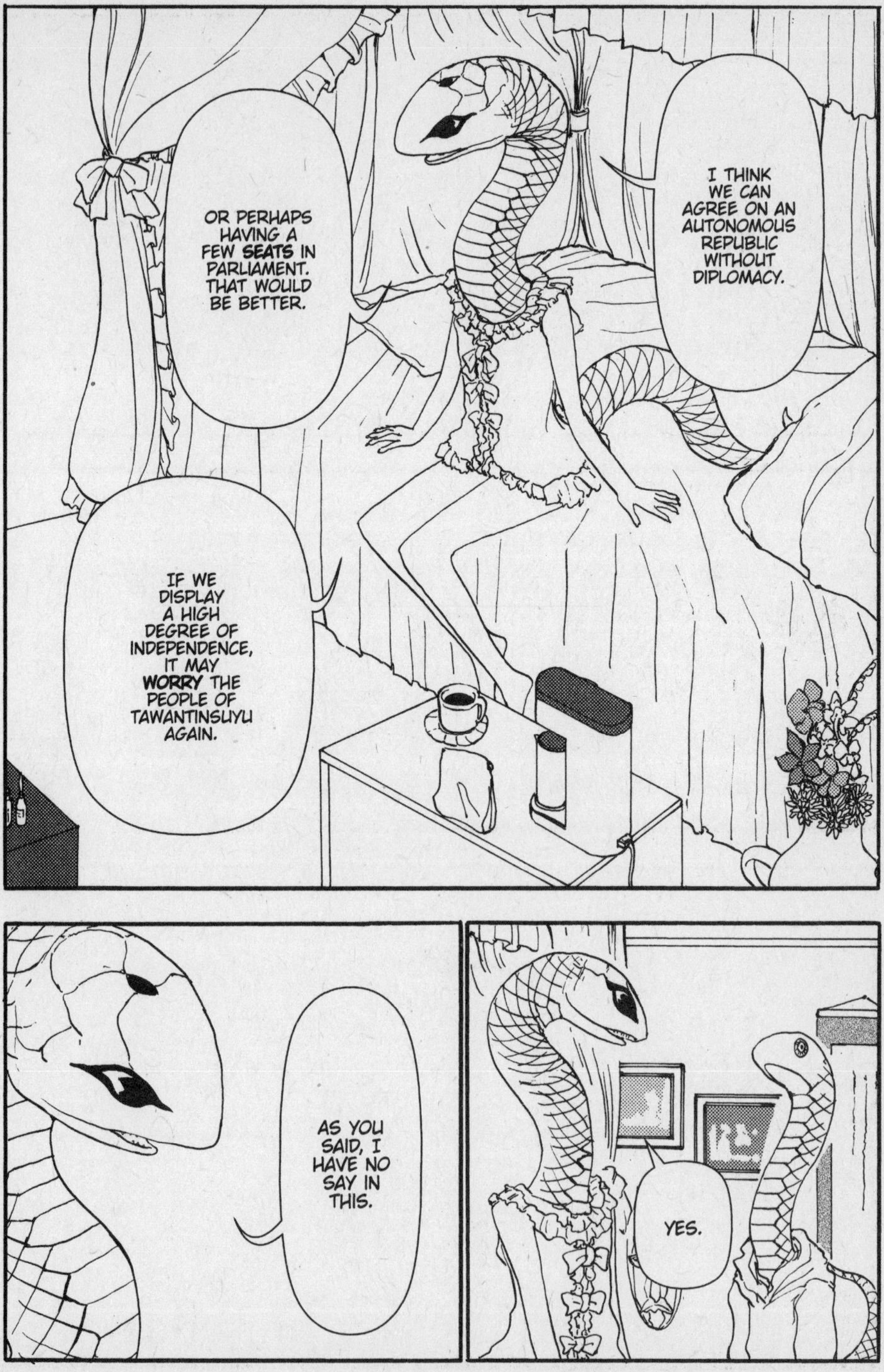
I THINK WE CAN AGREE ON AN AUTONOMOUS REPUBLIC WITHOUT DIPLOMACY.
OR PERHAPS HAVING A FEW **SEATS** IN PARLIAMENT. THAT WOULD BE BETTER.
IF WE DISPLAY A HIGH DEGREE OF INDEPENDENCE, IT MAY **WORRY** THE PEOPLE OF TAWANTINSUYU AGAIN.
YES.
AS YOU SAID, I HAVE NO SAY IN THIS.

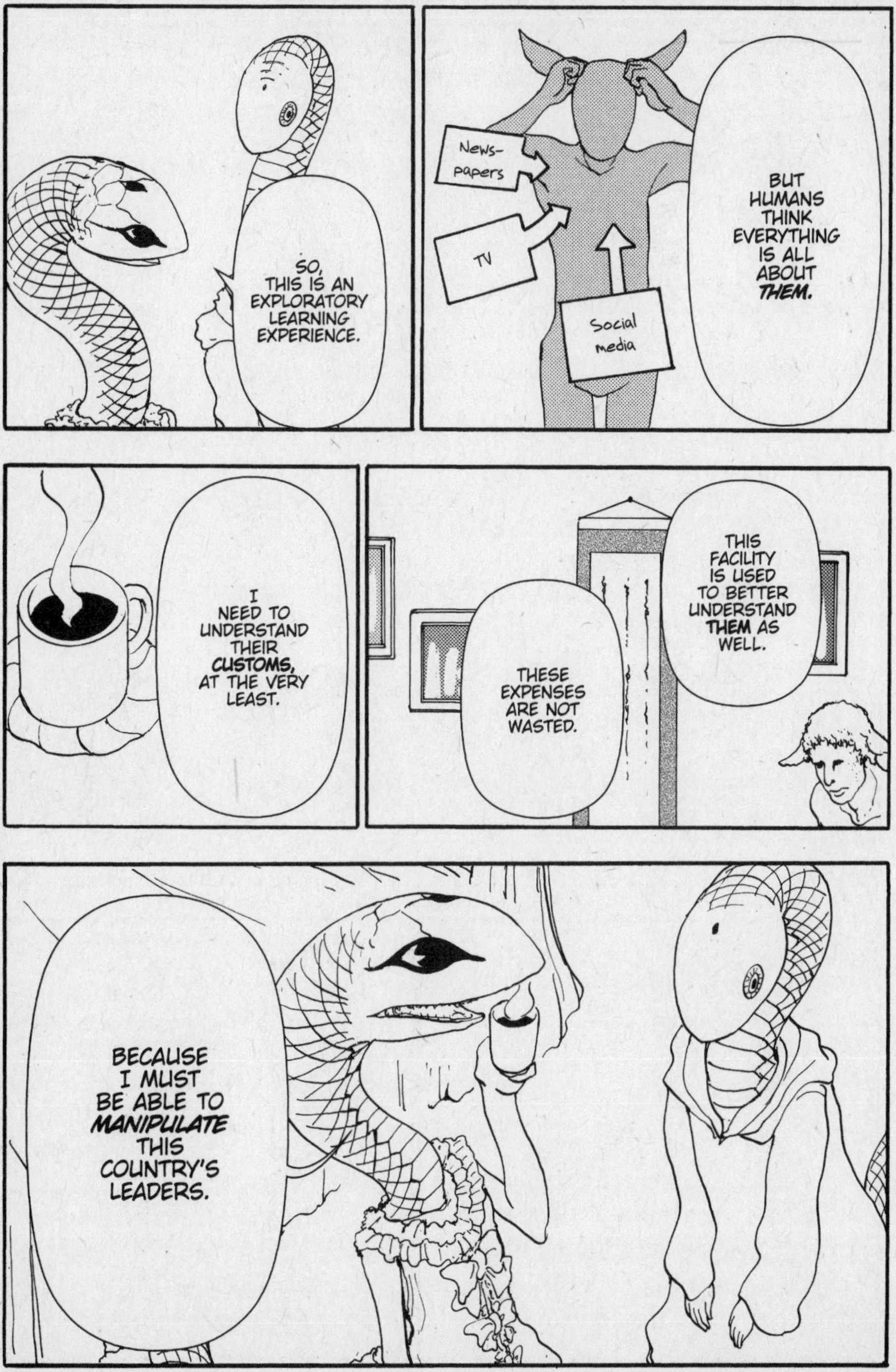
BUT HUMANS THINK EVERYTHING IS ALL ABOUT ***THEM.***
News-papers
TV
Social media
SO, THIS IS AN EXPLORATORY LEARNING EXPERIENCE.
THIS FACILITY IS USED TO BETTER UNDERSTAND **THEM** AS WELL.
THESE EXPENSES ARE NOT WASTED.
I NEED TO UNDERSTAND THEIR ***CUSTOMS,*** AT THE VERY LEAST.
BECAUSE I MUST BE ABLE TO ***MANIPULATE*** THIS COUNTRY'S LEADERS.

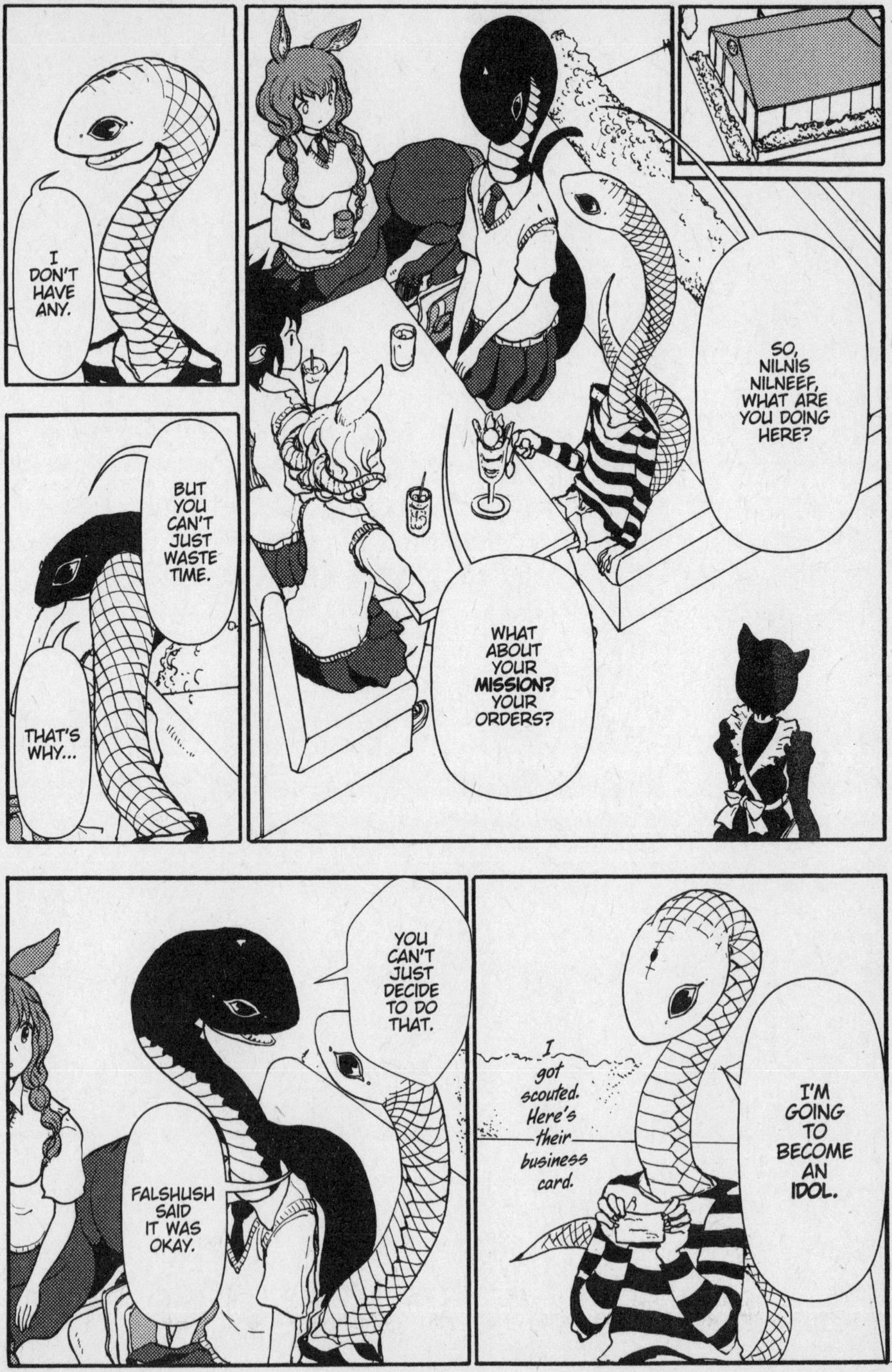
SO, NILNIS NILNEEF, WHAT ARE YOU DOING HERE?
WHAT ABOUT YOUR MISSION? YOUR ORDERS?
I DON'T HAVE ANY.
BUT YOU CAN'T JUST WASTE TIME.
THAT'S WHY...
I'M GOING TO BECOME AN IDOL.
I got scouted. Here's their business card.
YOU CAN'T JUST DECIDE TO DO THAT.
FALSHUSH SAID IT WAS OKAY.

A CentaUr's Life

UNDERSTANDING ANTARCTICANS: PART 4

WE DO NOT HAVE ACCESS TO MEDICAL RECORDS OR AUTOPSY REPORTS FOR ANTARCTICANS, AND THIS COUPLED WITH THEIR SECRECY MEANS THAT WE DON'T HAVE MUCH SPECIFIC INFORMATION ABOUT THEIR PHYSIOLOGY. WE CAN SPECULATE, HOWEVER, BASED ON THEIR OBSERVABLE CHARACTERISTICS AND THE SPOTTY INFORMATION WE'VE BEEN ABLE TO GLEAN FROM ANTARCTICANS THEMSELVES AND PEOPLE WHO HAVE INTERACTED WITH THEM.

ANTARCTICANS WERE PREVIOUSLY CALLED "ANTARCTIC SNAKE PEOPLE," WHICH IS NOW CONSIDERED IMPOLITE. THEY WERE OFTEN CAST AS MONSTERS IN LOW-BUDGET HORROR MOVIES, BUT THAT KIND OF TYPECASTING LIKELY LED TO INCORRECT PUBLIC PERCEPTIONS.

WE CURRENTLY CLASSIFY ANTARCTICANS INTO TWO SUBSPECIES KNOWN AS INTELLECTUAL AND WARRIOR. THE INTELLECTUAL SUBSPECIES IS GENERALLY PHYSICALLY SMALLER, HAS ONLY A SINGLE PAIR OF ARMS, AND IS BIPEDAL WITH A TAIL. THE WARRIOR SUBSPECIES IS GENERALLY LARGER AND MORE MUSCULAR, HAS TWO PAIRS OF ARMS, AND THE ENTIRE LOWER BODY RESEMBLES THAT OF A SNAKE. DESPITE THE DIFFERENCES IN THE LOWER BODY, BOTH SUBSPECIES STAND AND MOVE UPRIGHT. TO OUR KNOWLEDGE, ALL ANTARCTICANS ARE FEMALE AND ARE CONSIDERED CHILDREN OF THE "QUEEN." THIS KIND OF EUSOCIAL STRUCTURE HAS BEEN OBSERVED IN MAMMALS AND INSECTS (I.E. NAKED MOLE RATS, ANTS, BEES AND TERMITES), BUT NOT AMONG REPTILES—THOUGH, IT IS UNCERTAIN WHETHER ANTARCTICANS TRULY BELONG TO THAT GROUP. ALTHOUGH THEIR APPEARANCE STRONGLY IMPLIES RELATION TO DIAPSIDS, OTHER EVIDENCE MAKES IT UNLIKELY THAT THEY SHARE THE COLD-BLOODED TRAIT. FOR EXAMPLE, THE HIGH LEVEL OF INTELLIGENCE THAT THEY EXHIBIT DEMANDS A STABLE TEMPERATURE IN THEIR BRAINS, AND THE WARMTH IN THEIR HANDSHAKES IS CLEARLY INDICATIVE OF A HOMEOTHERMIC NATURE. THERE IS A CONVINCING THEORY, HOWEVER, THAT DINOSAURS MAY HAVE BEEN HOMEOTHERMIC; THEIR DESCENDANTS, MODERN BIRDS, ARE CERTAINLY KNOWN TO BE HOMEOTHERMIC AS WELL. THE ANCESTOR OF THE ALLIGATOR IS BELIEVED TO HAVE BEEN AN ACTIVE FOUR-CHAMBERED HOMEOTHERMIC QUADRUPED, WITH MODERN ALLIGATORS HAVING DIVERGED FROM THEIR ANCESTORS DUE TO A REVERSION TO AN AQUATIC HABITAT AND A PREDATORY NATURE.

ALTHOUGH ANTARCTICANS ARE CALLED SNAKEFOLK, THEY CANNOT BE CLASSIFIED INTO THE GROUP OF SCALED REPTILES THAT MODERN SNAKES AND LIZARDS BELONG TO. WE BELIEVE THAT THEY INSTEAD BELONG TO THE ARCHOSAUR FAMILY, WHICH INCLUDES ALLIGATORS, DINOSAURS, AND SIMILAR CREATURES. HOWEVER, THEIR PHYSICAL STRUCTURE IS NOT DEMONSTRATIVE OF THEIR RELATION TO DINOSAURS.

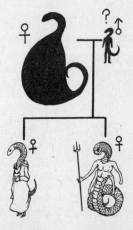

INTELLECTUAL
SUBSPECIES

WARRIOR
SUBSPECIES

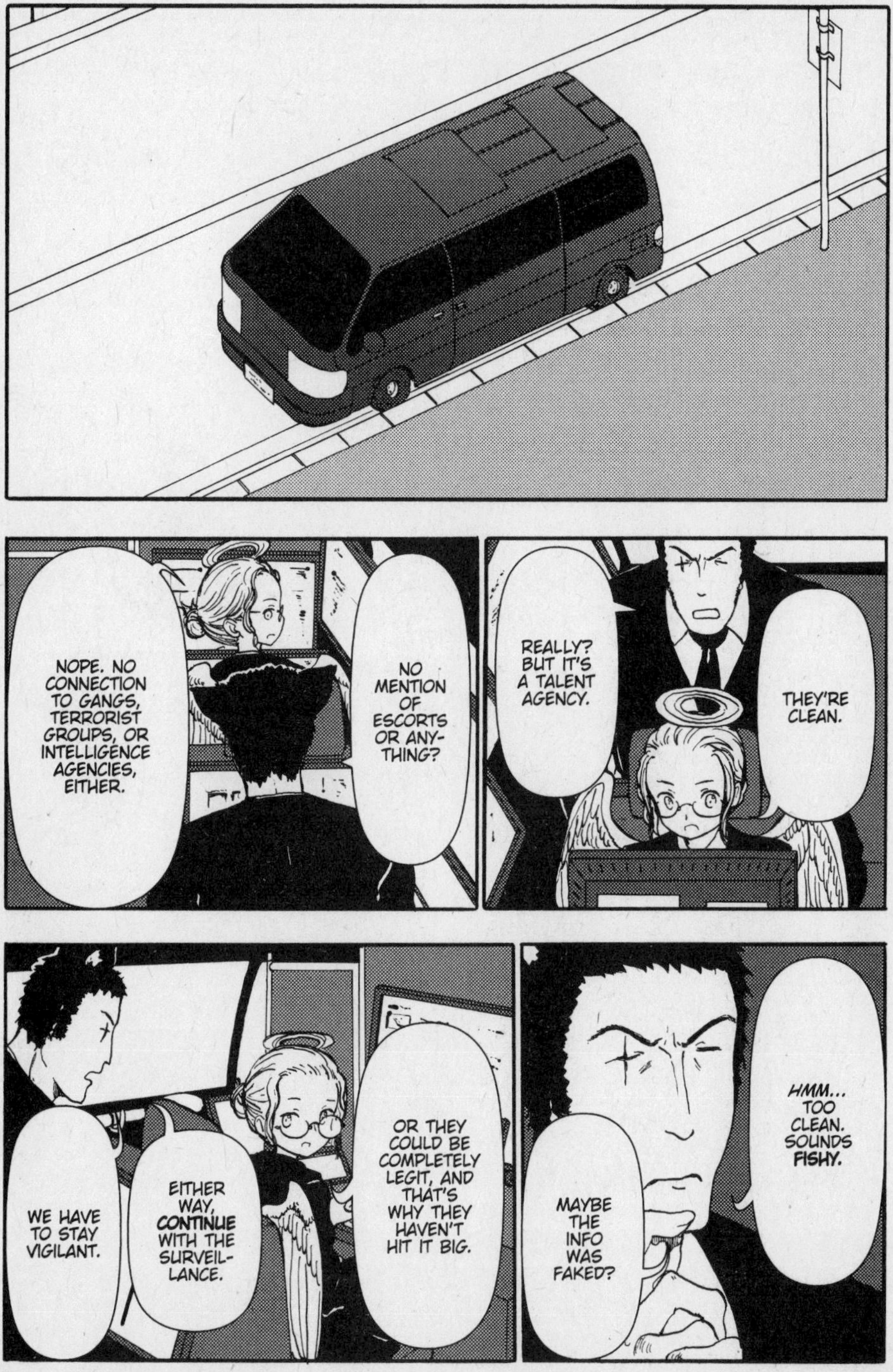
THEY'RE CLEAN.
REALLY? BUT IT'S A TALENT AGENCY.
NO MENTION OF ESCORTS OR ANY-THING?
NOPE. NO CONNECTION TO GANGS, TERRORIST GROUPS, OR INTELLIGENCE AGENCIES, EITHER.
HMM... TOO CLEAN. SOUNDS **FISHY.**
MAYBE THE INFO WAS FAKED?
OR THEY COULD BE COMPLETELY LEGIT, AND THAT'S WHY THEY HAVEN'T HIT IT BIG.
EITHER WAY, **CONTINUE** WITH THE SURVEIL-LANCE.
WE HAVE TO STAY VIGILANT.

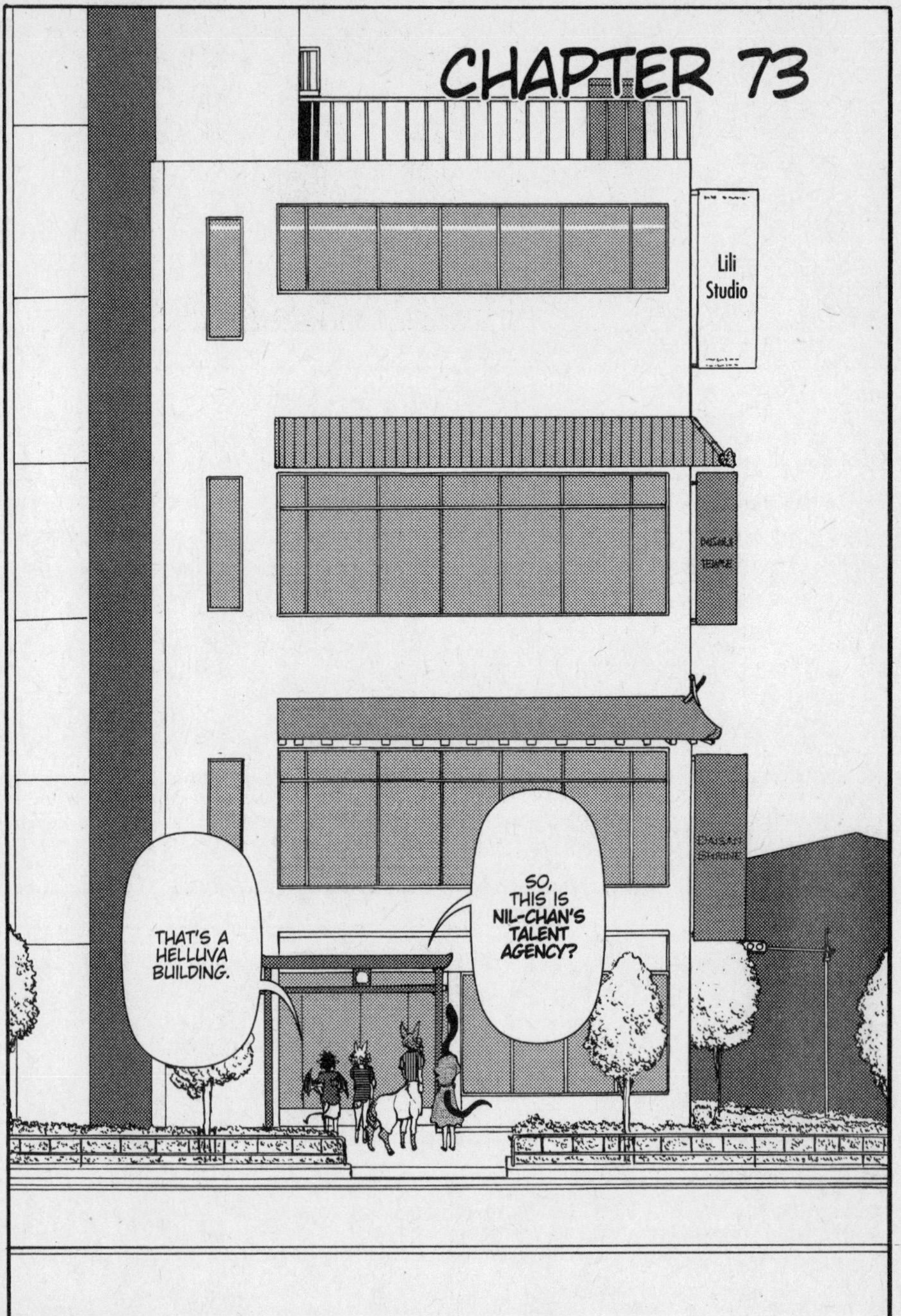
CHAPTER 73
Lili Studio
SO, THIS IS NIL-CHAN'S TALENT AGENCY?
THAT'S A HELLUVA BUILDING.

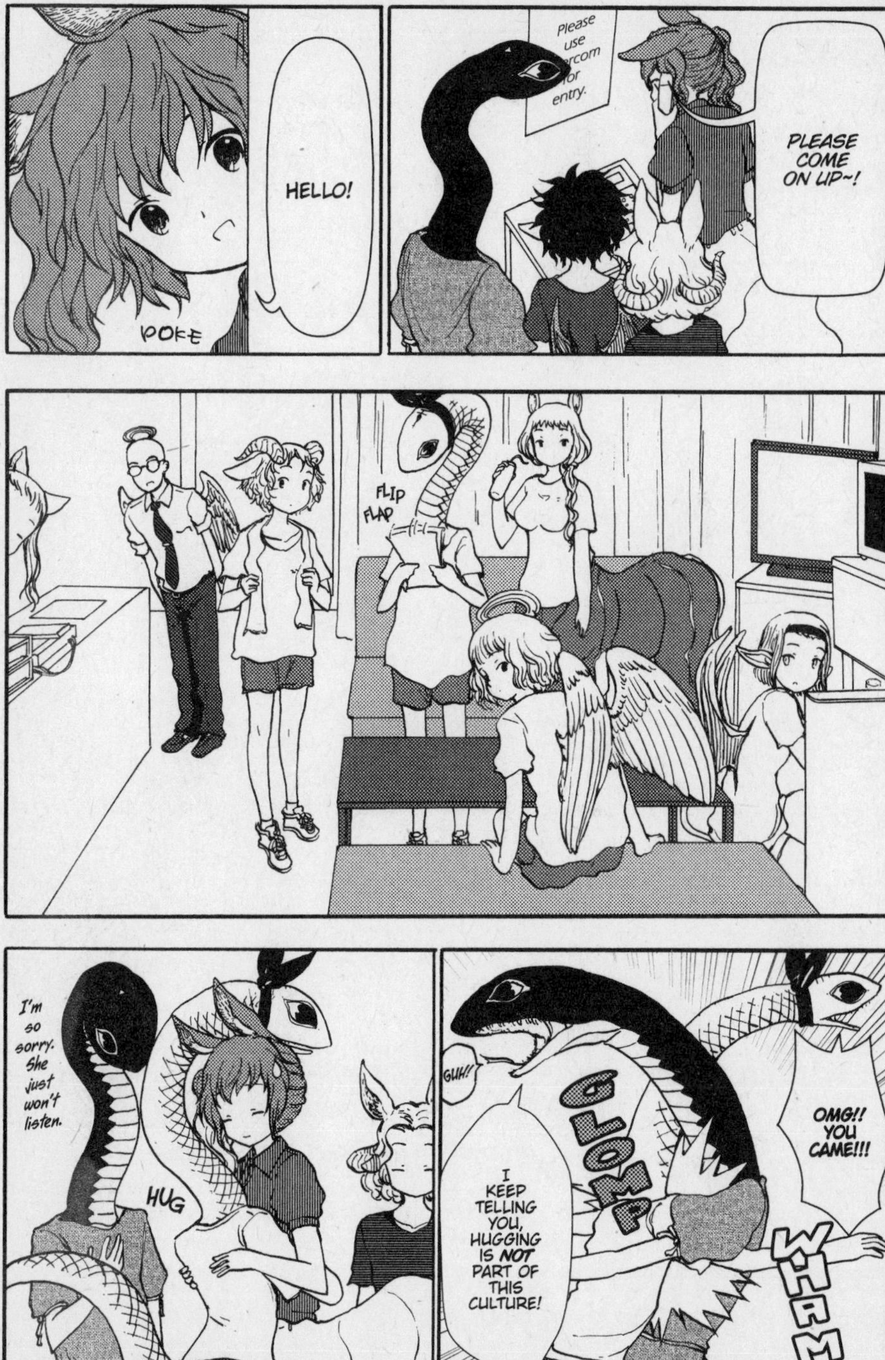
Please use rcom for entry.
PLEASE COME ON UP~!
HELLO!
POKE
FLIP FLAP
OMG!! YOU CAME!!!
GLOMP
WHAM
GUH!!
I KEEP TELLING YOU, HUGGING IS NOT PART OF THIS CULTURE!
I'm so sorry. She just won't listen.
HUG

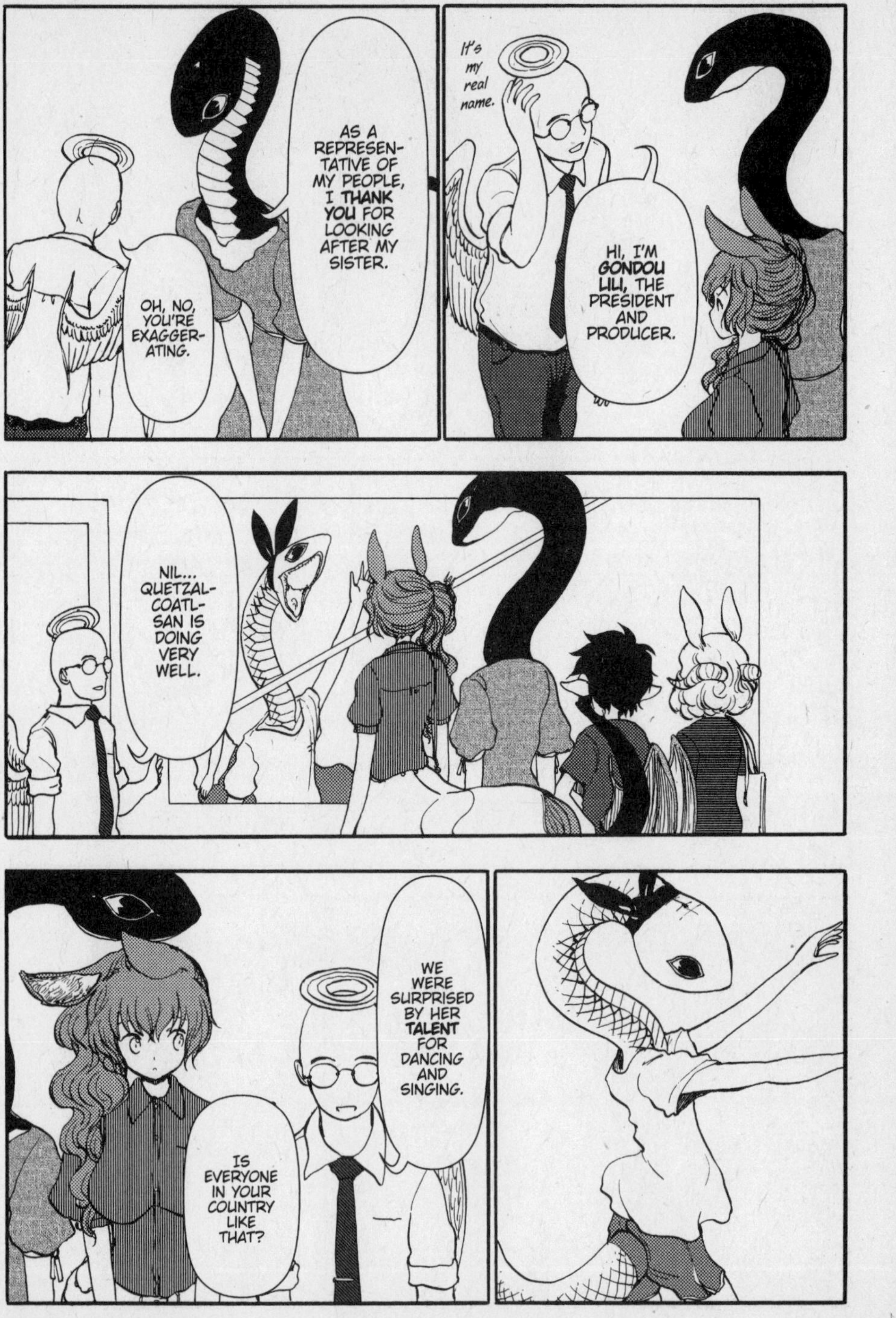
HI, I'M **GONDOU LILI,** THE PRESIDENT AND PRODUCER.
It's my real name.
AS A REPRESENTATIVE OF MY PEOPLE, I **THANK YOU** FOR LOOKING AFTER MY SISTER.
OH, NO, YOU'RE EXAGGERATING.
NIL... QUETZALCOATL-SAN IS DOING VERY WELL.
WE WERE SURPRISED BY HER **TALENT** FOR DANCING AND SINGING.
IS EVERYONE IN YOUR COUNTRY LIKE THAT?

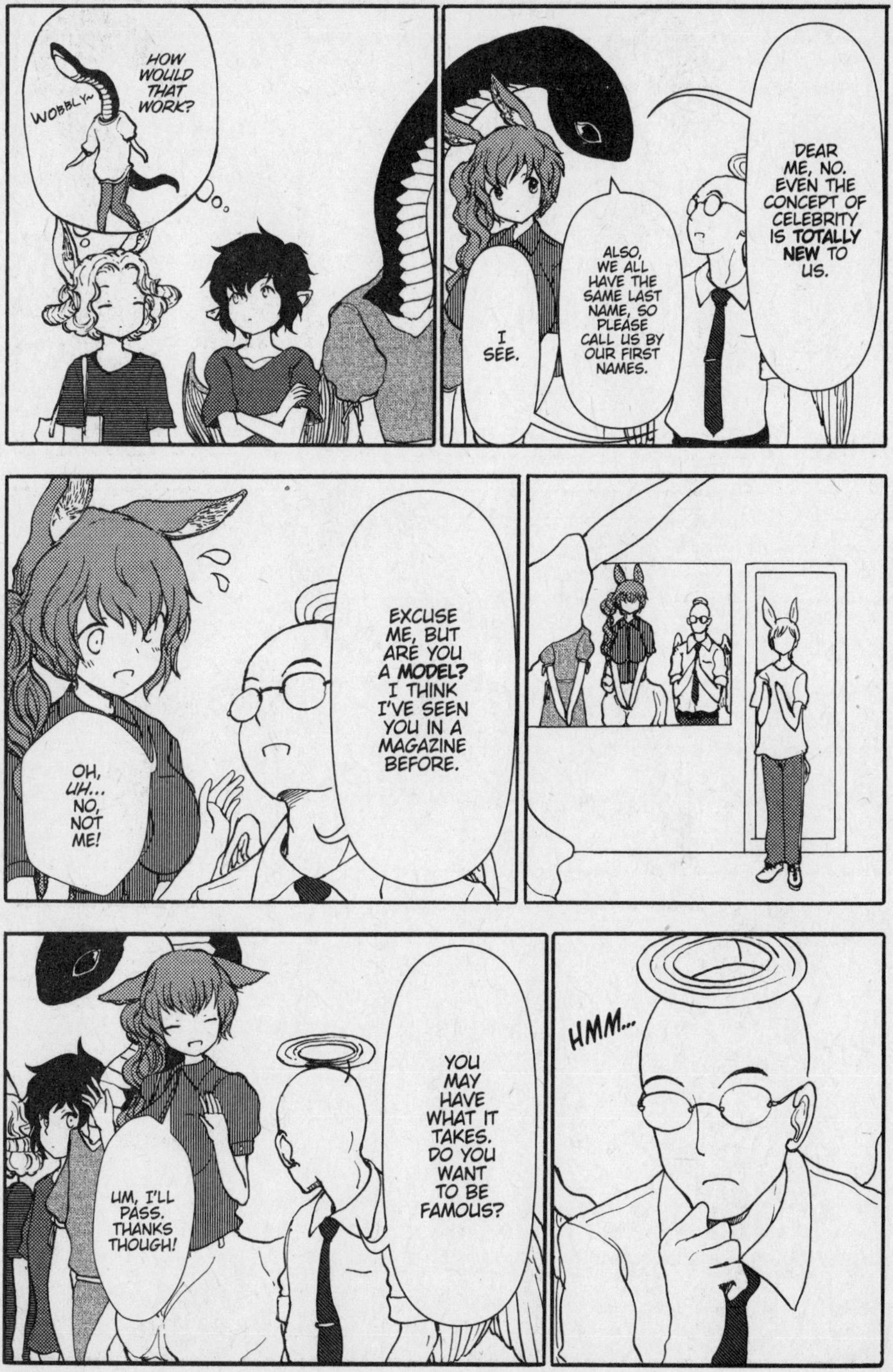
DEAR ME, NO. EVEN THE CONCEPT OF CELEBRITY IS **TOTALLY NEW** TO US.
ALSO, WE ALL HAVE THE SAME LAST NAME, SO PLEASE CALL US BY OUR FIRST NAMES.
I SEE.
HOW WOULD THAT WORK?
WOBBLY~
EXCUSE ME, BUT ARE YOU A **MODEL?** I THINK I'VE SEEN YOU IN A MAGAZINE BEFORE.
OH, UH... NO, NOT ME!
HMM...
YOU MAY HAVE WHAT IT TAKES. DO YOU WANT TO BE FAMOUS?
UM, I'LL PASS. THANKS THOUGH!

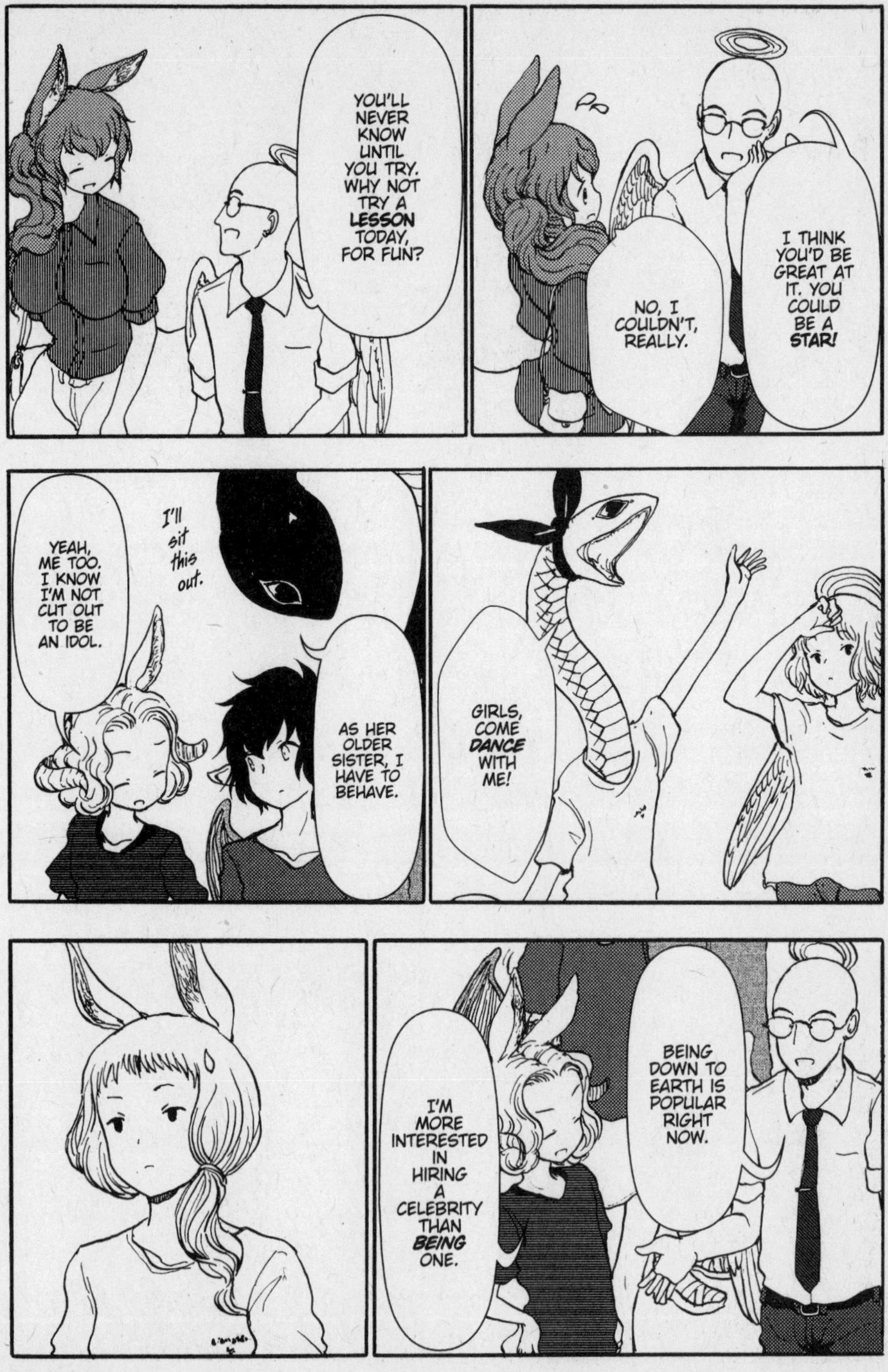
I THINK YOU'D BE GREAT AT IT. YOU COULD BE A **STAR!**
NO, I COULDN'T, REALLY.
YOU'LL NEVER KNOW UNTIL YOU TRY. WHY NOT TRY A **LESSON** TODAY, FOR FUN?
GIRLS, COME ***DANCE*** WITH ME!
AS HER OLDER SISTER, I HAVE TO BEHAVE.
I'll sit this out.
YEAH, ME TOO. I KNOW I'M NOT CUT OUT TO BE AN IDOL.
BEING DOWN TO EARTH IS POPULAR RIGHT NOW.
I'M MORE INTERESTED IN HIRING A CELEBRITY THAN ***BEING*** ONE.

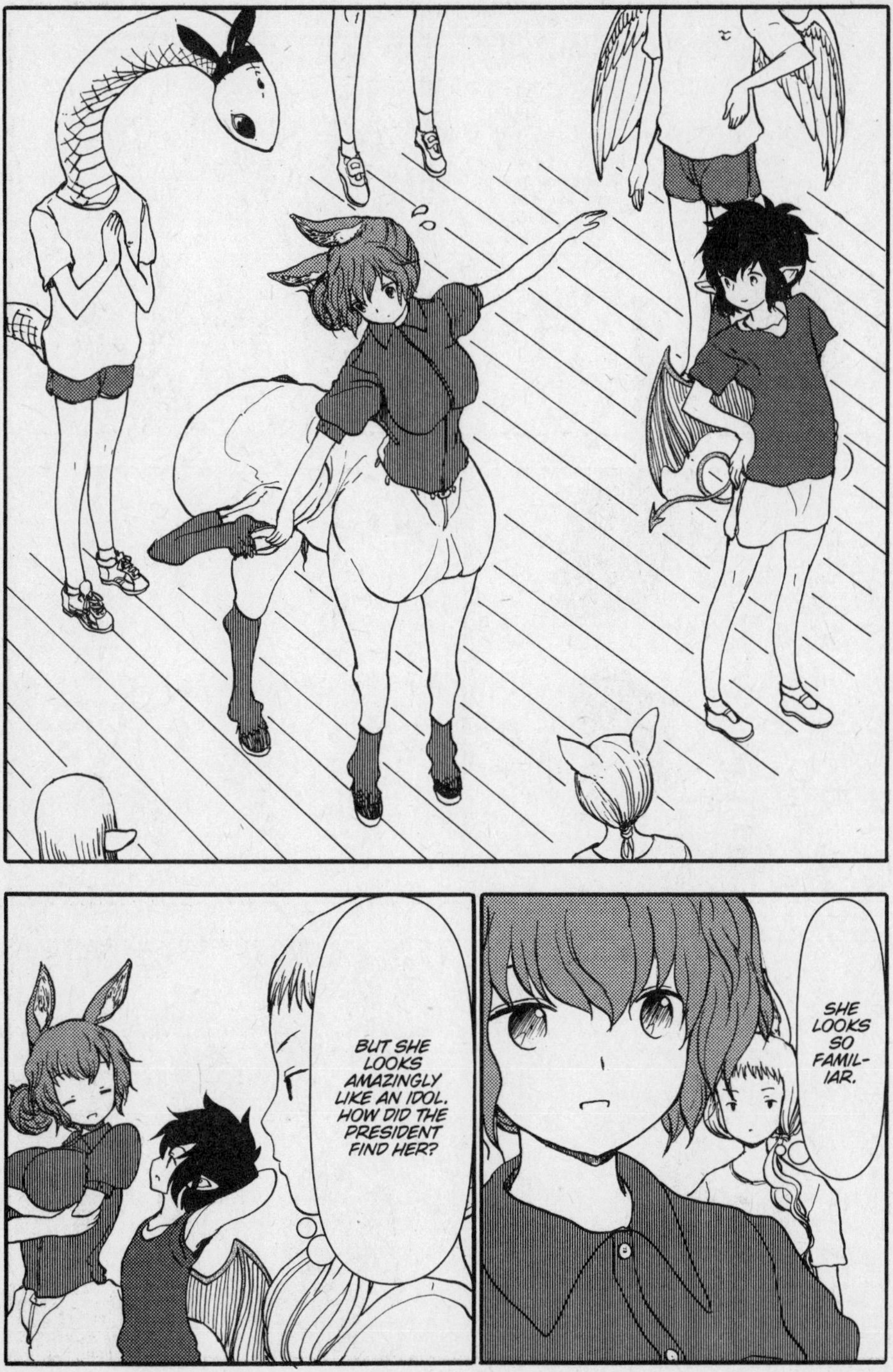
SHE LOOKS SO FAMIL-IAR.
BUT SHE LOOKS AMAZINGLY LIKE AN IDOL. HOW DID THE PRESIDENT FIND HER?

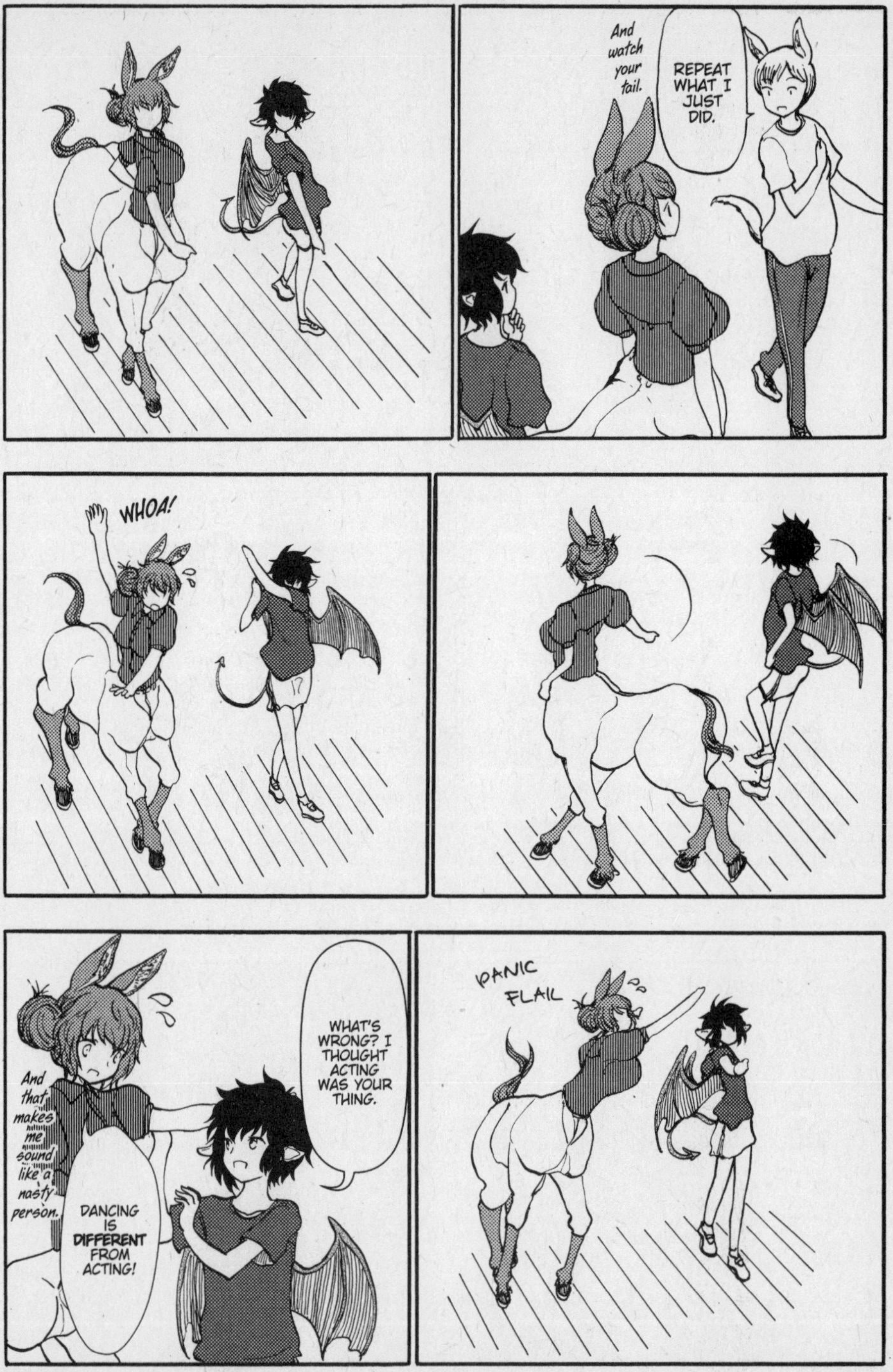
REPEAT WHAT I JUST DID.
And watch your tail.
WHOA!
PANIC
FLAIL
WHAT'S WRONG? I THOUGHT ACTING WAS YOUR THING.
DANCING IS **DIFFERENT** FROM ACTING!
And that makes me sound like a nasty person.

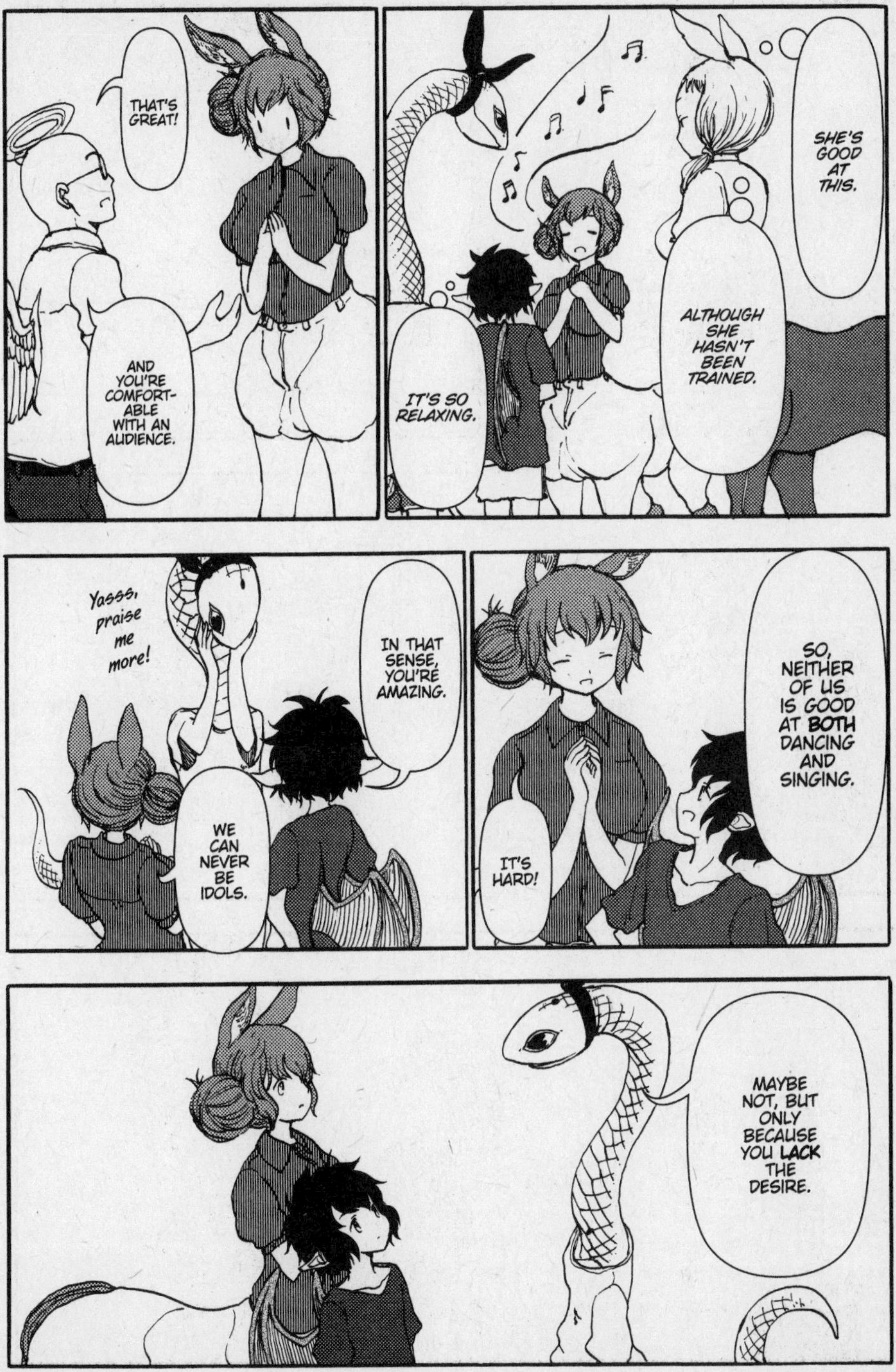
SHE'S GOOD AT THIS.
ALTHOUGH SHE HASN'T BEEN TRAINED.
IT'S SO RELAXING.
THAT'S GREAT!
AND YOU'RE COMFORTABLE WITH AN AUDIENCE.
SO, NEITHER OF US IS GOOD AT **BOTH** DANCING AND SINGING.
IT'S HARD!
IN THAT SENSE, YOU'RE AMAZING.
Yasss, praise me more!
WE CAN NEVER BE IDOLS.
MAYBE NOT, BUT ONLY BECAUSE YOU **LACK** THE DESIRE.

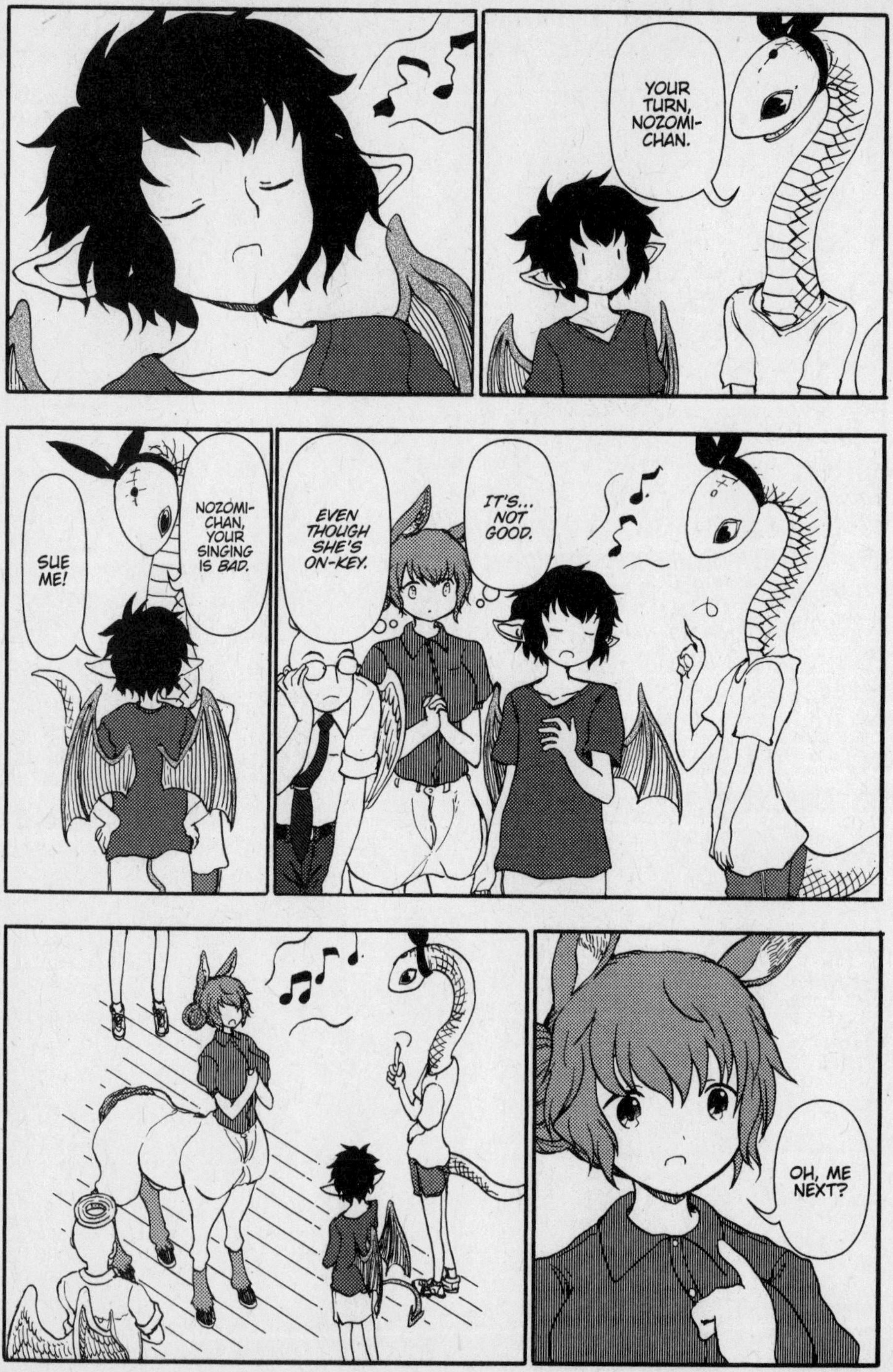
YOUR TURN, NOZOMI-CHAN.
IT'S... NOT GOOD.
EVEN THOUGH SHE'S ON-KEY.
NOZOMI-CHAN, YOUR SINGING IS *BAD*.
SUE ME!
OH, ME NEXT?

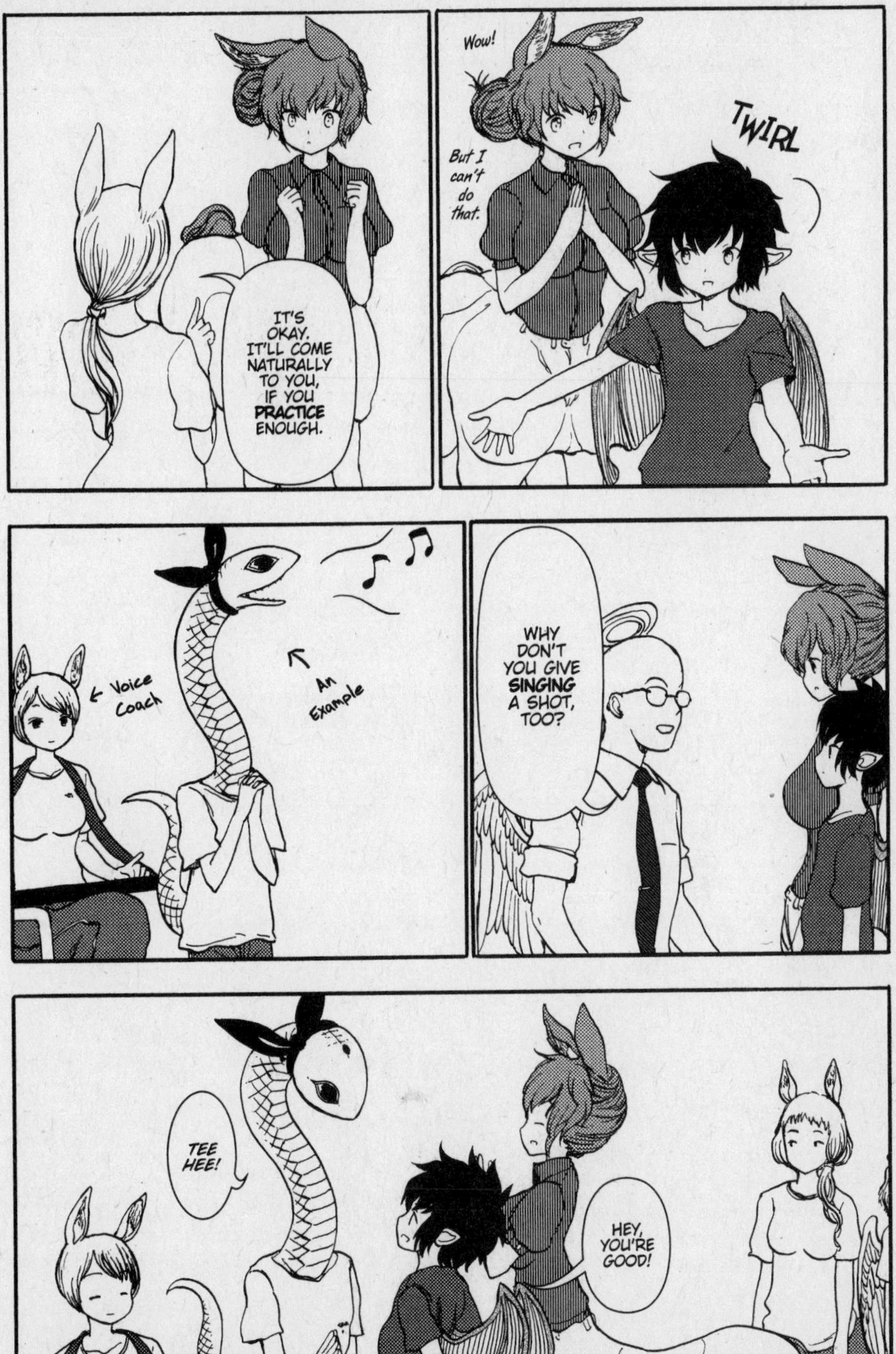
Wow!
But I can't do that.
TWIRL
IT'S OKAY. IT'LL COME NATURALLY TO YOU, IF YOU **PRACTICE** ENOUGH.
WHY DON'T YOU GIVE **SINGING** A SHOT, TOO?
← Voice Coach
An Example
HEY, YOU'RE GOOD!
TEE HEE!

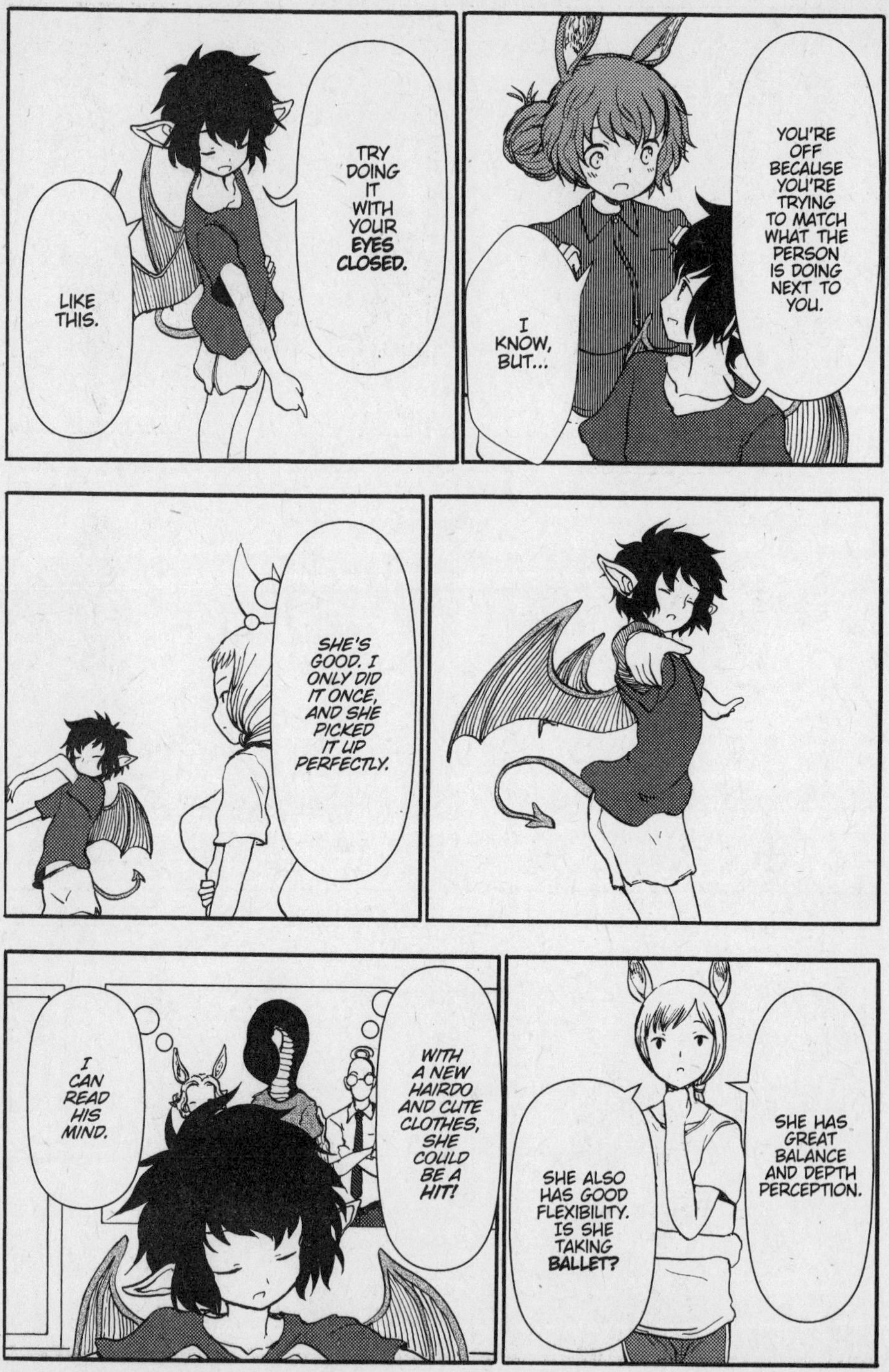
YOU'RE OFF BECAUSE YOU'RE TRYING TO MATCH WHAT THE PERSON IS DOING NEXT TO YOU.
I KNOW, BUT...
TRY DOING IT WITH YOUR EYES CLOSED.
LIKE THIS.
SHE'S GOOD. I ONLY DID IT ONCE, AND SHE PICKED IT UP PERFECTLY.
SHE HAS GREAT BALANCE AND DEPTH PERCEPTION.
SHE ALSO HAS GOOD FLEXIBILITY. IS SHE TAKING BALLET?
WITH A NEW HAIRDO AND CUTE CLOTHES, SHE COULD BE A HIT!
I CAN READ HIS MIND.

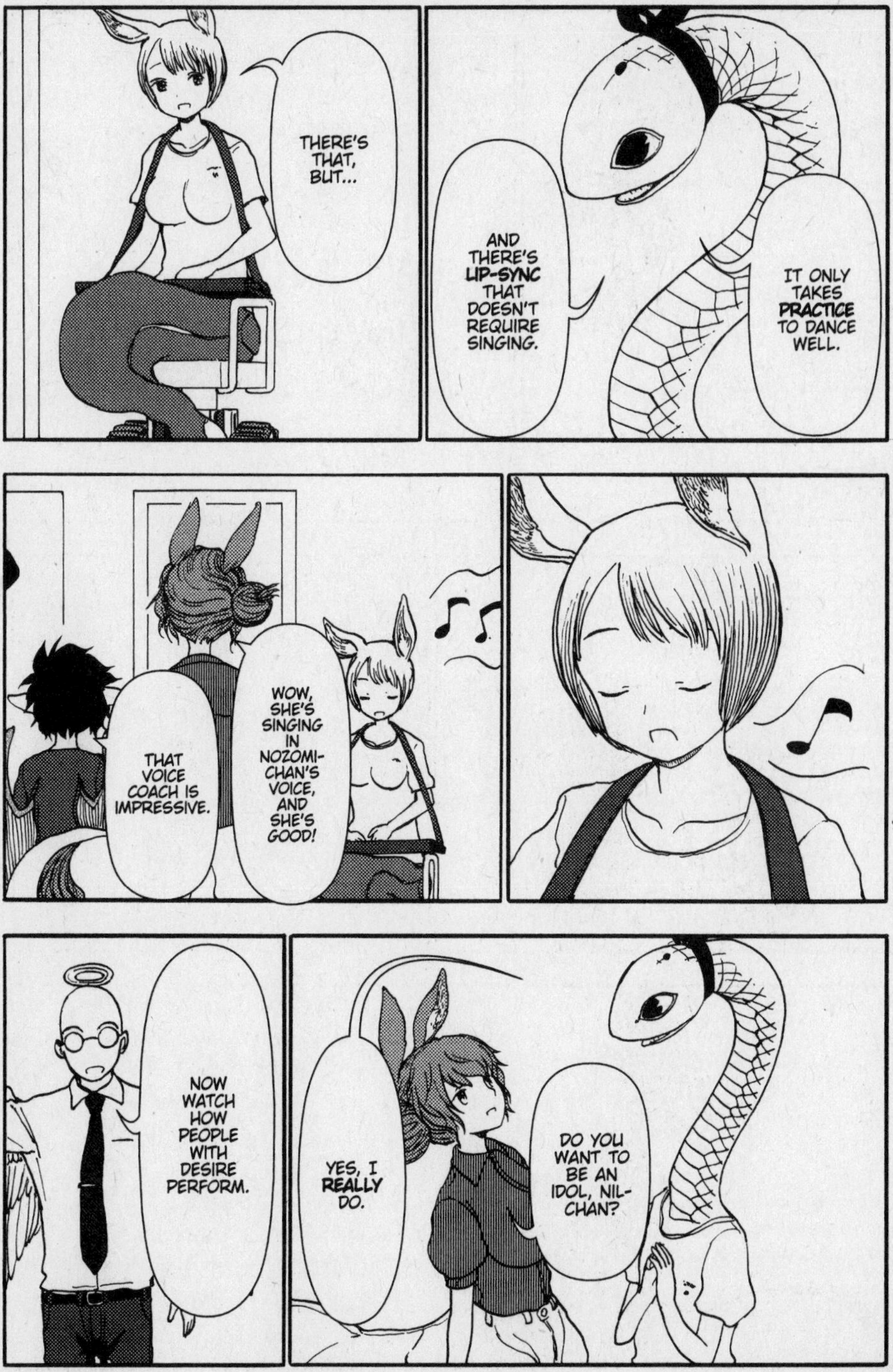
IT ONLY TAKES PRACTICE TO DANCE WELL.
AND THERE'S LIP-SYNC THAT DOESN'T REQUIRE SINGING.
THERE'S THAT, BUT...
WOW, SHE'S SINGING IN NOZOMI-CHAN'S VOICE, AND SHE'S GOOD!
THAT VOICE COACH IS IMPRESSIVE.
DO YOU WANT TO BE AN IDOL, NIL-CHAN?
YES, I REALLY DO.
NOW WATCH HOW PEOPLE WITH DESIRE PERFORM.

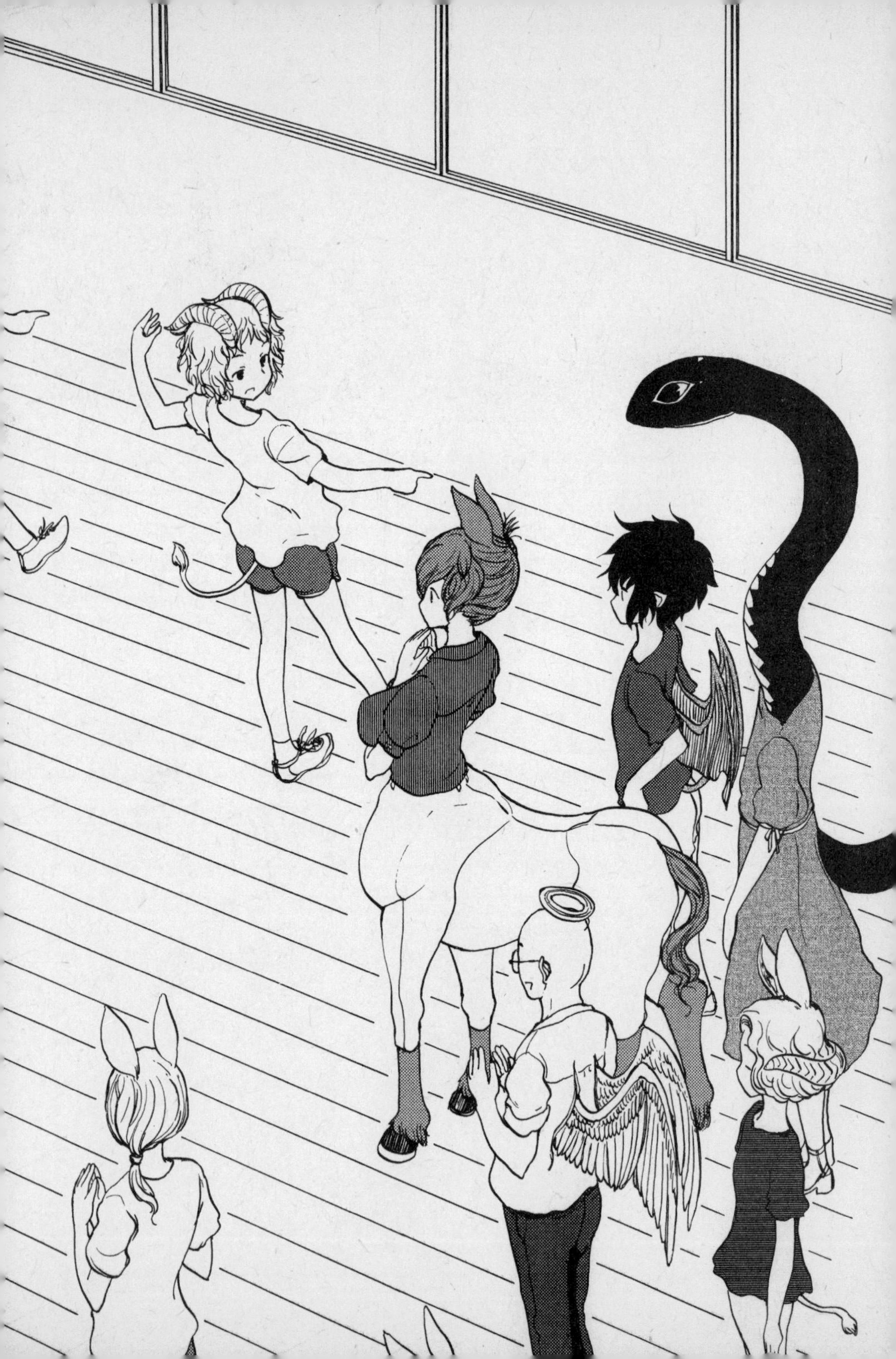

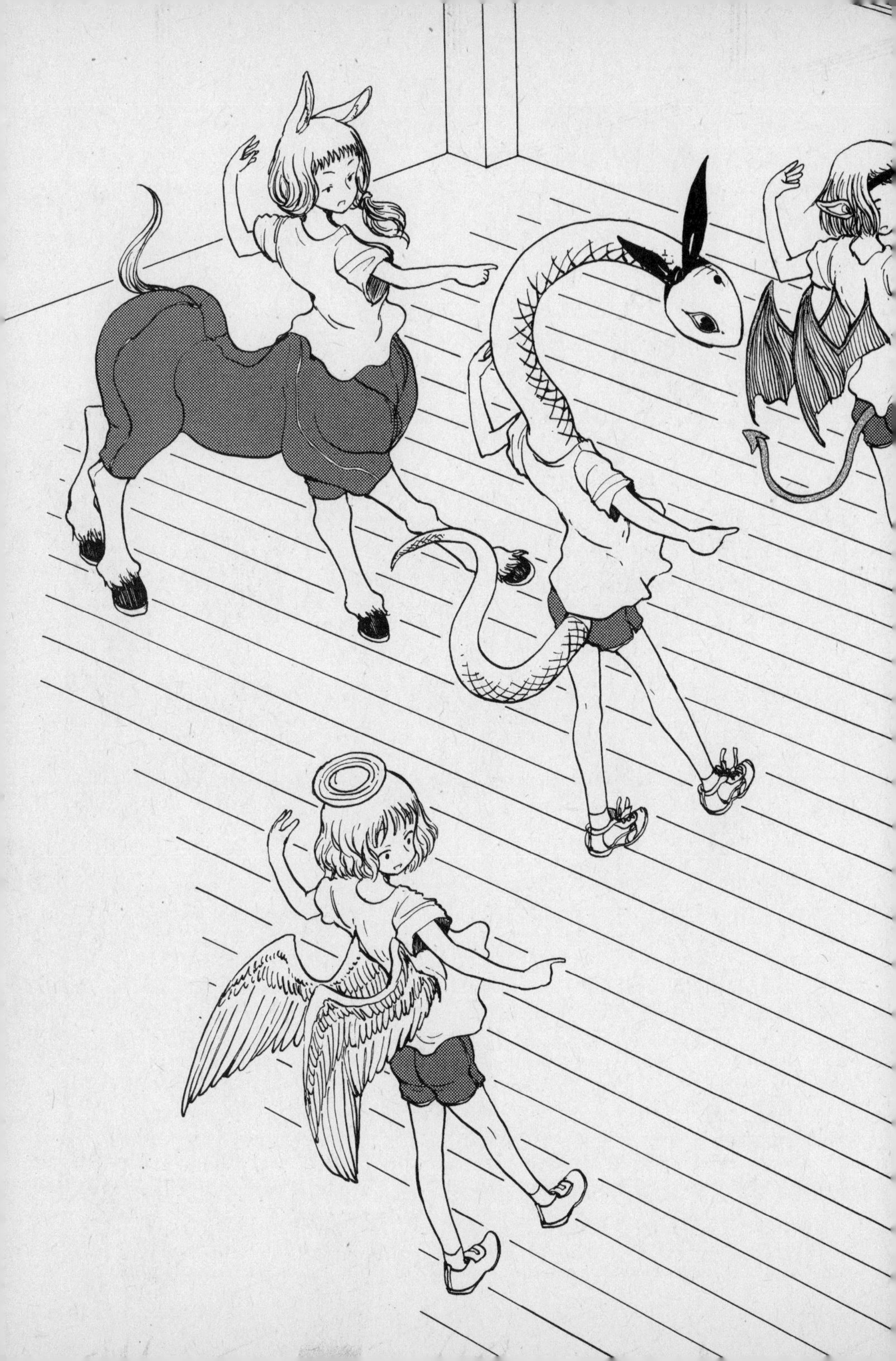

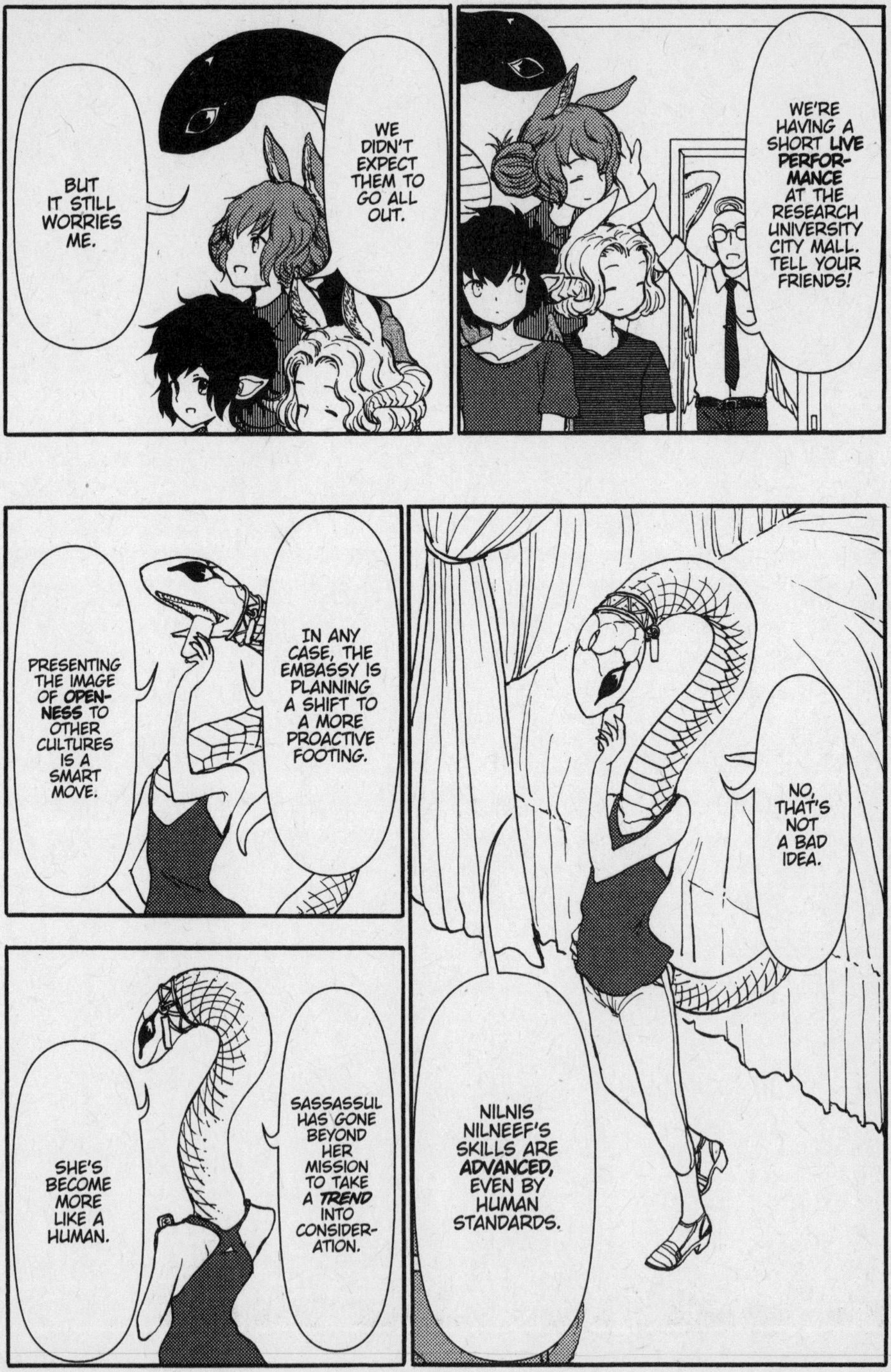
WE'RE HAVING A SHORT LIVE PERFORMANCE AT THE RESEARCH UNIVERSITY CITY MALL. TELL YOUR FRIENDS!
WE DIDN'T EXPECT THEM TO GO ALL OUT.
BUT IT STILL WORRIES ME.
NO, THAT'S NOT A BAD IDEA.
NILNIS NILNEEF'S SKILLS ARE ADVANCED, EVEN BY HUMAN STANDARDS.
IN ANY CASE, THE EMBASSY IS PLANNING A SHIFT TO A MORE PROACTIVE FOOTING.
PRESENTING THE IMAGE OF OPENNESS TO OTHER CULTURES IS A SMART MOVE.
SASSASSUL HAS GONE BEYOND HER MISSION TO TAKE A TREND INTO CONSIDERATION.
SHE'S BECOME MORE LIKE A HUMAN.

A Centaur's Life

UNDERSTANDING ANTARCTICANS: PART 5

THE ANTARCTICAN SOCIAL STRUCTURE SEEMS
TO SHARE EUSOCIAL TRAITS WITH CREATURES
LIKE ANTS AND BEES, SUCH AS THE COOPERATIVE
REARING OF YOUNG AND WHAT APPEARS TO BE AN
OVERWHELMINGLY FEMALE SOCIETY IN WHICH ONLY
THE QUEEN REPRODUCES. IT'S IMPORTANT TO NOTE,
HOWEVER, THAT ANTARCTICANS DO SEEM TO HAVE A
MUCH GREATER SENSE OF INDIVIDUAL IDENTITY THAN
IS EXHIBITED BY OTHER EUSOCIAL CREATURES. THOUGH
HUMANS MAY PERCEIVE THEIR SOCIETY AS RIGID AND
TOTALITARIAN, WE CANNOT DENY THAT MEMBERS OF
THE INTELLECTUAL SUBSPECIES HAVE DEMONSTRATED
THAT THEY THINK AS INDIVIDUALS AND OPERATE AT
THEIR OWN DISCRETION, EVEN GOING SO FAR AS TO
SHOW EMOTION, ALBEIT INFREQUENTLY. (OF COURSE,
ANTS AND BEES MAY ALSO HAVE THEIR OWN INDIVIDUAL
MINDS OR EMOTIONS, BUT WE HAVE NO WAY TO KNOW.)
GIVEN THAT ALL ANTARCTICANS THAT INTERACT WITH
HUMANS ARE IN DIPLOMATIC ROLES, WE CAN ASSUME
THAT THEY ARE PURSUING A UNIFIED PURPOSE FOR
THEIR GOVERNMENT; IT'S POSSIBLE THAT WE PERCEIVE
THEM AS TOTALITARIAN BECAUSE WE ONLY SEE ONE
FACET OF THEIR CIVILIZATION. THEY COULD BE JUST
AS INDIVIDUALISTIC AS HUMANS.

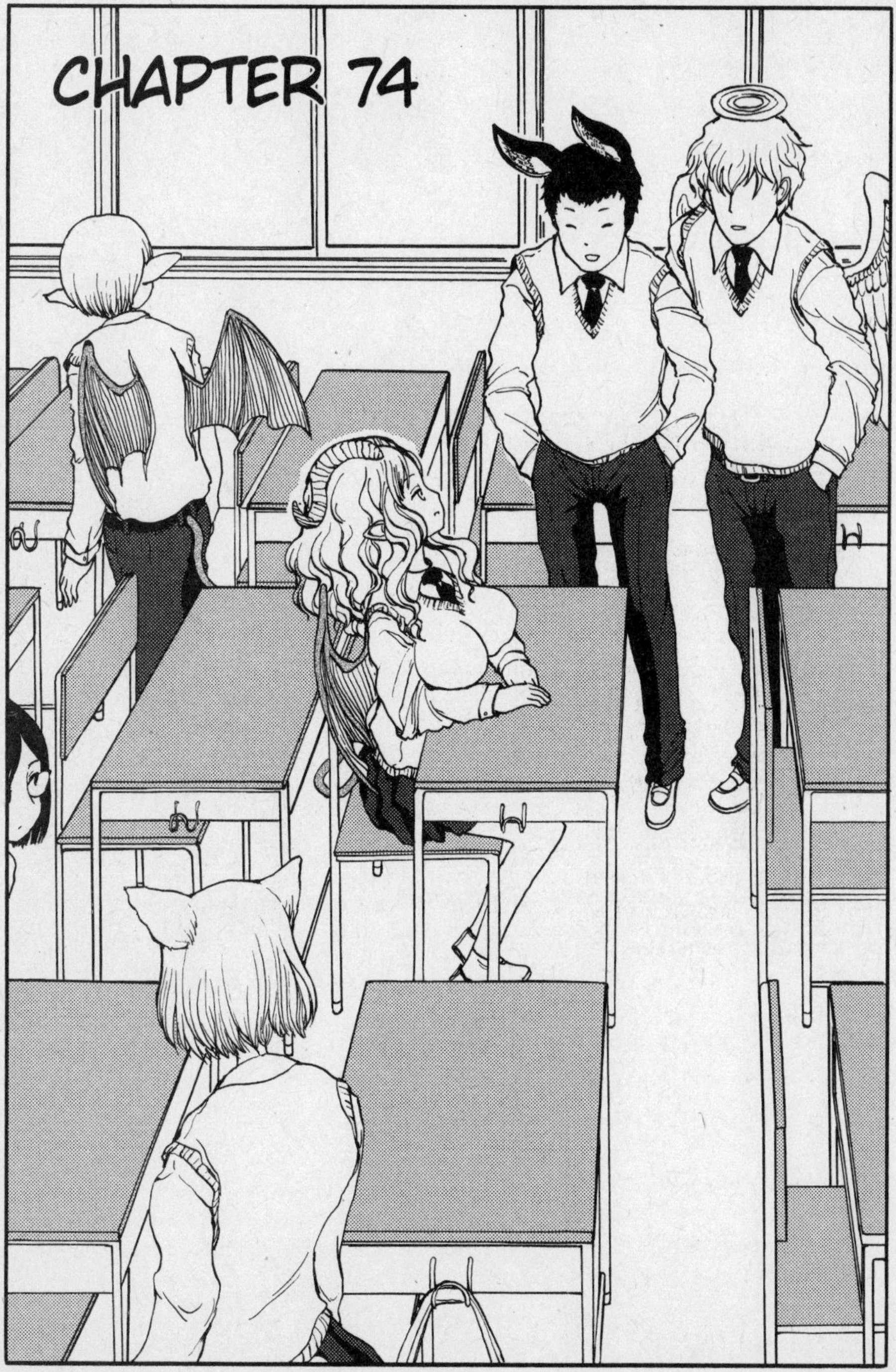
CHAPTER 74

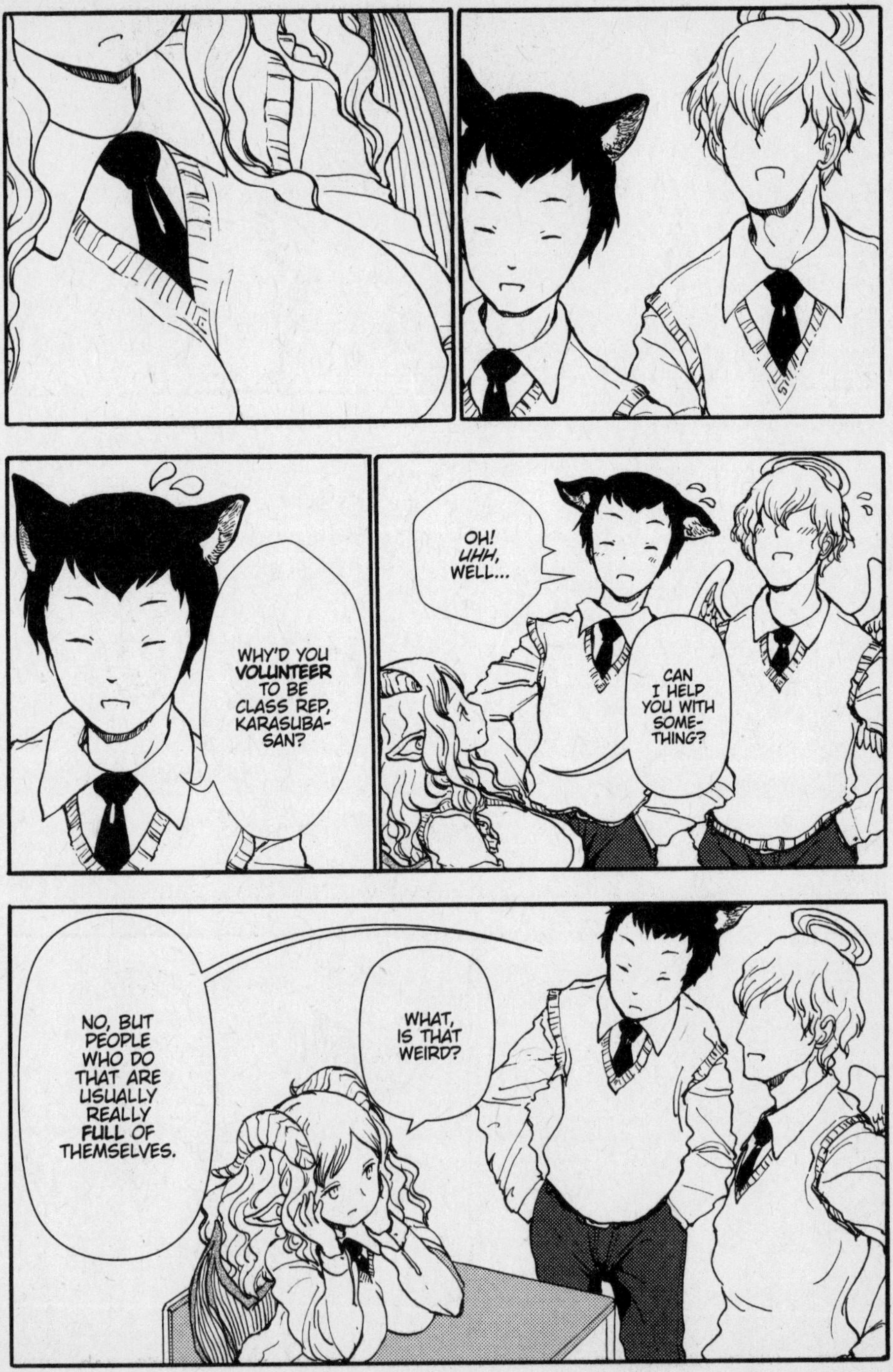
CAN I HELP YOU WITH SOME-THING?
OH! UHH, WELL...
WHY'D YOU **VOLUNTEER** TO BE CLASS REP, KARASUBA-SAN?
WHAT, IS THAT WEIRD?
NO, BUT PEOPLE WHO DO THAT ARE USUALLY REALLY **FULL** OF THEMSELVES.

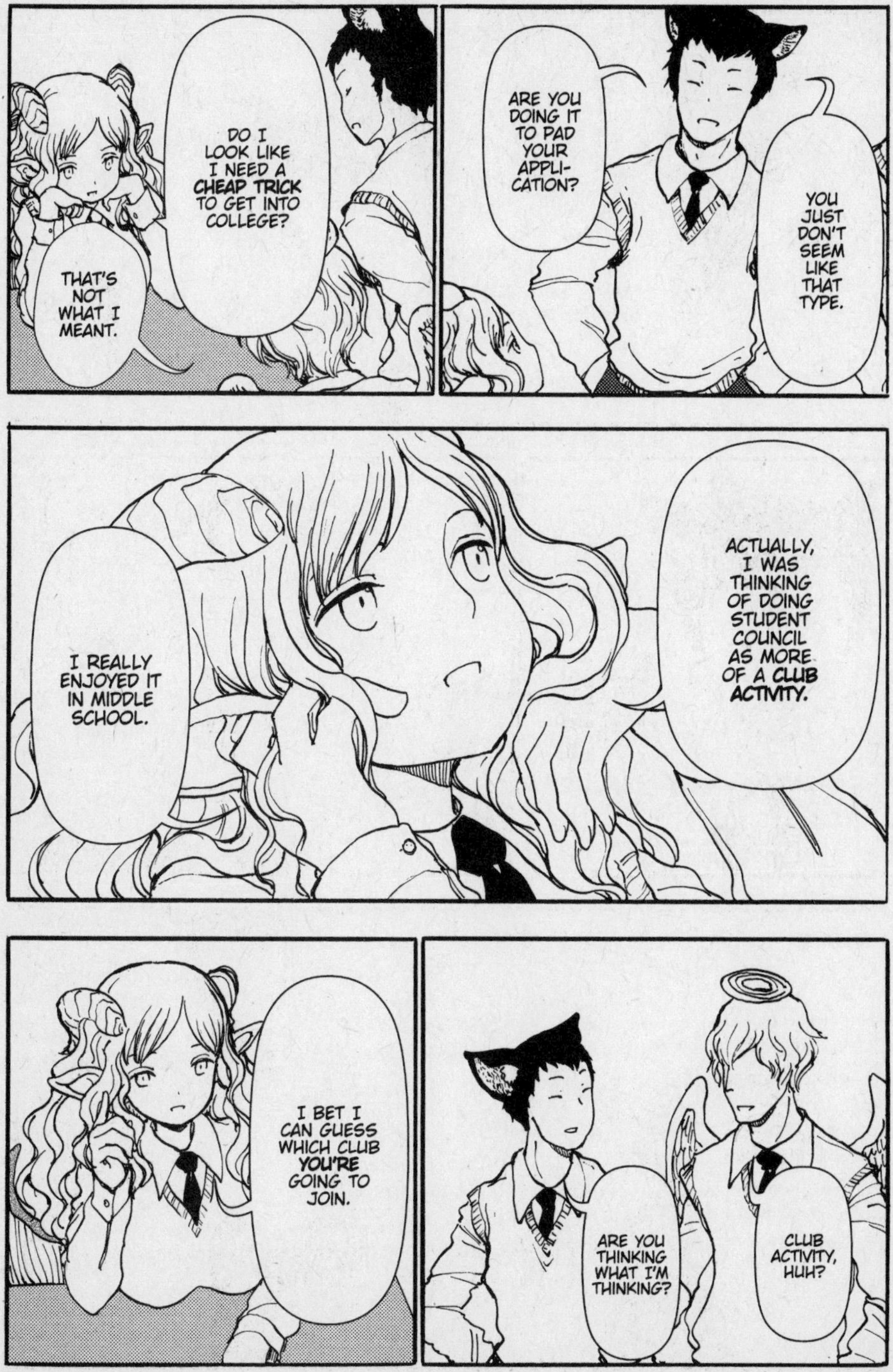
ARE YOU DOING IT TO PAD YOUR APPLICATION?
YOU JUST DON'T SEEM LIKE THAT TYPE.
DO I LOOK LIKE I NEED A **CHEAP TRICK** TO GET INTO COLLEGE?
THAT'S NOT WHAT I MEANT.
ACTUALLY, I WAS THINKING OF DOING STUDENT COUNCIL AS MORE OF A **CLUB ACTIVITY.**
I REALLY ENJOYED IT IN MIDDLE SCHOOL.
CLUB ACTIVITY, HUH?
ARE YOU THINKING WHAT I'M THINKING?
I BET I CAN GUESS WHICH CLUB **YOU'RE** GOING TO JOIN.

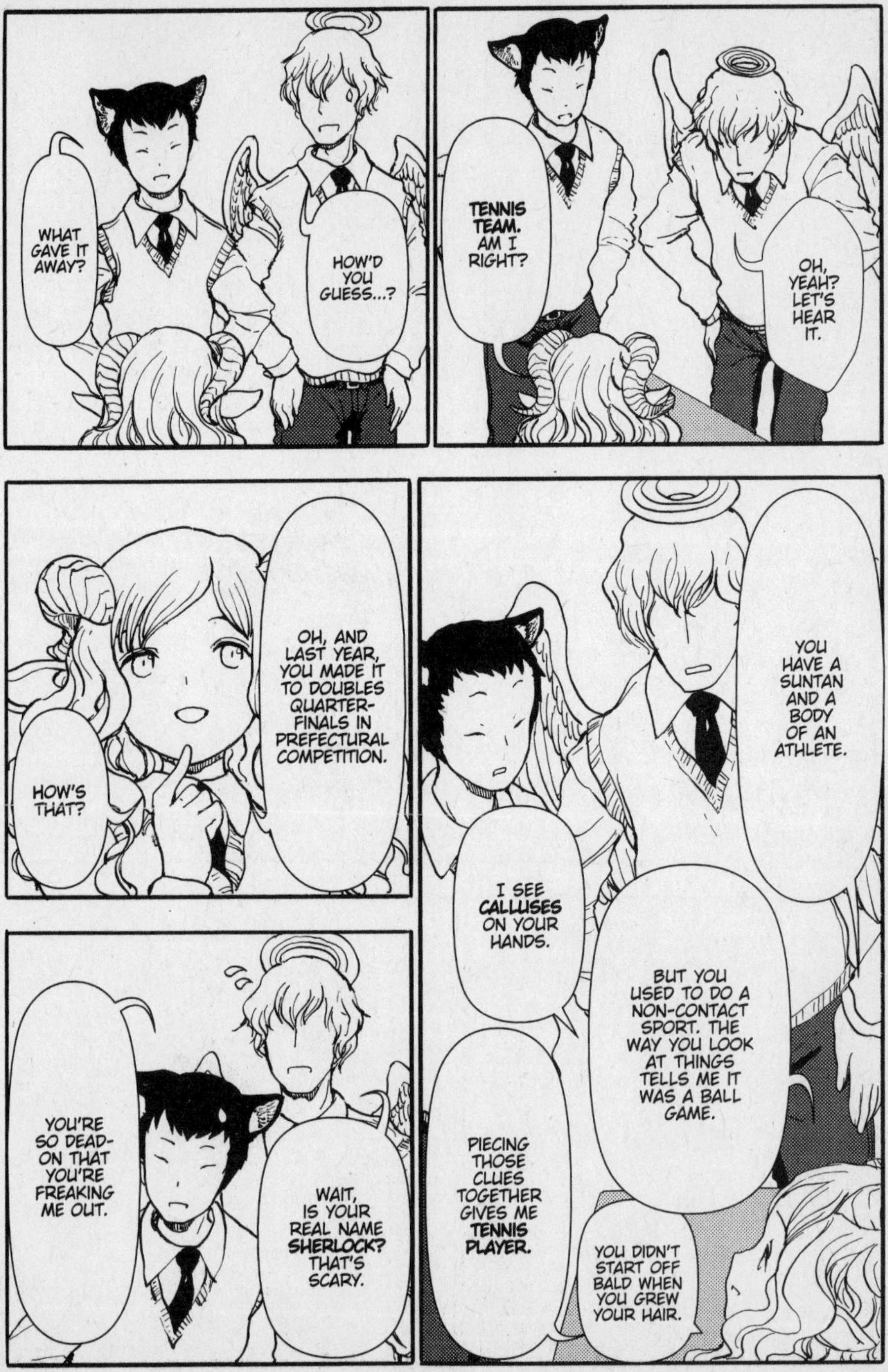
TENNIS TEAM. AM I RIGHT?
OH, YEAH? LET'S HEAR IT.
HOW'D YOU GUESS...?
WHAT GAVE IT AWAY?
YOU HAVE A SUNTAN AND A BODY OF AN ATHLETE.
I SEE CALLUSES ON YOUR HANDS.
BUT YOU USED TO DO A NON-CONTACT SPORT. THE WAY YOU LOOK AT THINGS TELLS ME IT WAS A BALL GAME.
PIECING THOSE CLUES TOGETHER GIVES ME TENNIS PLAYER.
YOU DIDN'T START OFF BALD WHEN YOU GREW YOUR HAIR.
OH, AND LAST YEAR, YOU MADE IT TO DOUBLES QUARTER-FINALS IN PREFECTURAL COMPETITION.
HOW'S THAT?
WAIT, IS YOUR REAL NAME SHERLOCK? THAT'S SCARY.
YOU'RE SO DEAD-ON THAT YOU'RE FREAKING ME OUT.

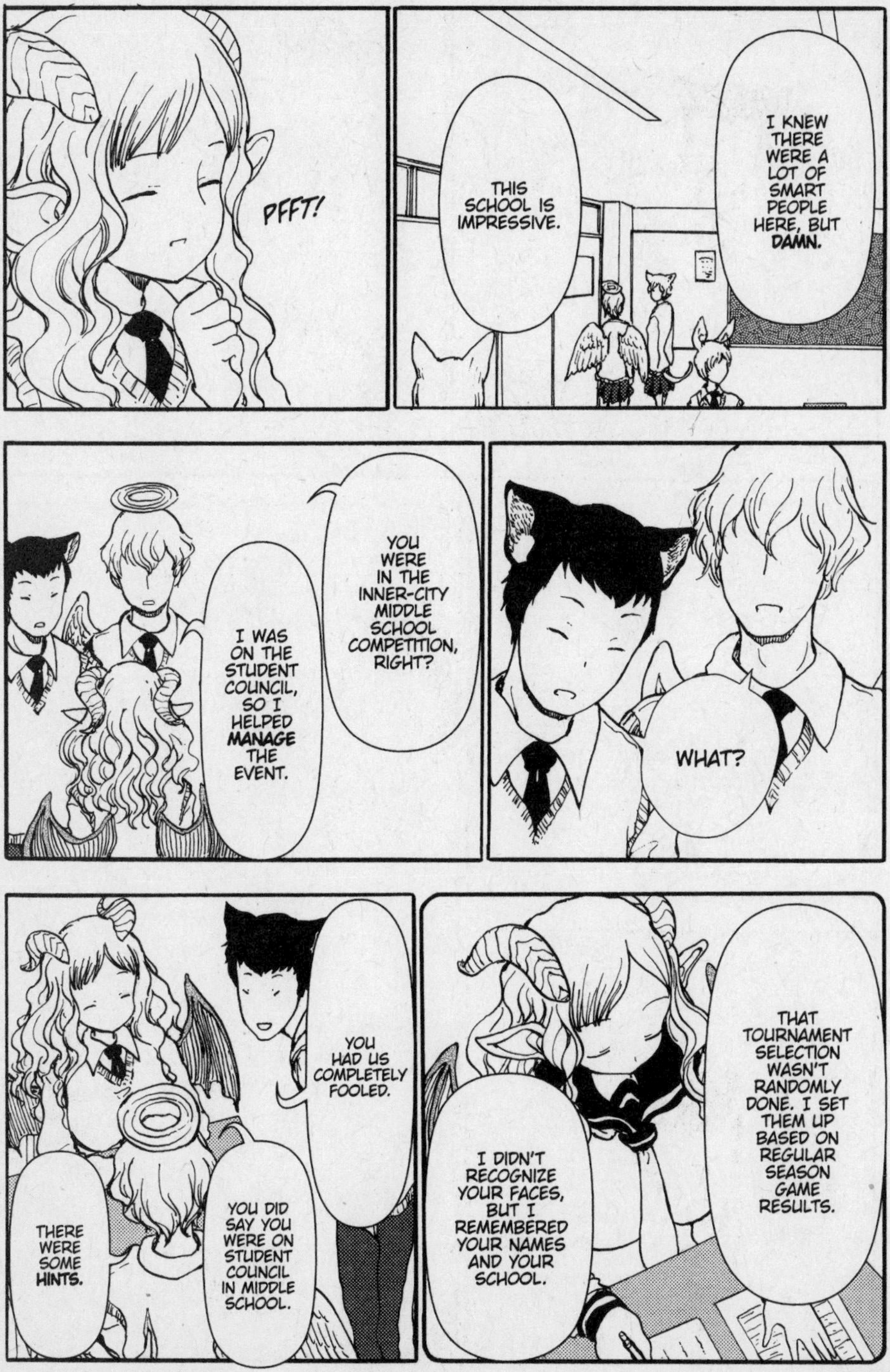
I KNEW THERE WERE A LOT OF SMART PEOPLE HERE, BUT DAMN.
THIS SCHOOL IS IMPRESSIVE.
PFFT!
WHAT?
YOU WERE IN THE INNER-CITY MIDDLE SCHOOL COMPETITION, RIGHT?
I WAS ON THE STUDENT COUNCIL, SO I HELPED MANAGE THE EVENT.
THAT TOURNAMENT SELECTION WASN'T RANDOMLY DONE. I SET THEM UP BASED ON REGULAR SEASON GAME RESULTS.
I DIDN'T RECOGNIZE YOUR FACES, BUT I REMEMBERED YOUR NAMES AND YOUR SCHOOL.
YOU HAD US COMPLETELY FOOLED.
YOU DID SAY YOU WERE ON STUDENT COUNCIL IN MIDDLE SCHOOL.
THERE WERE SOME HINTS.

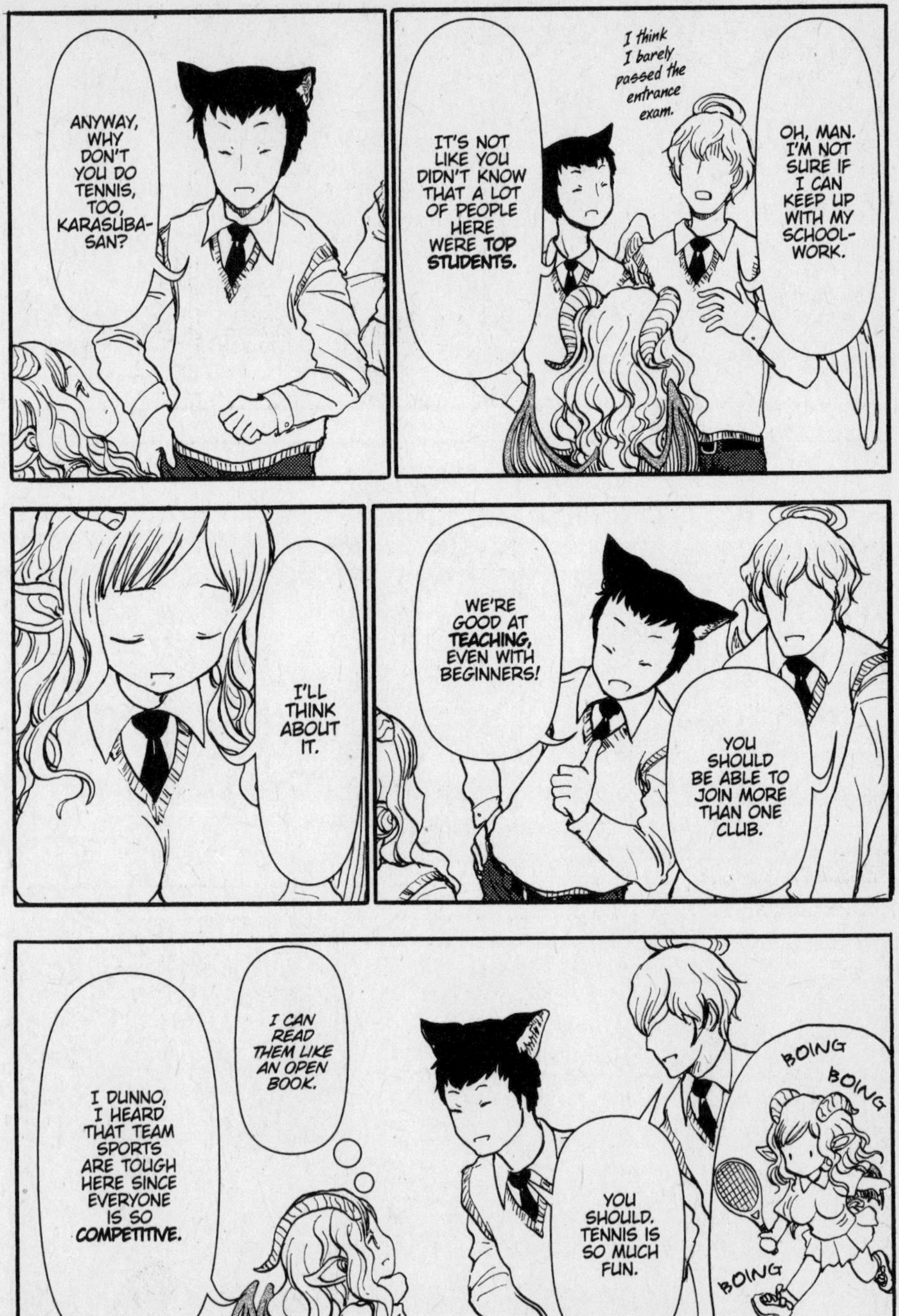

OH, MAN. I'M NOT SURE IF I CAN KEEP UP WITH MY SCHOOLWORK.
I think I barely passed the entrance exam.
IT'S NOT LIKE YOU DIDN'T KNOW THAT A LOT OF PEOPLE HERE WERE TOP STUDENTS.
ANYWAY, WHY DON'T YOU DO TENNIS, TOO, KARASUBA-SAN?
WE'RE GOOD AT TEACHING, EVEN WITH BEGINNERS!
YOU SHOULD BE ABLE TO JOIN MORE THAN ONE CLUB.
I'LL THINK ABOUT IT.
BOING
BOING
BOING
YOU SHOULD. TENNIS IS SO MUCH FUN.
I CAN READ THEM LIKE AN OPEN BOOK.
I DUNNO, I HEARD THAT TEAM SPORTS ARE TOUGH HERE SINCE EVERYONE IS SO COMPETITIVE.

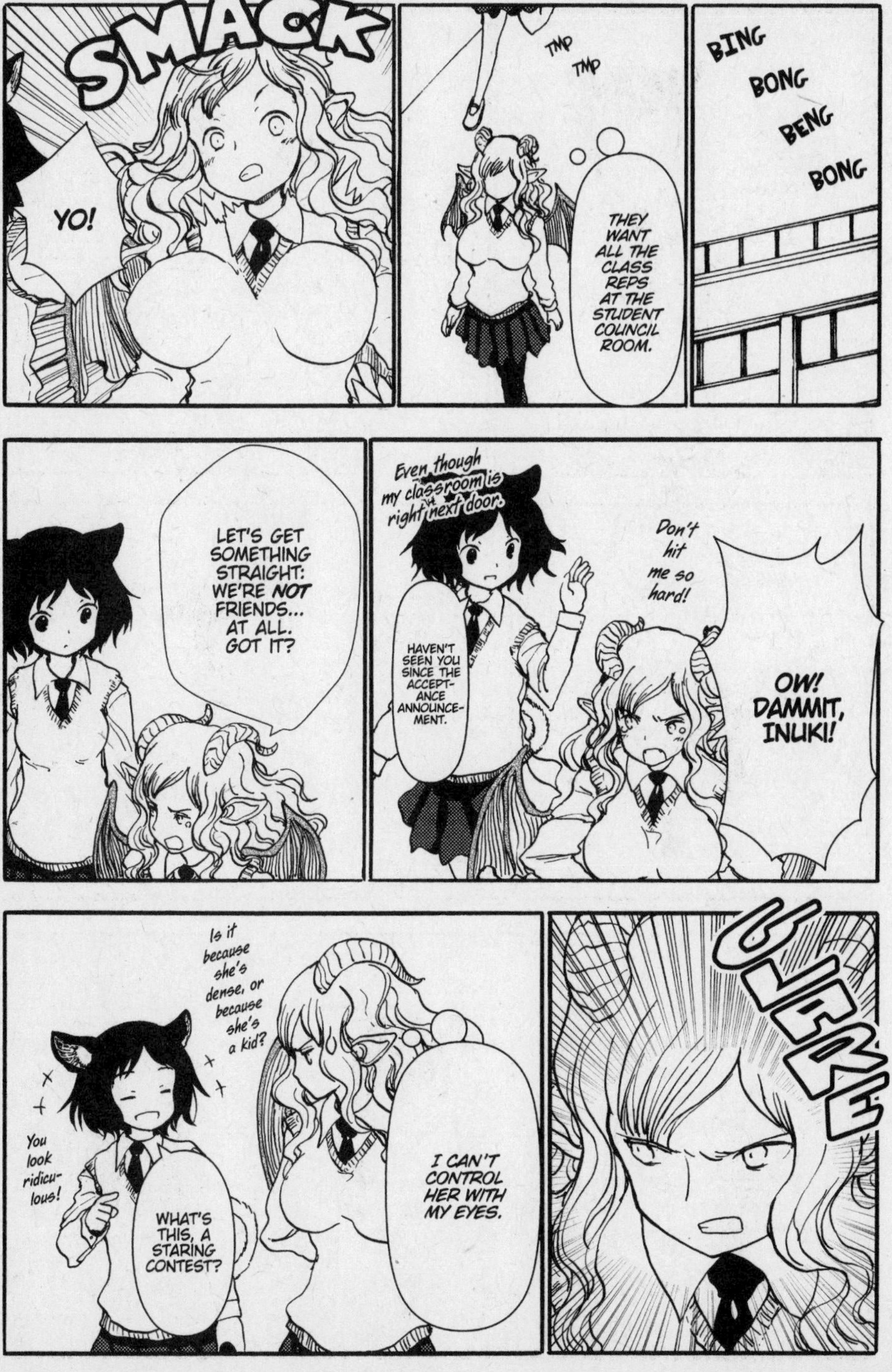
BING
BONG
BENG
BONG
TMP
TMP
THEY WANT ALL THE CLASS REPS AT THE STUDENT COUNCIL ROOM.
SMACK
YO!
OW! DAMMIT, INUKI!
Don't hit me so hard!
Even though my classroom is right next door.
HAVEN'T SEEN YOU SINCE THE ACCEPT-ANCE ANNOUNCE-MENT.
LET'S GET SOMETHING STRAIGHT: WE'RE *NOT* FRIENDS... AT ALL. GOT IT?
GLARE
I CAN'T CONTROL HER WITH MY EYES.
Is it because she's dense, or because she's a kid?
WHAT'S THIS, A STARING CONTEST?
You look ridicu-lous!

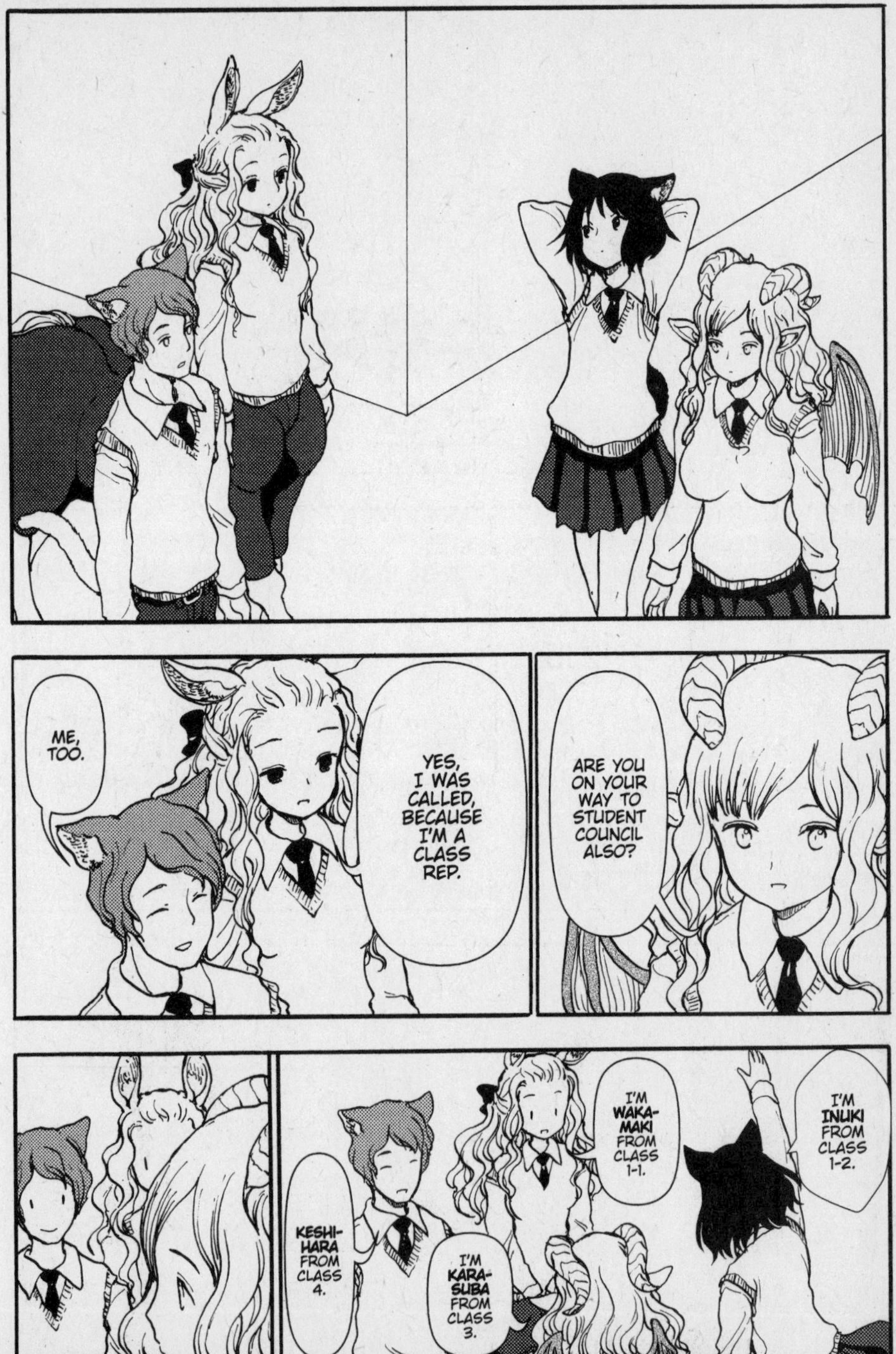
ARE YOU ON YOUR WAY TO STUDENT COUNCIL ALSO?
YES, I WAS CALLED, BECAUSE I'M A CLASS REP.
ME, TOO.
I'M **INUKI** FROM CLASS 1-2.
I'M **WAKA-MAKI** FROM CLASS 1-1.
I'M **KARA-SUBA** FROM CLASS 3.
KESHI-HARA FROM CLASS 4.

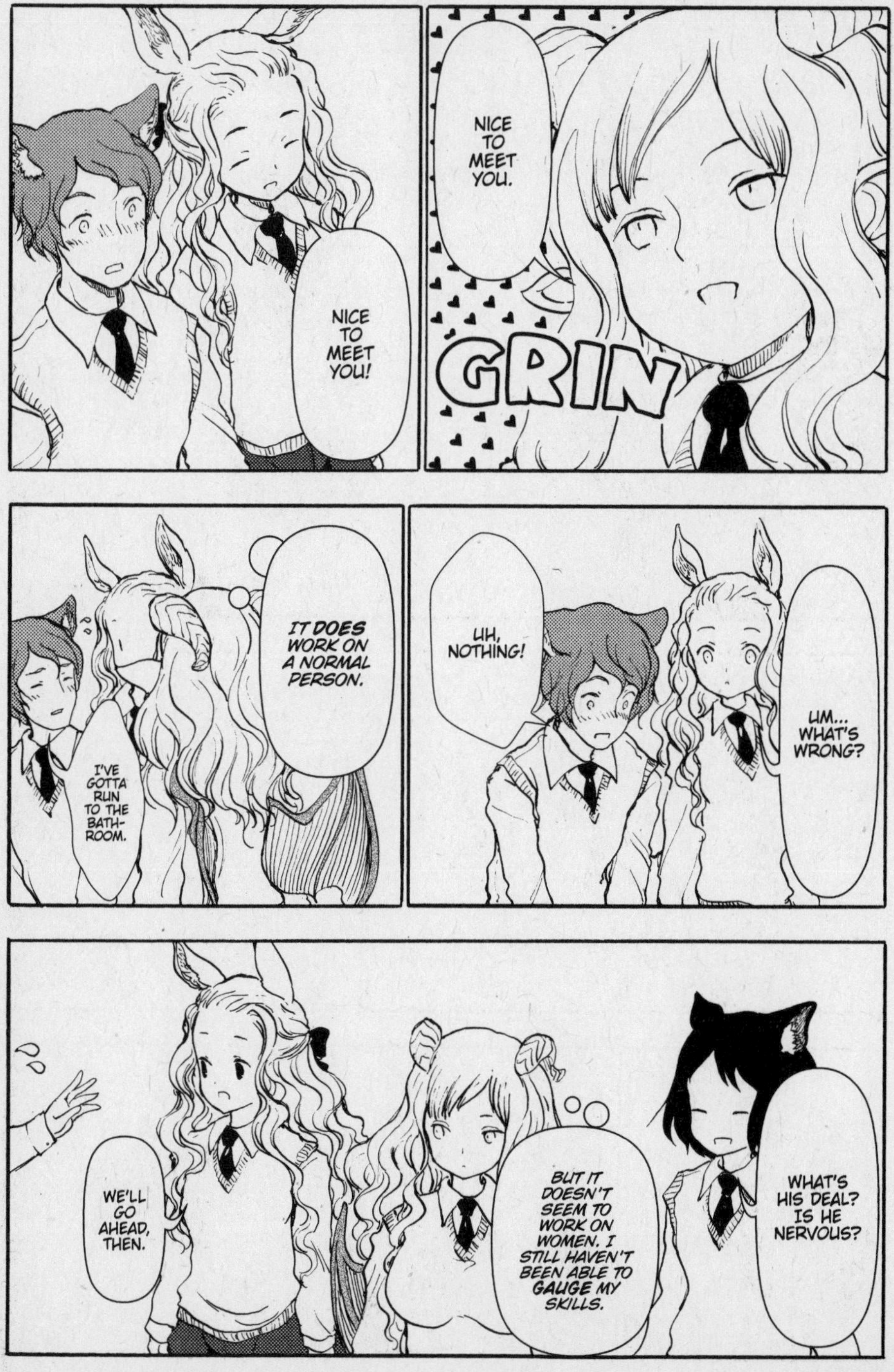
NICE TO MEET YOU.
GRIN
NICE TO MEET YOU!
UM... WHAT'S WRONG?
UH, NOTHING!
IT DOES WORK ON A NORMAL PERSON.
I'VE GOTTA RUN TO THE BATHROOM.
WHAT'S HIS DEAL? IS HE NERVOUS?
BUT IT DOESN'T SEEM TO WORK ON WOMEN. I STILL HAVEN'T BEEN ABLE TO GAUGE MY SKILLS.
WE'LL GO AHEAD, THEN.

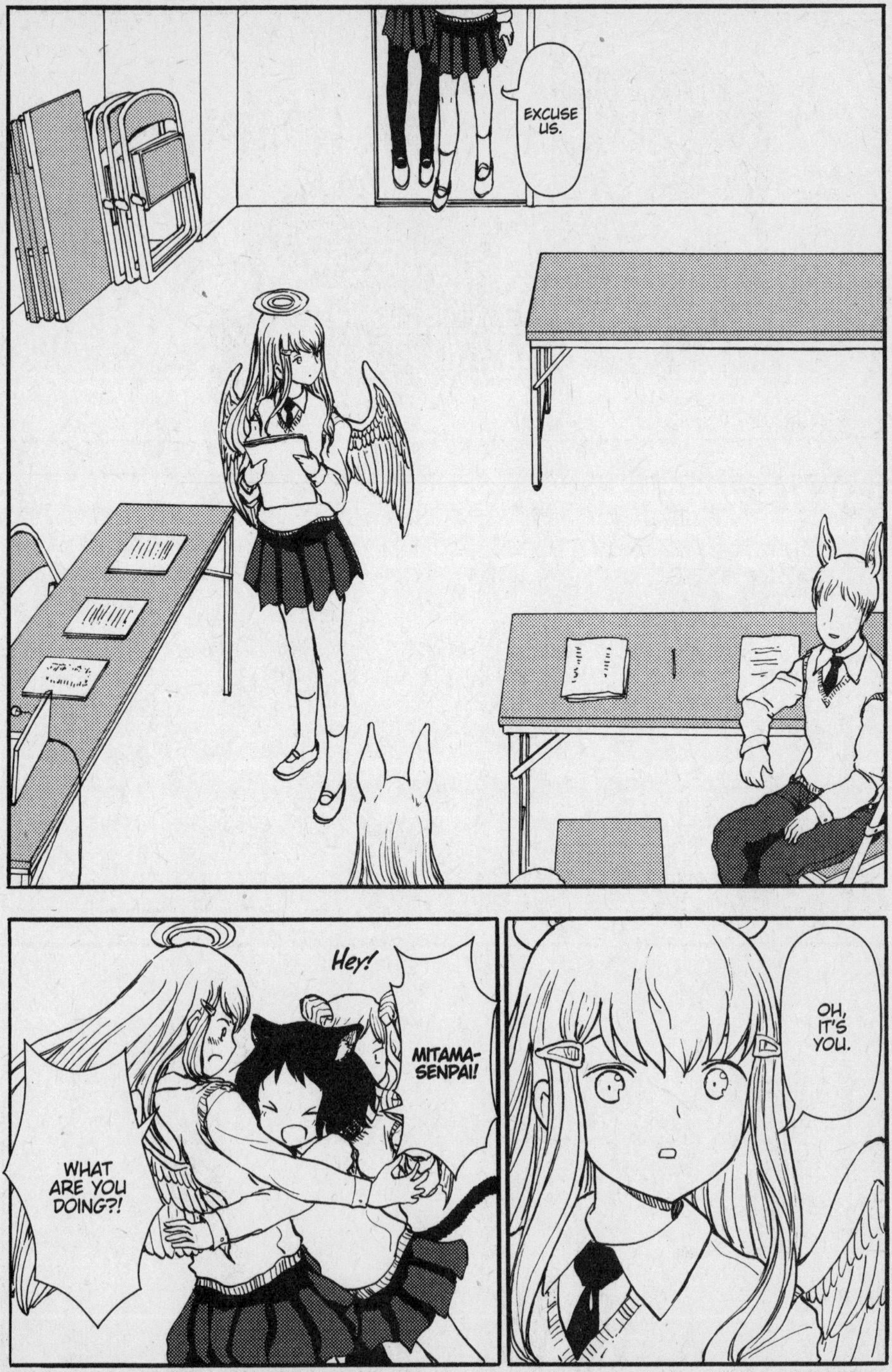
EXCUSE US.
OH, IT'S YOU.
Hey!
MITAMA-SENPAI!
WHAT ARE YOU DOING?!

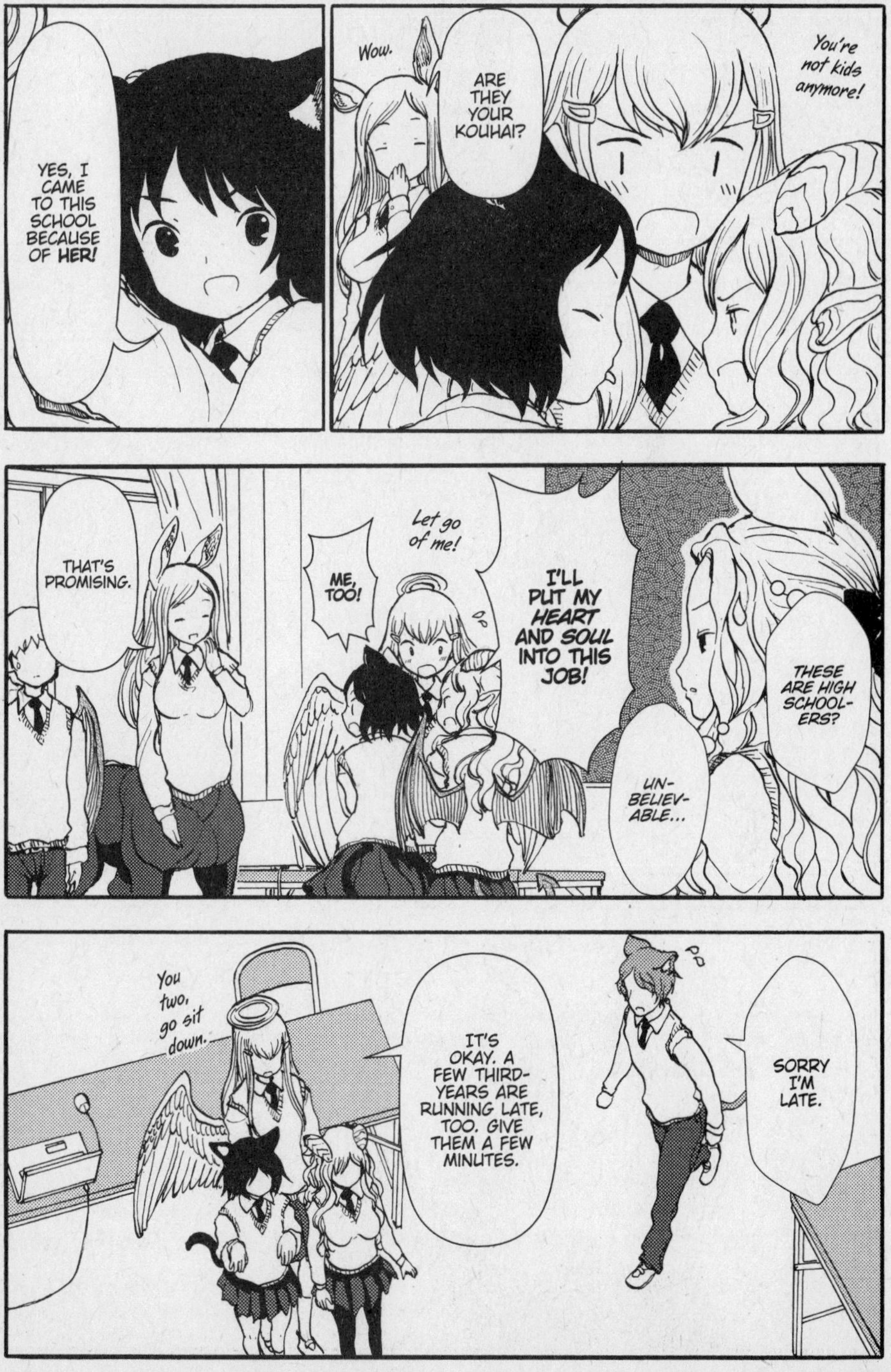
You're not kids anymore!
ARE THEY YOUR KOUHAI?
Wow.
YES, I CAME TO THIS SCHOOL BECAUSE OF HER!
THESE ARE HIGH SCHOOLERS?
UN-BELIEVABLE...
I'LL PUT MY HEART AND SOUL INTO THIS JOB!
Let go of me!
ME, TOO!
THAT'S PROMISING.
SORRY I'M LATE.
IT'S OKAY. A FEW THIRD-YEARS ARE RUNNING LATE, TOO. GIVE THEM A FEW MINUTES.
You two, go sit down.

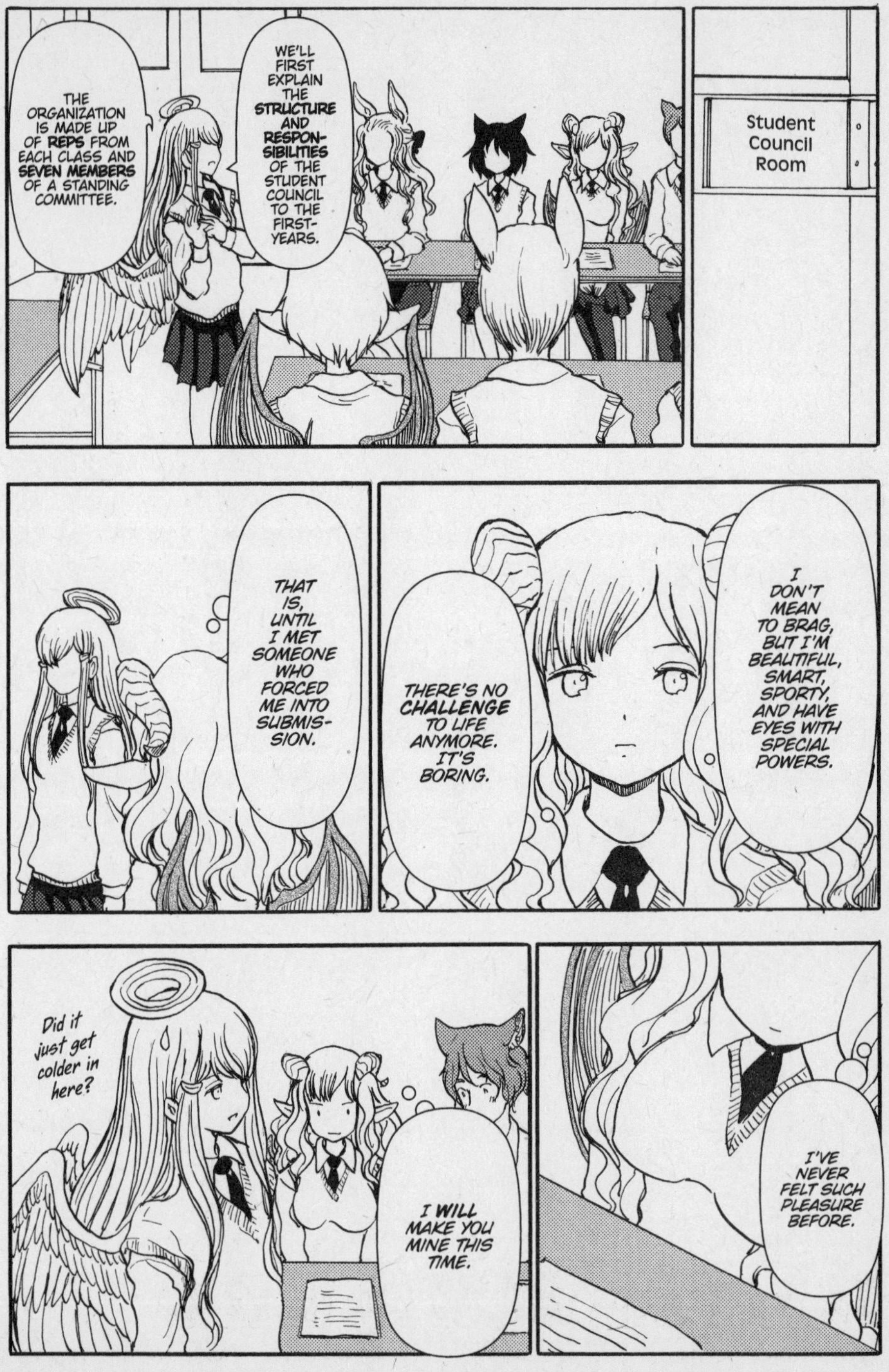
Student Council Room
WE'LL FIRST EXPLAIN THE STRUCTURE AND RESPONSIBILITIES OF THE STUDENT COUNCIL TO THE FIRST-YEARS.
THE ORGANIZATION IS MADE UP OF REPS FROM EACH CLASS AND SEVEN MEMBERS OF A STANDING COMMITTEE.
I DON'T MEAN TO BRAG, BUT I'M BEAUTIFUL, SMART, SPORTY, AND HAVE EYES WITH SPECIAL POWERS.
THERE'S NO CHALLENGE TO LIFE ANYMORE. IT'S BORING.
THAT IS, UNTIL I MET SOMEONE WHO FORCED ME INTO SUBMISSION.
I'VE NEVER FELT SUCH PLEASURE BEFORE.
I WILL MAKE YOU MINE THIS TIME.
Did it just get colder in here?

A Centaur's Life

UNDERSTANDING ANTARCTICANS: PART 6

AN CONTRAST TO THE INDIVIDUALITY
SHOWN BY THEIR COUNTERPARTS,
MEMBERS OF THE WARRIOR SUBSPECIES
SEEM FAR MORE COLLECTIVIST: THEY'VE
BEEN OBSERVED FOLLOWING ORDERS FROM
THE INTELLECTUAL SUBSPECIES; THEY NEVER
COMPLAIN OR DISOBEY; THEY SHOW NO VISIBLE
SIGNS OF EMOTION OR WILL. IT'S CLEAR,
HOWEVER, THAT THEY'RE NOT JUST ROBOTS—
EACH INDIVIDUAL MAKES HER OWN DECISIONS
ON HOW TO EXECUTE ORDERS AND CARRIES
OUT NONSPECIFIC TASKS USING HER OWN
AUTONOMOUS THOUGHT AND JUDGMENT.
THIS MAY LEAD SOME TO THINK OF THEM
AS SLAVES, BUT IT IS UNWISE TO APPLY
OUR IDEOLOGY TO OTHER CIVILIZATIONS.
WE LIVE IN AN ENLIGHTENED ERA THAT DOES
NOT PERMIT SUCH UNCIVILIZED BEHAVIOR
AS FORCING OTHER RACES TO CONFORM TO
OUR STANDARDS, AS WE DID IN CENTURIES PAST.
REGARDLESS, THE COMPARISON IS UNFAIR,
AS HUMAN SLAVES CLEARLY HAVE EMOTION
AND INTENTION WHERE THE ANTARCTICAN
WARRIOR SUBSPECIES HAS SHOWN NONE.

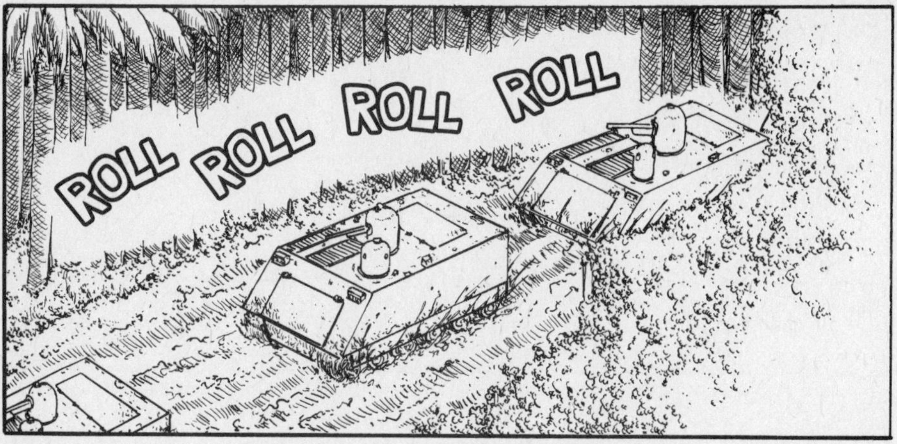
ROLL ROLL ROLL ROLL

CHAPTER 75

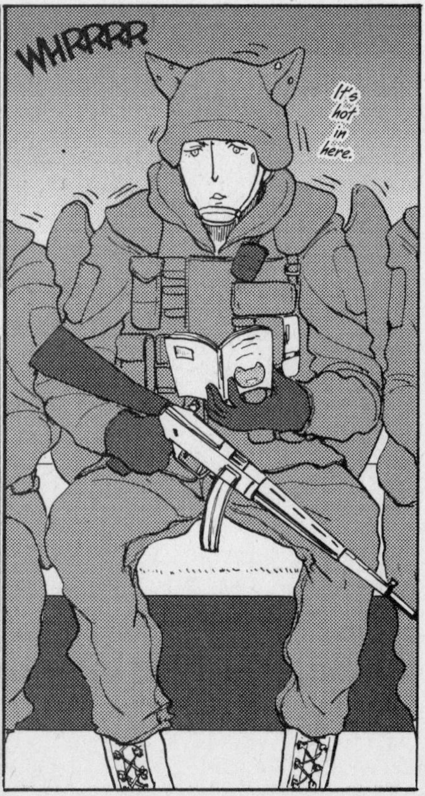
WHRRRR
It's hot in here.

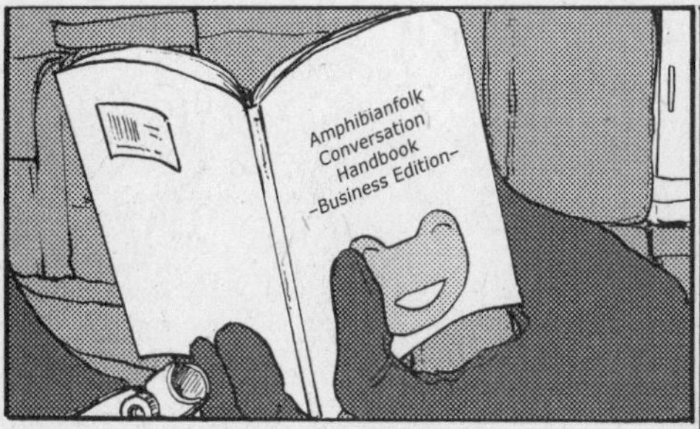
Amphibianfolk Conversation Handbook ~Business Edition~

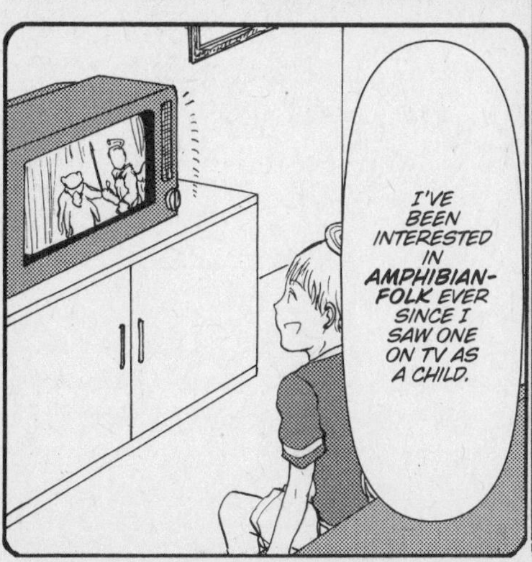
I'VE BEEN INTERESTED IN AMPHIBIAN-FOLK EVER SINCE I SAW ONE ON TV AS A CHILD.

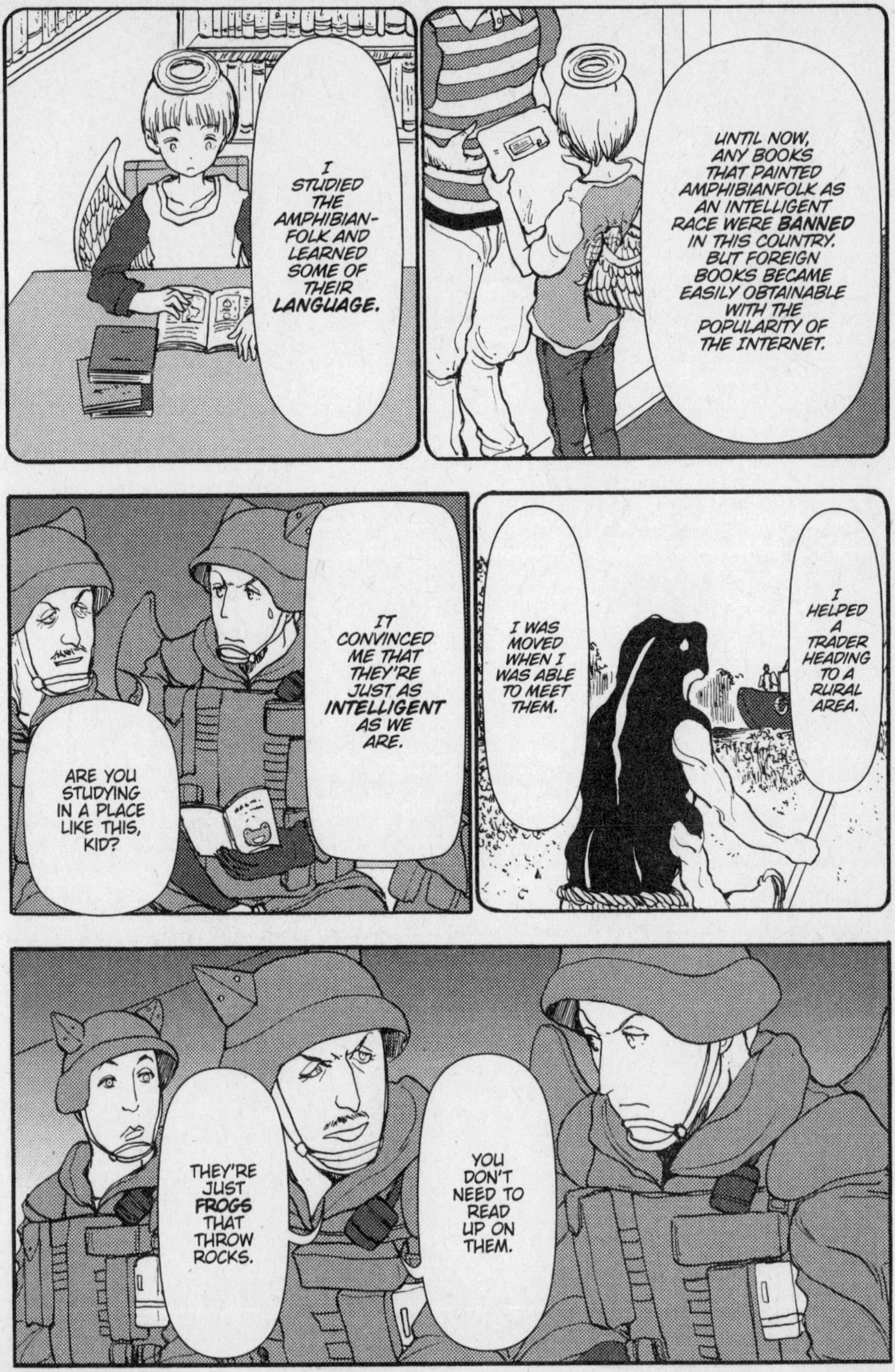
UNTIL NOW, ANY BOOKS THAT PAINTED AMPHIBIANFOLK AS AN INTELLIGENT RACE WERE **BANNED** IN THIS COUNTRY. BUT FOREIGN BOOKS BECAME EASILY OBTAINABLE WITH THE POPULARITY OF THE INTERNET.
I STUDIED THE AMPHIBIAN-FOLK AND LEARNED SOME OF THEIR **LANGUAGE.**
I HELPED A TRADER HEADING TO A RURAL AREA.
I WAS MOVED WHEN I WAS ABLE TO MEET THEM.
IT CONVINCED ME THAT THEY'RE JUST AS **INTELLIGENT** AS WE ARE.
ARE YOU STUDYING IN A PLACE LIKE THIS, KID?
YOU DON'T NEED TO READ UP ON THEM.
THEY'RE JUST **FROGS** THAT THROW ROCKS.

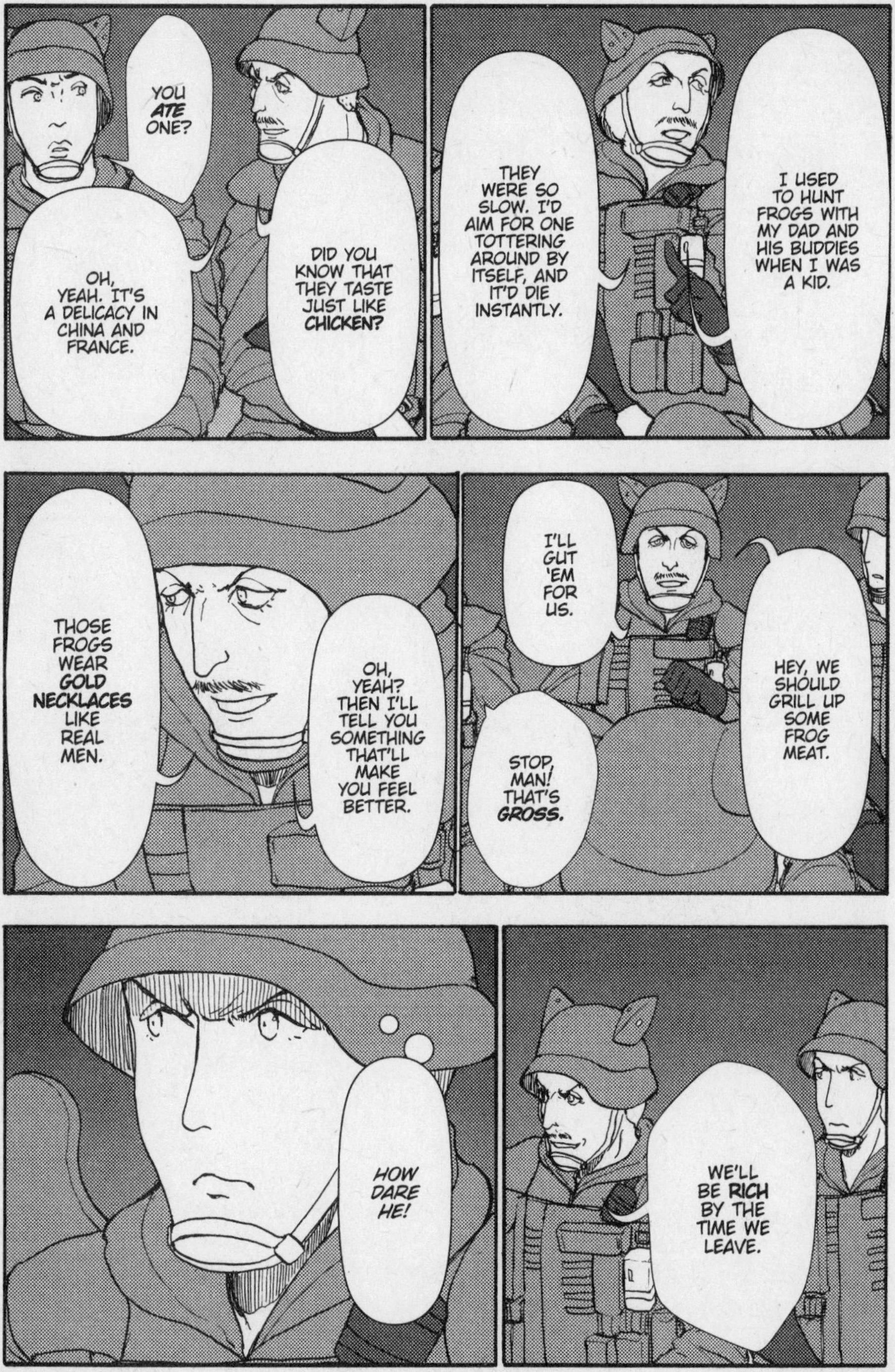
I USED TO HUNT FROGS WITH MY DAD AND HIS BUDDIES WHEN I WAS A KID.
THEY WERE SO SLOW. I'D AIM FOR ONE TOTTERING AROUND BY ITSELF, AND IT'D DIE INSTANTLY.
YOU **ATE** ONE?
DID YOU KNOW THAT THEY TASTE JUST LIKE **CHICKEN?**
OH, YEAH. IT'S A DELICACY IN CHINA AND FRANCE.
HEY, WE SHOULD GRILL UP SOME FROG MEAT.
I'LL GUT 'EM FOR US.
STOP, MAN! THAT'S ***GROSS.***
OH, YEAH? THEN I'LL TELL YOU SOMETHING THAT'LL MAKE YOU FEEL BETTER.
THOSE FROGS WEAR **GOLD NECKLACES** LIKE REAL MEN.
WE'LL BE **RICH** BY THE TIME WE LEAVE.
HOW DARE HE!

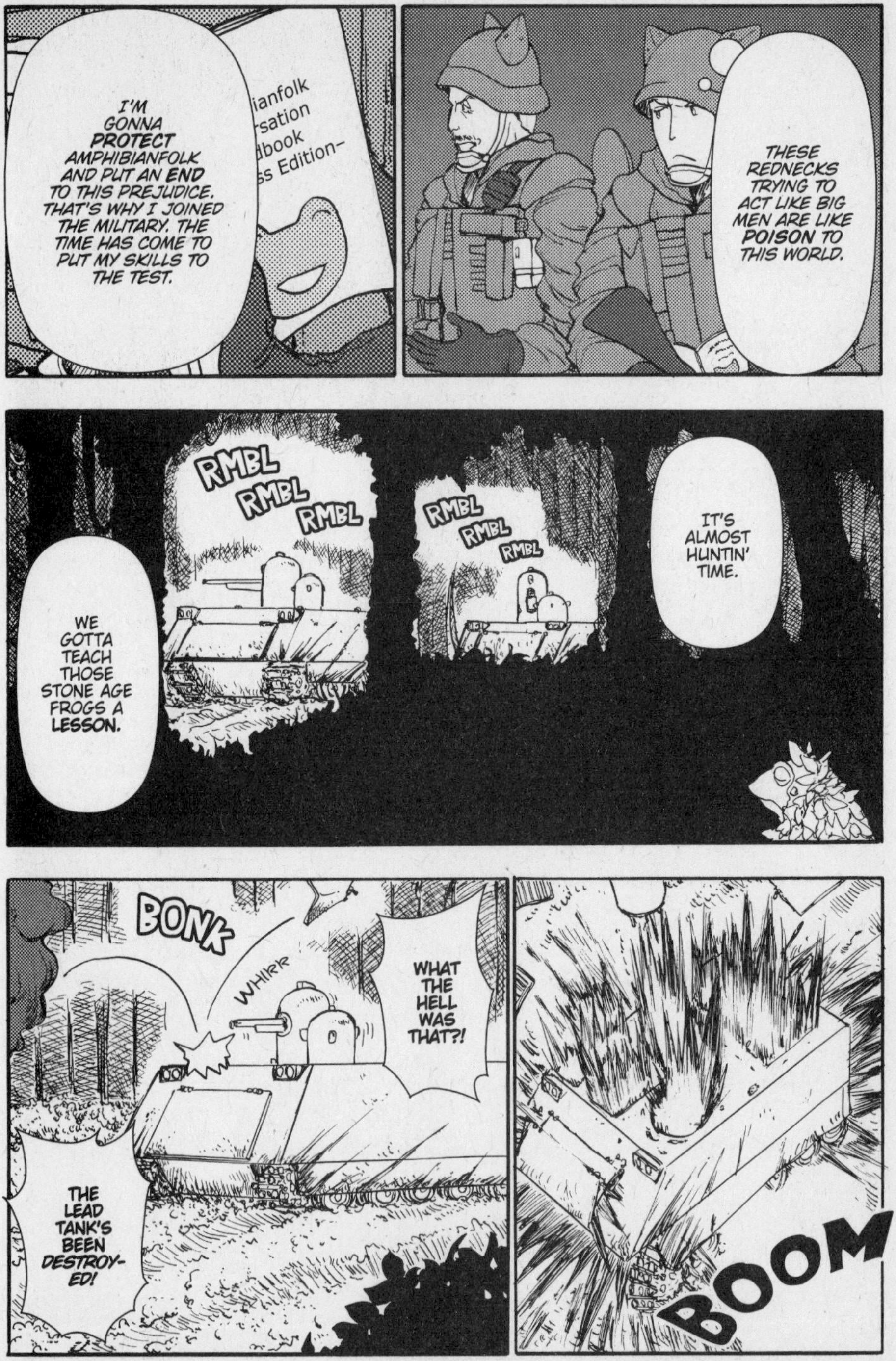
THESE REDNECKS TRYING TO ACT LIKE BIG MEN ARE LIKE POISON TO THIS WORLD.
I'M GONNA PROTECT AMPHIBIANFOLK AND PUT AN END TO THIS PREJUDICE. THAT'S WHY I JOINED THE MILITARY. THE TIME HAS COME TO PUT MY SKILLS TO THE TEST.
IT'S ALMOST HUNTIN' TIME.
RMBL RMBL RMBL
RMBL RMBL RMBL
WE GOTTA TEACH THOSE STONE AGE FROGS A LESSON.
BOOM
BONK
WHIRR
WHAT THE HELL WAS THAT?!
THE LEAD TANK'S BEEN DESTROYED!

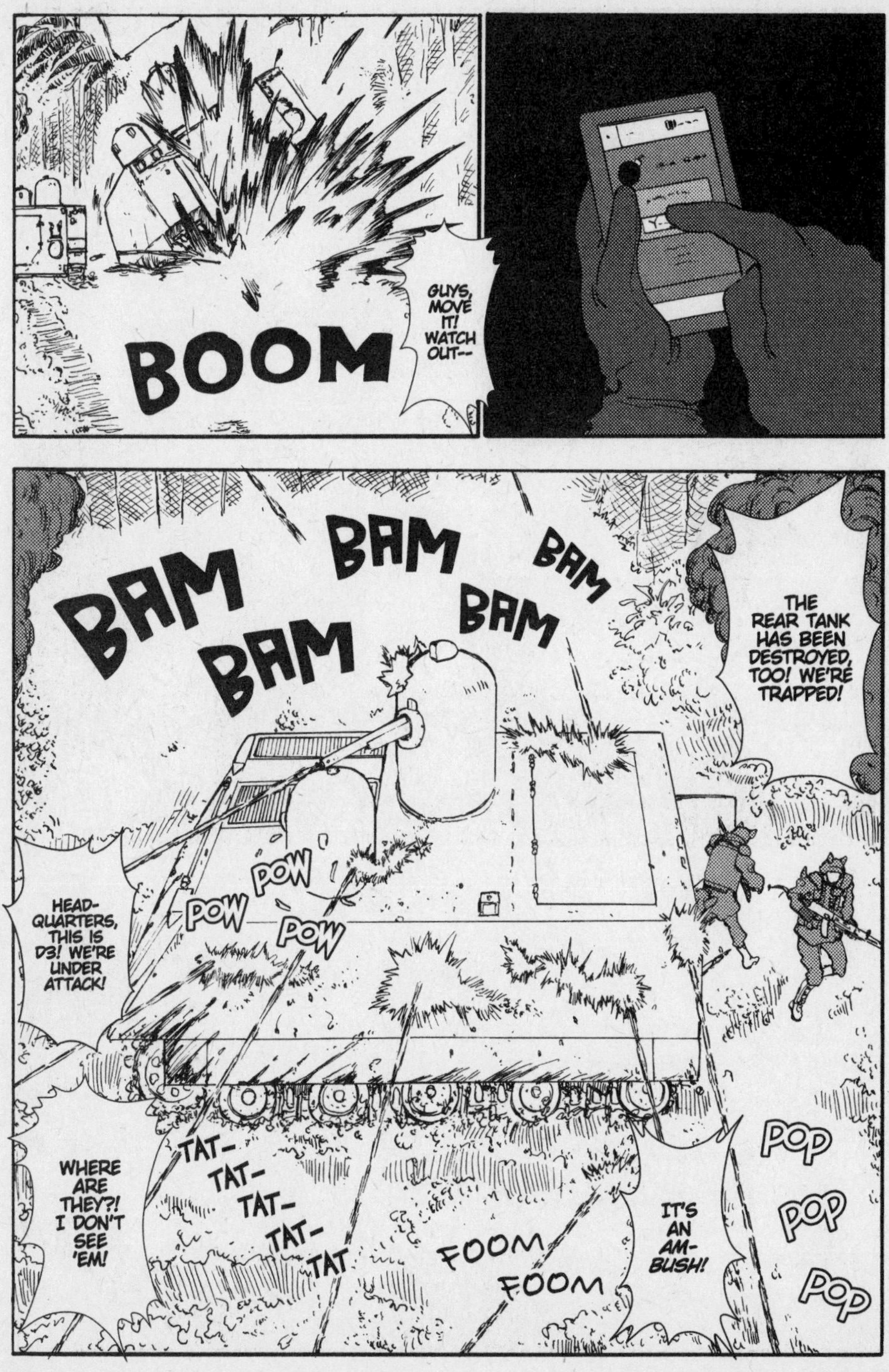
GUYS, MOVE IT! WATCH OUT--
BOOM
THE REAR TANK HAS BEEN DESTROYED, TOO! WE'RE TRAPPED!
BAM
BAM
BAM BAM
BAM
HEAD-QUARTERS, THIS IS D3! WE'RE UNDER ATTACK!
POW
POW
POW
POP
POP
POP
IT'S AN AM-BUSH!
FOOM
FOOM
TAT-TAT-TAT-TAT-TAT
WHERE ARE THEY?! I DON'T SEE 'EM!

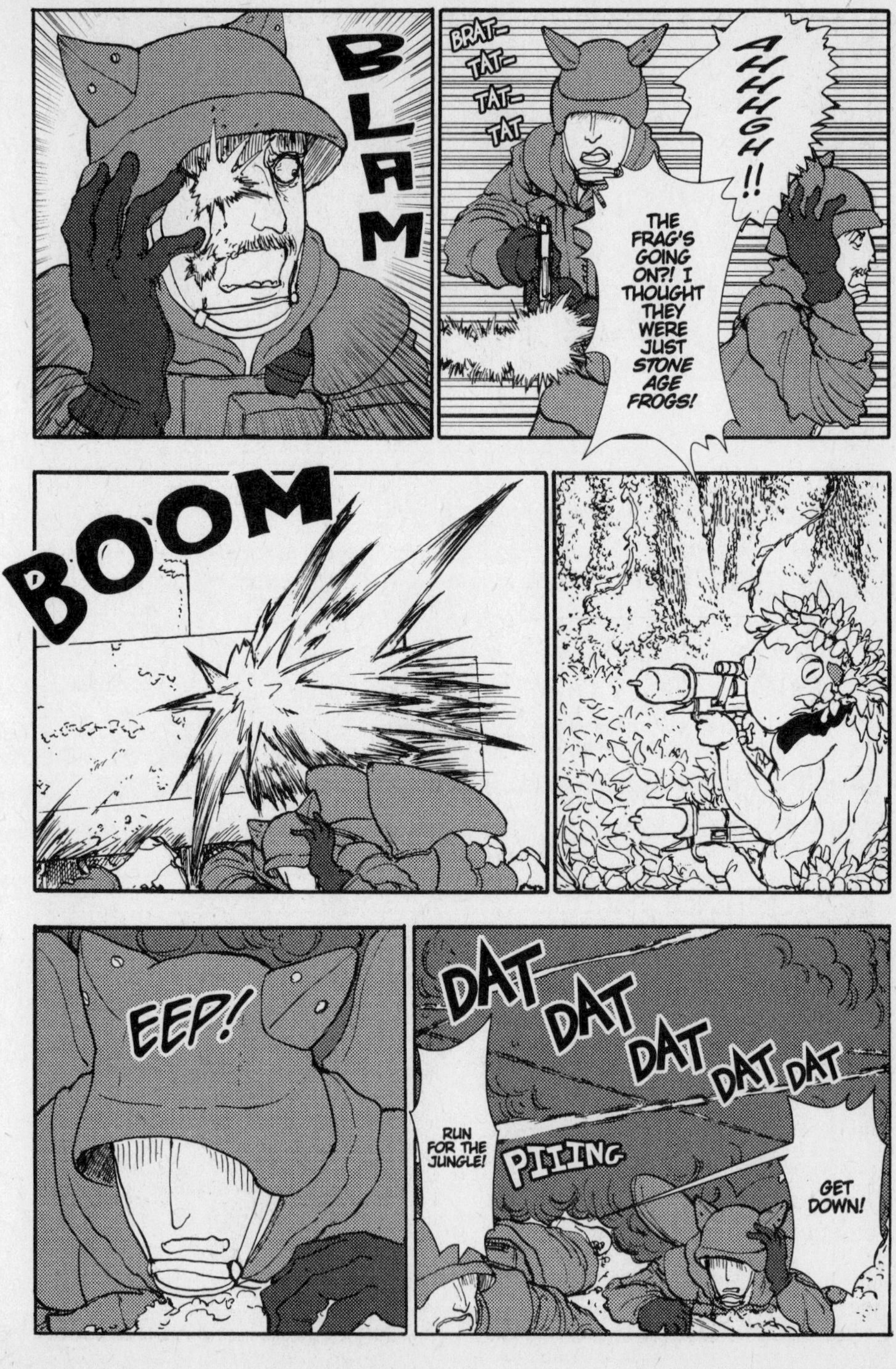

BRAT-TAT-TAT-TAT
AHHHHGH!!
THE FRAG'S GOING ON?! I THOUGHT THEY WERE JUST STONE AGE FROGS!
BLAM
BOOM
DAT DAT DAT DAT DAT
GET DOWN!
RUN FOR THE JUNGLE!
PIIING
EEP!

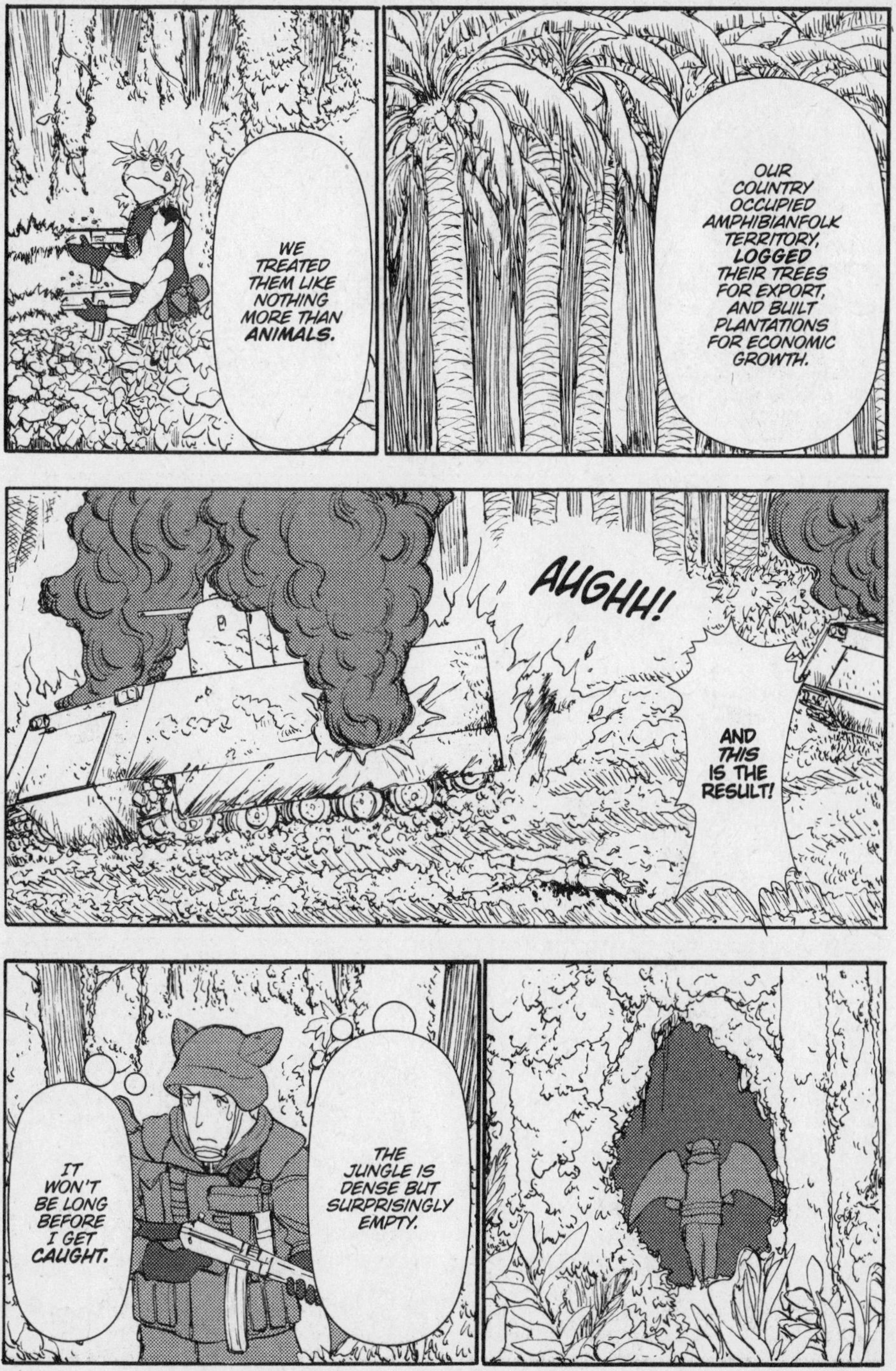
OUR COUNTRY OCCUPIED AMPHIBIANFOLK TERRITORY, LOGGED THEIR TREES FOR EXPORT, AND BUILT PLANTATIONS FOR ECONOMIC GROWTH.
WE TREATED THEM LIKE NOTHING MORE THAN ANIMALS.
AUGHH!
AND THIS IS THE RESULT!
THE JUNGLE IS DENSE BUT SURPRISINGLY EMPTY.
IT WON'T BE LONG BEFORE I GET CAUGHT.

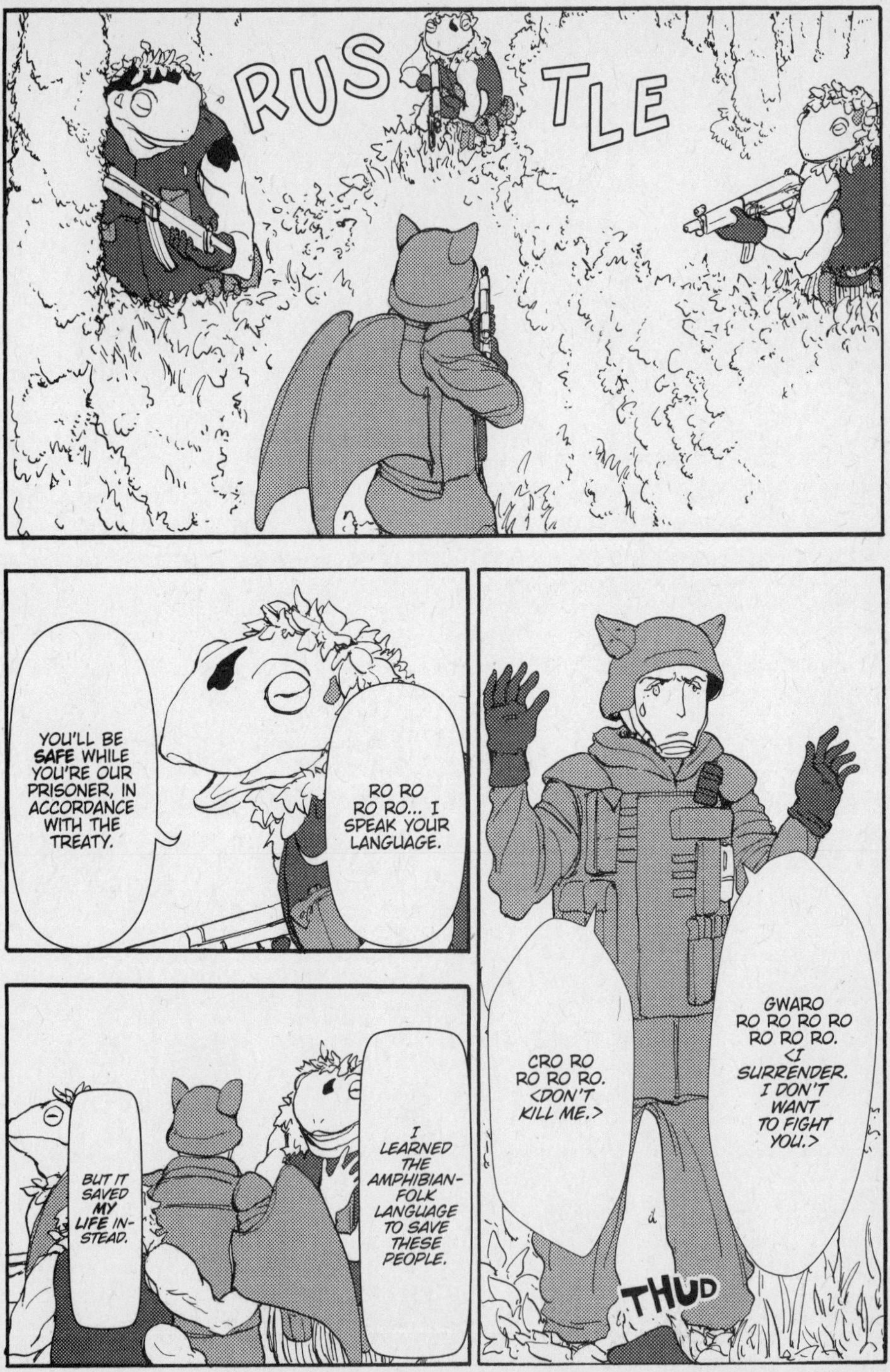
RUSTLE
GWARO RO RO RO RO RO RO RO. <I SURRENDER. I DON'T WANT TO FIGHT YOU.>
CRO RO RO RO RO. <DON'T KILL ME.>
THUD
RO RO RO RO... I SPEAK YOUR LANGUAGE.
YOU'LL BE SAFE WHILE YOU'RE OUR PRISONER, IN ACCORDANCE WITH THE TREATY.
I LEARNED THE AMPHIBIAN-FOLK LANGUAGE TO SAVE THESE PEOPLE.
BUT IT SAVED MY LIFE INSTEAD.

A CentaUr's Life

UNDERSTANDING ANTARCTICANS: PART 7

HE PHYSICAL ABILITIES OF ANTARCTICANS ARE VERY DIFFERENT DEPENDING ON SUBSPECIES. THE INTELLECTUAL SUBSPECIES DISPLAYS A LEVEL OF PHYSICAL APTITUDE ROUGHLY EQUIVALENT TO A PERSON WITH A FAIRLY SEDENTARY LIFESTYLE, BUT WHETHER THIS INDICATES A NEGLECT OF THEIR HEALTH OR RESULTS IN ANY MEDICAL PROBLEMS IS UNKNOWN. THE ANTARCTICANS GO TO EXTREMES TO KEEP OUTSIDERS FROM ACCESSING THIS AND OTHER INFORMATION, PREVENTING US FROM EXPANDING OUR KNOWLEDGE OF THEIR RACE. SOME HAVE SPECULATED THAT SINCE NO ANTARCTICANS WITH OBVIOUS INFIRMITY OR DISABILITY HAVE BEEN ENCOUNTERED BY HUMANS, THEIR RACE MAY HAVE ADVANCED MEDICAL TECHNOLOGY, A GENETIC PREDISPOSITION FOR GOOD HEALTH, OR EVEN SOME UNKNOWN TECHNIQUE TO PROMOTE WELLNESS. ASIDE FROM THEIR APPARENT PHYSICAL INABILITY TO CHEW (AND LACK OF FOOD PREFERENCES, ALLERGIES, AND INTOLERANCES), THEIR DIET AND CONSUMPTION IS SIMILAR TO THAT OF HUMANS. THESE DIFFERENCES SUGGEST THE STRONG POSSIBILITY THAT THEY OBSERVE MEALTIME CUSTOMS AND RITUALS AND THAT THEY SWALLOW FOOD WHOLE, BUT WE DON'T KNOW IF OR HOW THEY DIGEST WHAT THEY CONSUME. THERE HAVE BEEN NO KNOWN ANTARCTICAN DEATHS FROM POISONS, WHICH MAY OR MAY NOT INDICATE SOME DEGREE OF TOLERANCE. THEY'RE QUITE SENSITIVE TO COLD DESPITE LIVING IN ANTARCTICA, BUT EXHIBIT A HIGH TOLERANCE TO HEAT AND HUMIDITY, WHICH MAY BE INDICATIVE OF CONDITIONS IN THEIR UNDERGROUND CITY.

THE WARRIOR SUBSPECIES SHOWS EXCEPTIONAL PHYSICAL PROWESS AND SENSORY ACUITY. THIS WAS PROVEN BY AN INCIDENT IN CANADA THAT INVOLVED AN ARMED, PSYCHOTIC MAN WHO BELIEVED A CLICHÉ CONSPIRACY THEORY ABOUT REPTILIANS MANIPULATING THE HUMAN WORLD. MEMBERS OF THE WARRIOR SUBSPECIES WHO WERE ACTING AS BODYGUARDS SENSED THE DANGER LONG BEFORE ANY HUMANS DID, AND MANAGED TO APPREHEND THE MAN BEFORE HE TRIED TO PULL THE TRIGGER.

CHAPTER 76

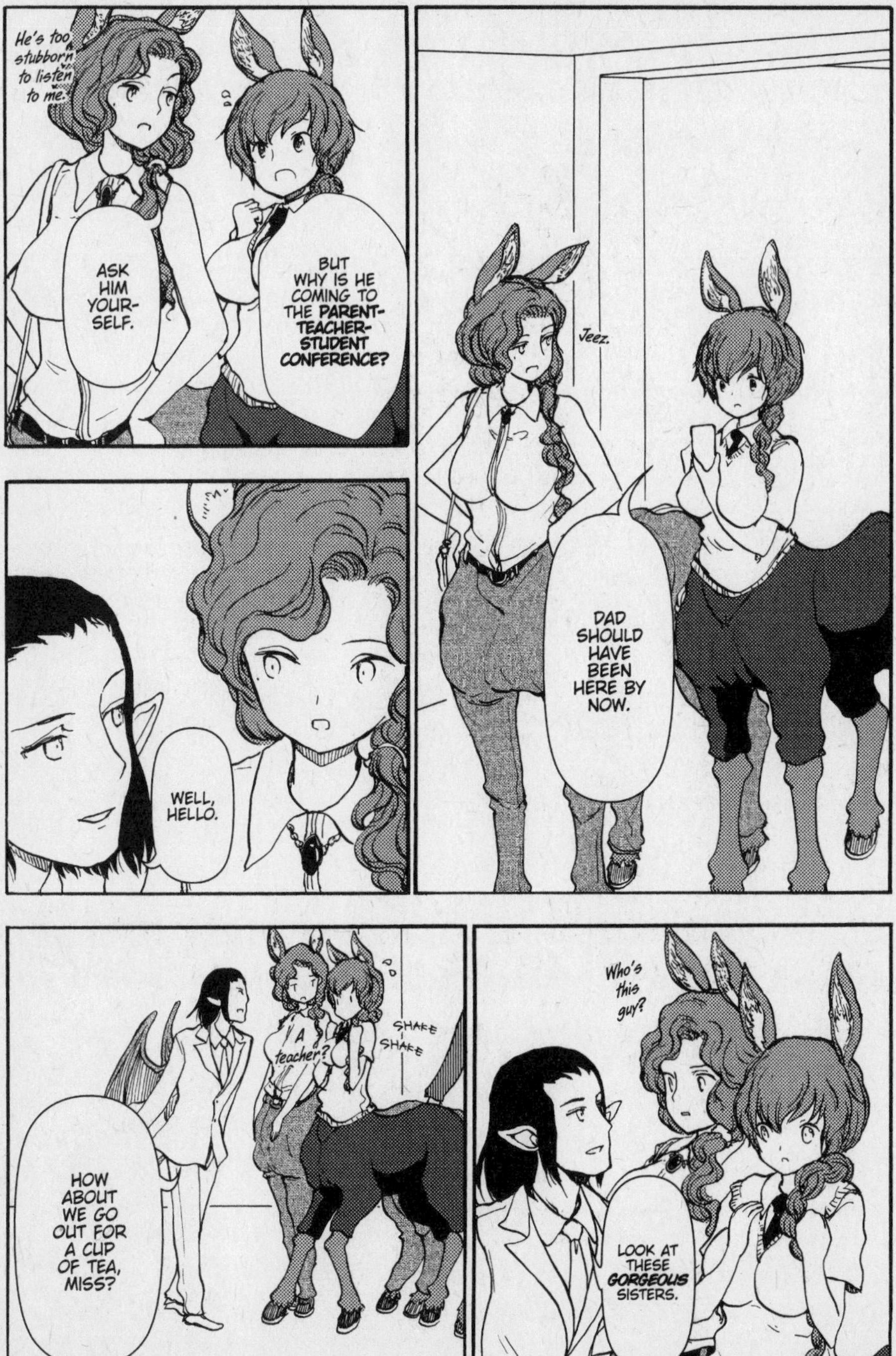
Jeez.
DAD SHOULD HAVE BEEN HERE BY NOW.
BUT WHY IS HE COMING TO THE PARENT-TEACHER-STUDENT CONFERENCE?
ASK HIM YOURSELF.
He's too stubborn to listen to me.
WELL, HELLO.
Who's this guy?
LOOK AT THESE GORGEOUS SISTERS.
A teacher?
SHAKE SHAKE
HOW ABOUT WE GO OUT FOR A CUP OF TEA, MISS?

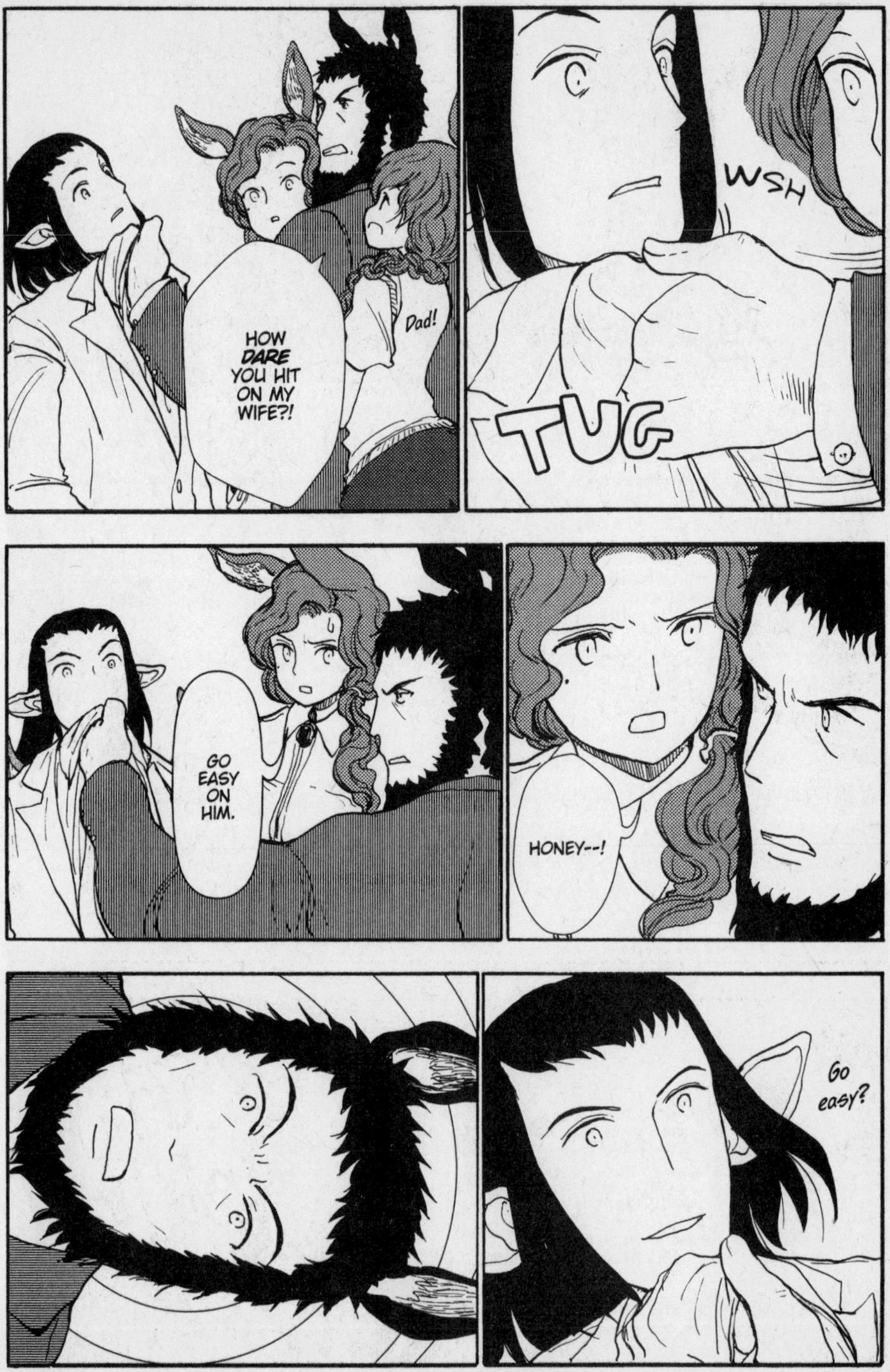
WSH
TUG
HOW DARE YOU HIT ON MY WIFE?!
Dad!
HONEY--!
GO EASY ON HIM.
Go easy?

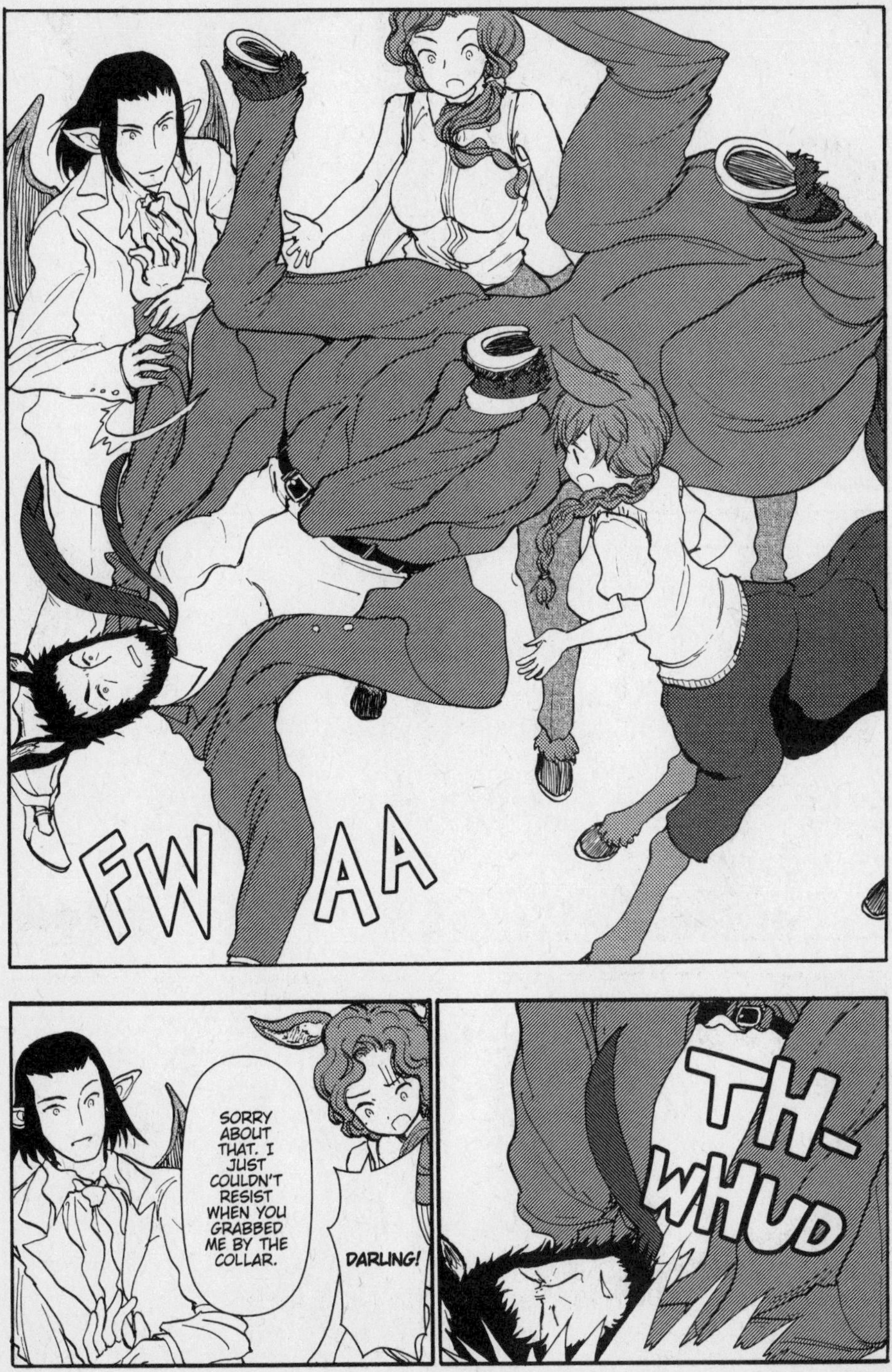
FW AA
TH-WHUD
SORRY ABOUT THAT. I JUST COULDN'T RESIST WHEN YOU GRABBED ME BY THE COLLAR.
DARLING!

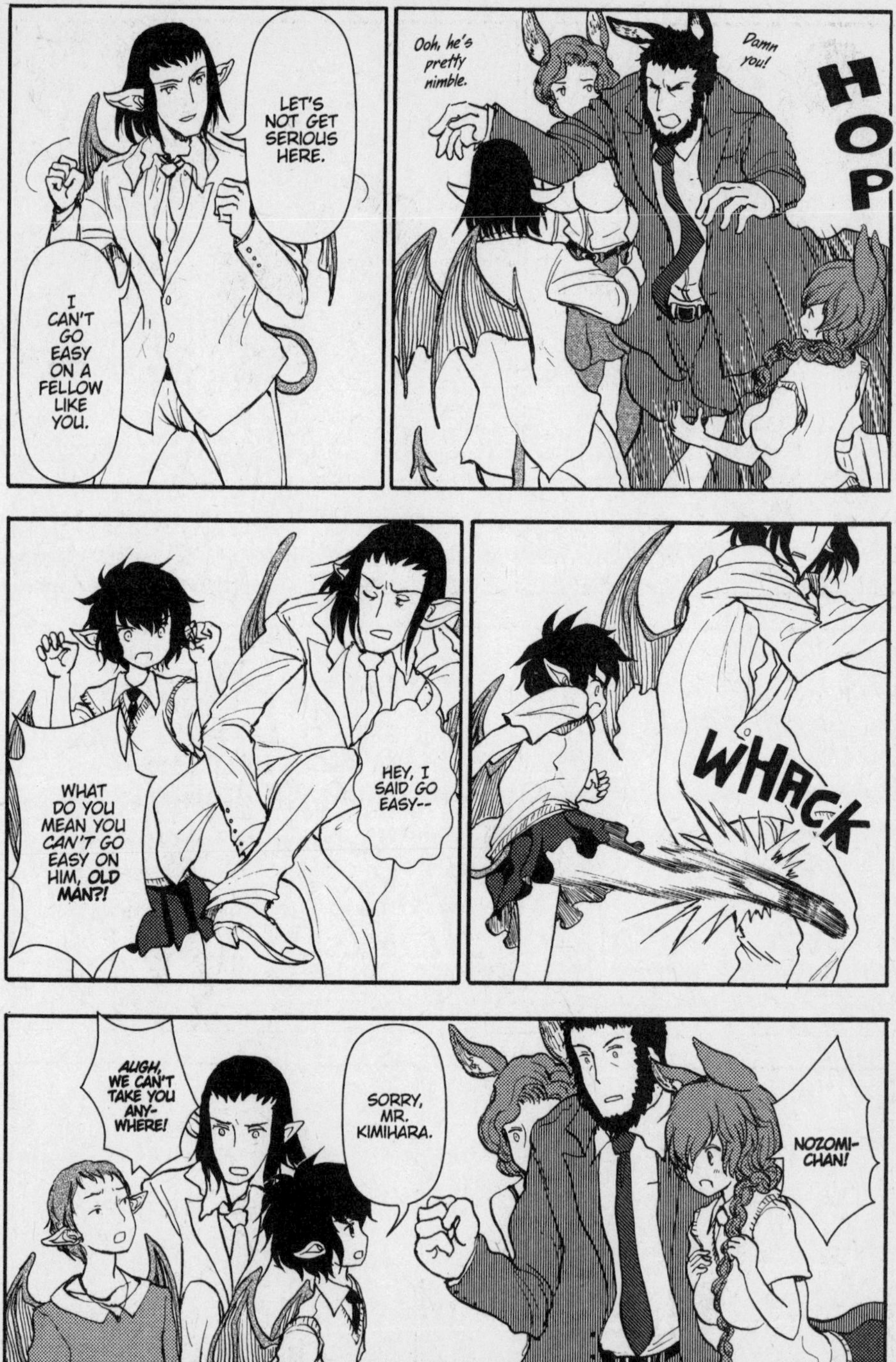
HOP HOP
Damn you!
Ooh, he's pretty nimble.
LET'S NOT GET SERIOUS HERE.
I CAN'T GO EASY ON A FELLOW LIKE YOU.
WHACK
HEY, I SAID GO EASY--
WHAT DO YOU MEAN YOU CAN'T GO EASY ON HIM, **OLD MAN?!**
NOZOMI-CHAN!
SORRY, MR. KIMIHARA.
AUGH, WE CAN'T TAKE YOU ANY-WHERE!

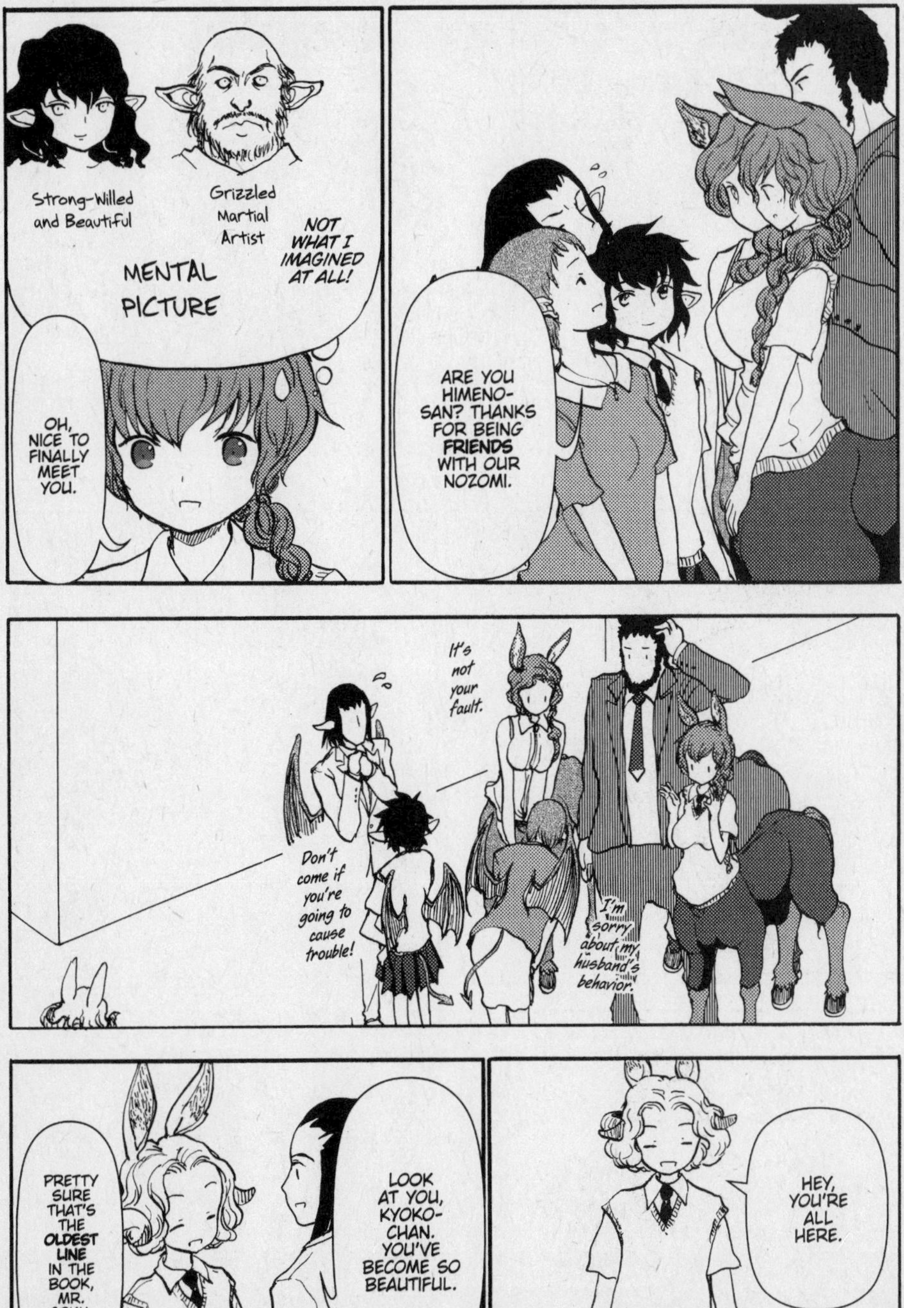
ARE YOU HIMENO-SAN? THANKS FOR BEING **FRIENDS** WITH OUR NOZOMI.
NOT WHAT I IMAGINED AT ALL!
Grizzled Martial Artist
Strong-Willed and Beautiful
MENTAL PICTURE
OH, NICE TO FINALLY MEET YOU.
It's not your fault.
I'm sorry about my husband's behavior.
Don't come if you're going to cause trouble!
HEY, YOU'RE ALL HERE.
LOOK AT YOU, KYOKO-CHAN. YOU'VE BECOME SO BEAUTIFUL.
PRETTY SURE THAT'S THE **OLDEST LINE** IN THE BOOK, MR. GOKU-RAKU.

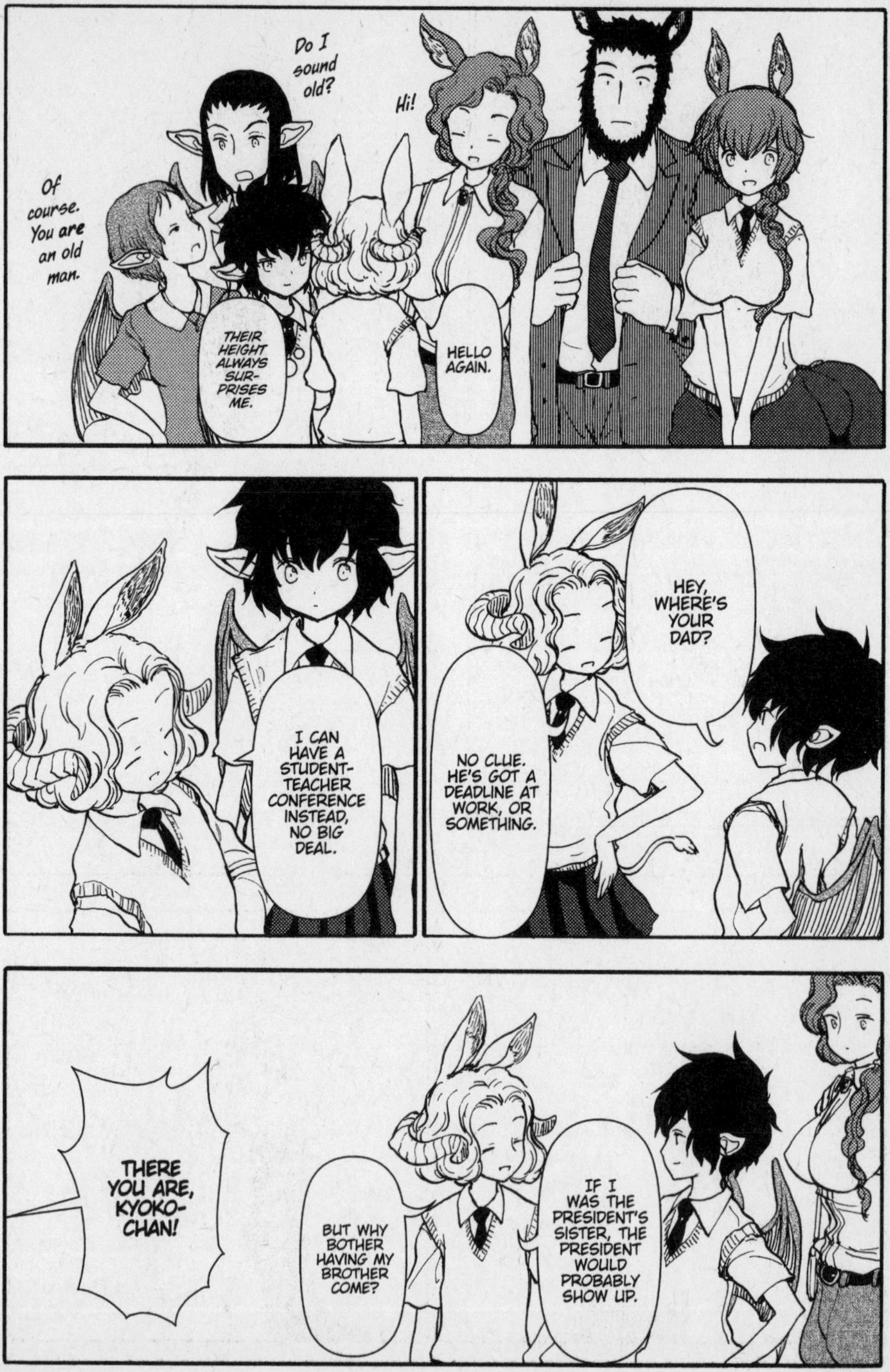

Hi!
HELLO AGAIN.
Do I sound old?
Of course. You are an old man.
THEIR HEIGHT ALWAYS SURPRISES ME.
HEY, WHERE'S YOUR DAD?
NO CLUE. HE'S GOT A DEADLINE AT WORK, OR SOMETHING.
I CAN HAVE A STUDENT-TEACHER CONFERENCE INSTEAD, NO BIG DEAL.
IF I WAS THE PRESIDENT'S SISTER, THE PRESIDENT WOULD PROBABLY SHOW UP.
BUT WHY BOTHER HAVING MY BROTHER COME?
THERE YOU ARE, KYOKO-CHAN!

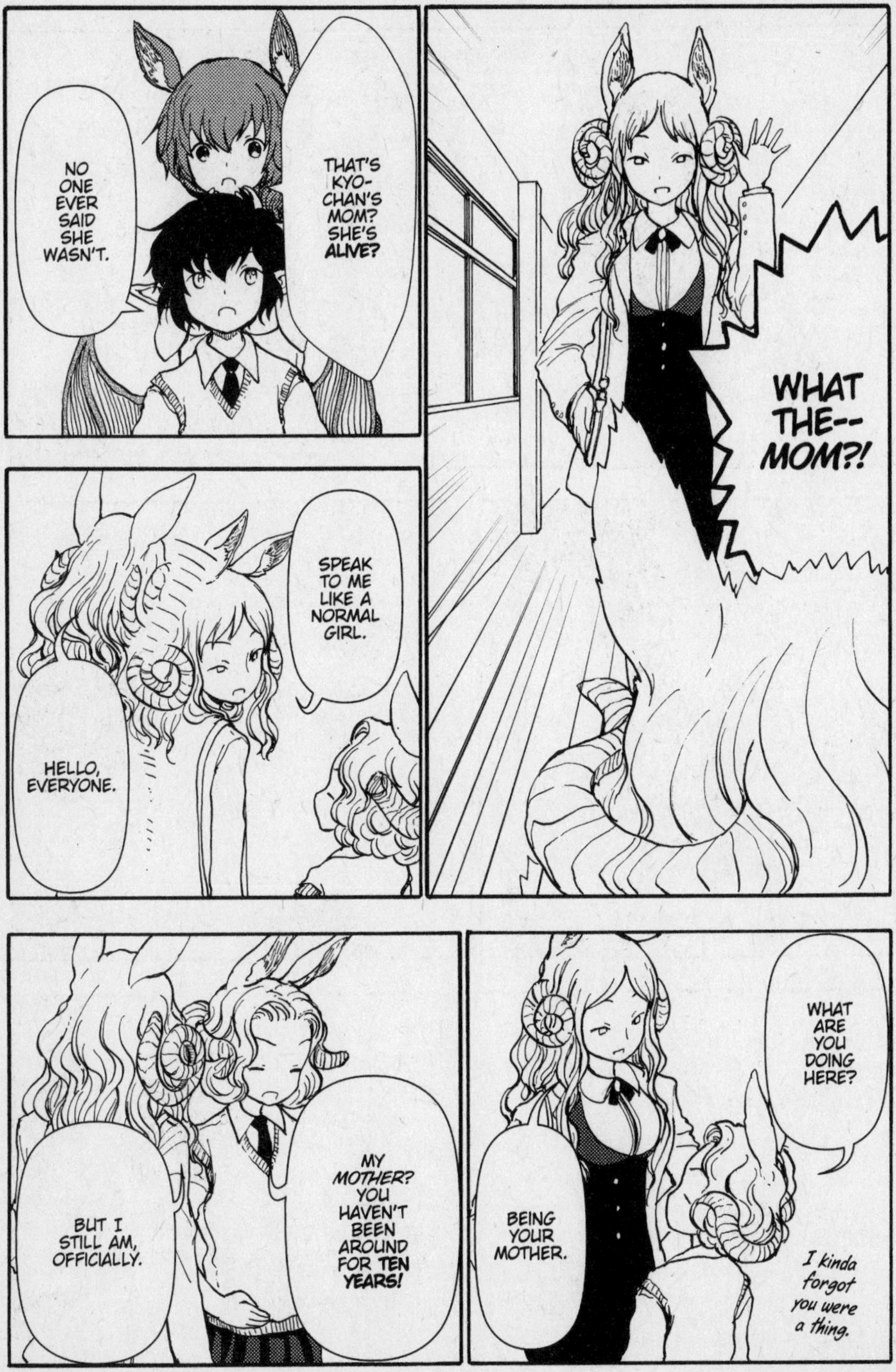
WHAT THE-- MOM?!
THAT'S KYO-CHAN'S MOM? SHE'S ALIVE?
NO ONE EVER SAID SHE WASN'T.
SPEAK TO ME LIKE A NORMAL GIRL.
HELLO, EVERYONE.
WHAT ARE YOU DOING HERE?
BEING YOUR MOTHER.
I kinda forgot you were a thing.
MY MOTHER? YOU HAVEN'T BEEN AROUND FOR TEN YEARS!
BUT I STILL AM, OFFICIALLY.

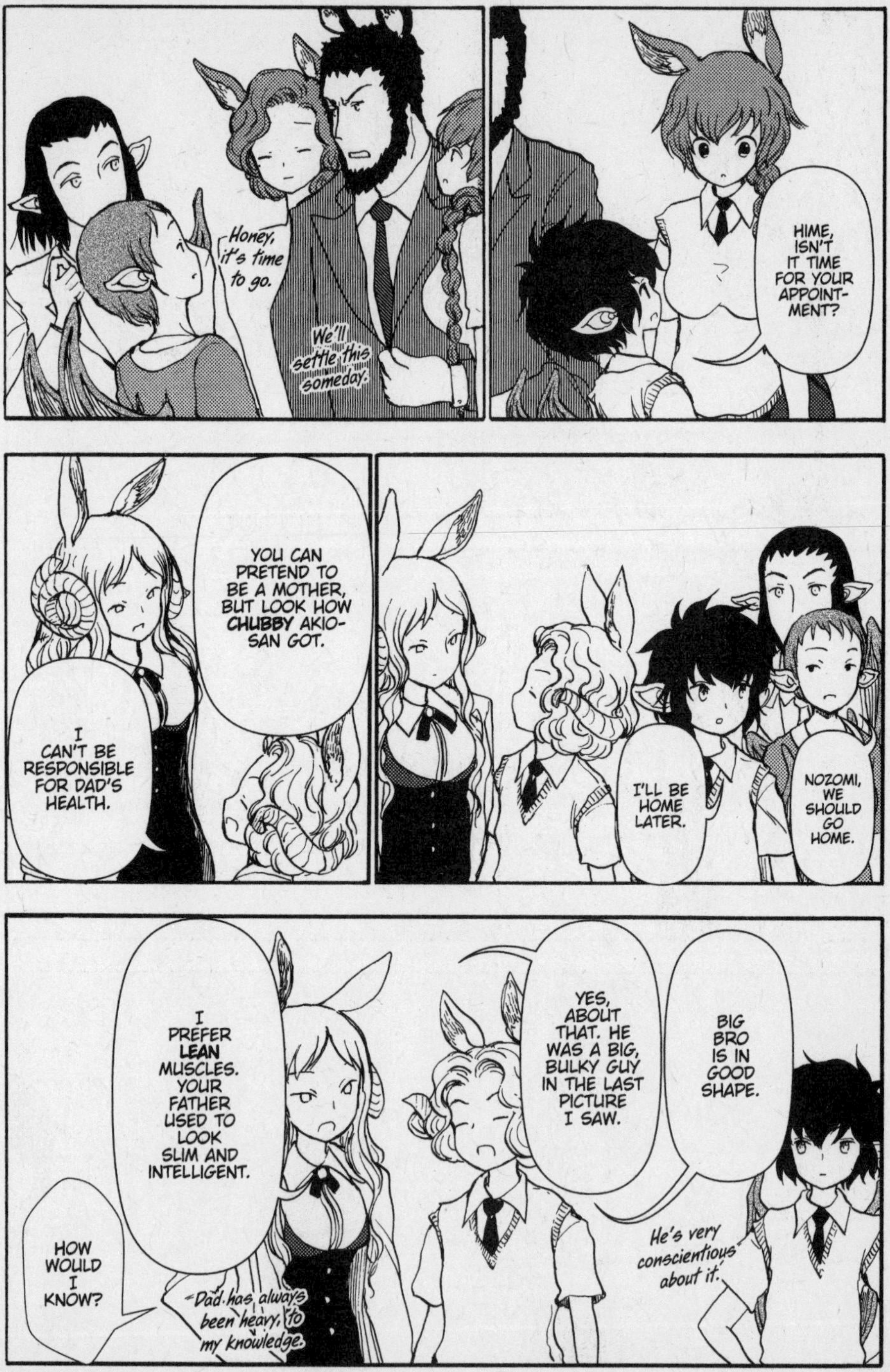
HIME, ISN'T IT TIME FOR YOUR APPOINTMENT?
Honey, it's time to go.
We'll settle this someday.
NOZOMI, WE SHOULD GO HOME.
I'LL BE HOME LATER.
YOU CAN PRETEND TO BE A MOTHER, BUT LOOK HOW CHUBBY AKIO-SAN GOT.
I CAN'T BE RESPONSIBLE FOR DAD'S HEALTH.
BIG BRO IS IN GOOD SHAPE.
YES, ABOUT THAT. HE WAS A BIG, BULKY GUY IN THE LAST PICTURE I SAW.
He's very conscientious about it.
I PREFER LEAN MUSCLES. YOUR FATHER USED TO LOOK SLIM AND INTELLIGENT.
Dad has always been heavy, to my knowledge.
HOW WOULD I KNOW?

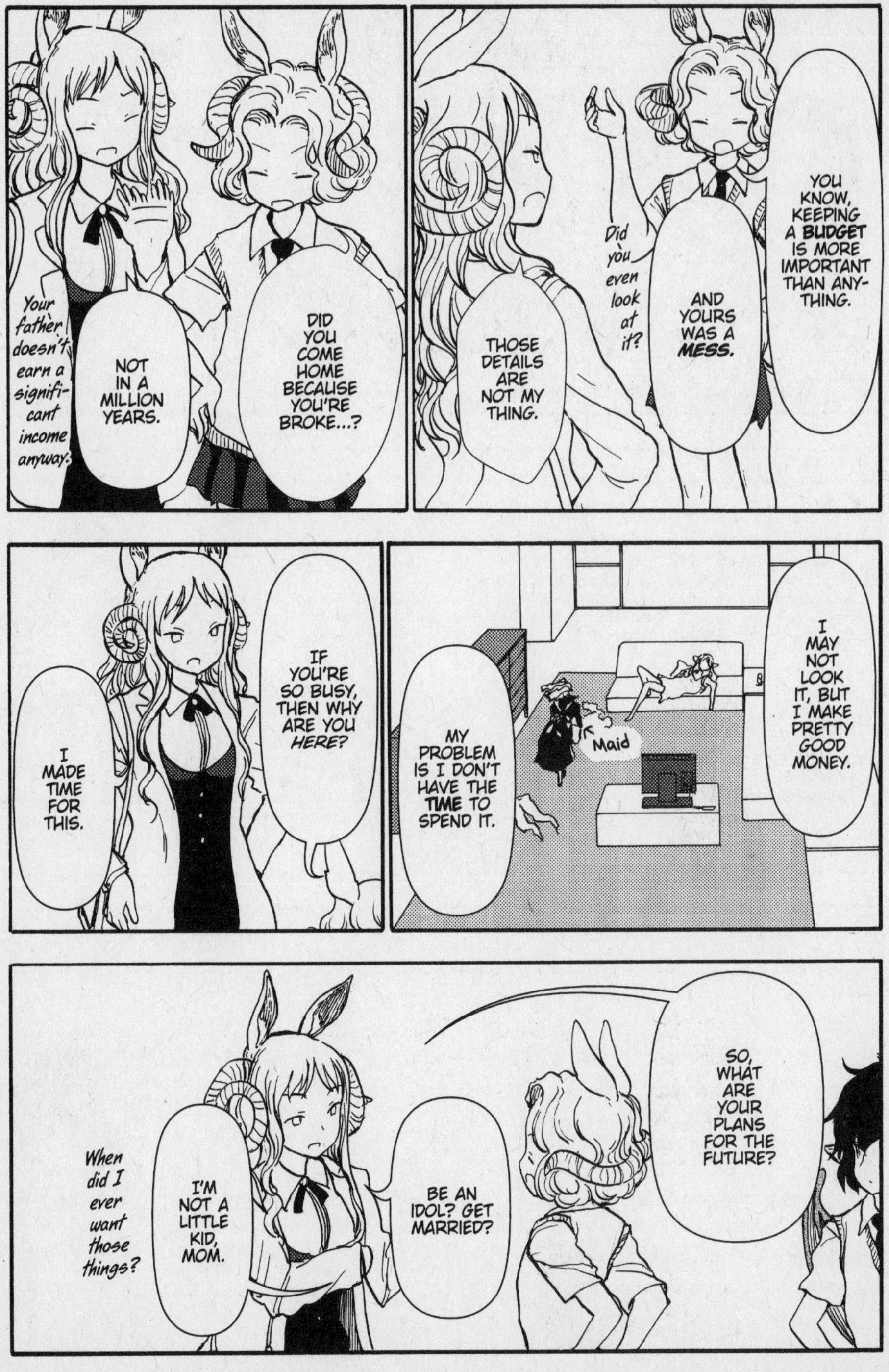
YOU KNOW, KEEPING A BUDGET IS MORE IMPORTANT THAN ANYTHING.
AND YOURS WAS A MESS.
Did you even look at it?
THOSE DETAILS ARE NOT MY THING.
DID YOU COME HOME BECAUSE YOU'RE BROKE...?
NOT IN A MILLION YEARS.
Your father doesn't earn a significant income anyway.
I MAY NOT LOOK IT, BUT I MAKE PRETTY GOOD MONEY.
Maid
MY PROBLEM IS I DON'T HAVE THE TIME TO SPEND IT.
IF YOU'RE SO BUSY, THEN WHY ARE YOU HERE?
I MADE TIME FOR THIS.
SO, WHAT ARE YOUR PLANS FOR THE FUTURE?
BE AN IDOL? GET MARRIED?
I'M NOT A LITTLE KID, MOM.
When did I ever want those things?

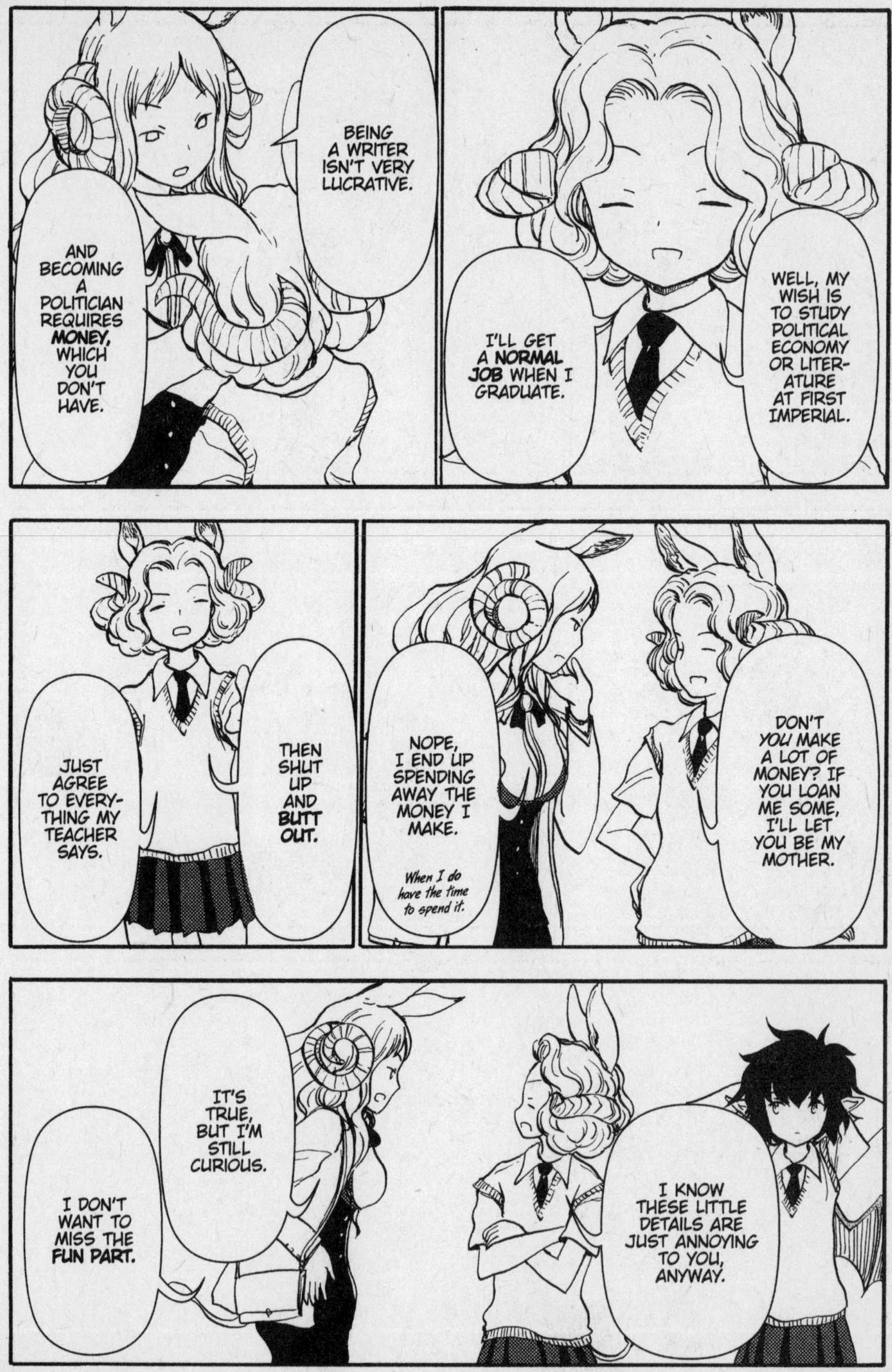
WELL, MY WISH IS TO STUDY POLITICAL ECONOMY OR LITER-ATURE AT FIRST IMPERIAL.
I'LL GET A **NORMAL JOB** WHEN I GRADUATE.
BEING A WRITER ISN'T VERY LUCRATIVE.
AND BECOMING A POLITICIAN REQUIRES **MONEY,** WHICH YOU DON'T HAVE.
DON'T *YOU* MAKE A LOT OF MONEY? IF YOU LOAN ME SOME, I'LL LET YOU BE MY MOTHER.
NOPE, I END UP SPENDING AWAY THE MONEY I MAKE.
When I do have the time to spend it.
THEN SHUT UP AND **BUTT OUT.**
JUST AGREE TO EVERY-THING MY TEACHER SAYS.
I KNOW THESE LITTLE DETAILS ARE JUST ANNOYING TO YOU, ANYWAY.
IT'S TRUE, BUT I'M STILL CURIOUS.
I DON'T WANT TO MISS THE **FUN PART.**

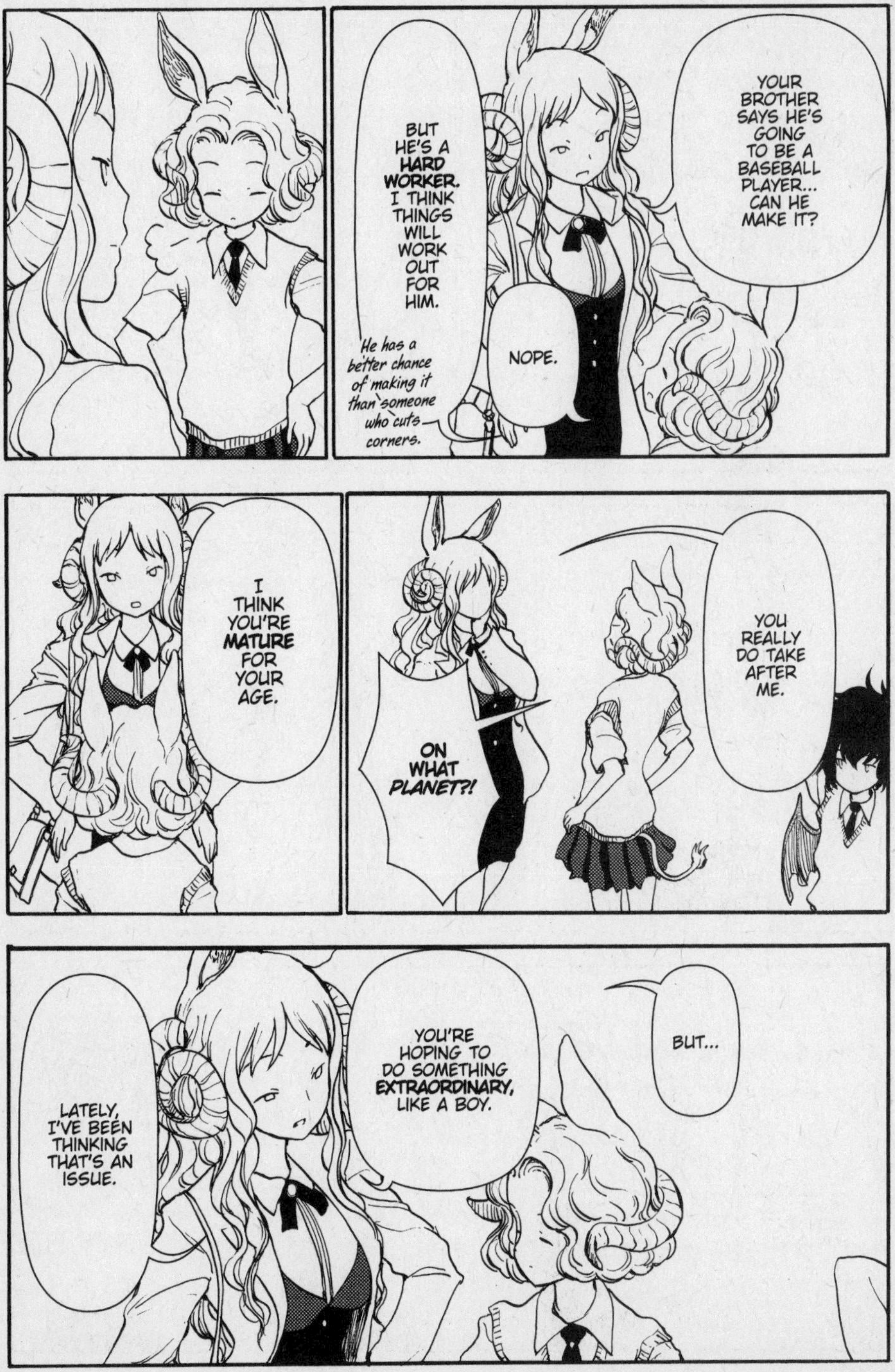
YOUR BROTHER SAYS HE'S GOING TO BE A BASEBALL PLAYER... CAN HE MAKE IT?
NOPE.
BUT HE'S A HARD WORKER. I THINK THINGS WILL WORK OUT FOR HIM.
He has a better chance of making it than someone who cuts corners.
YOU REALLY DO TAKE AFTER ME.
ON WHAT PLANET?!
I THINK YOU'RE MATURE FOR YOUR AGE.
BUT...
YOU'RE HOPING TO DO SOMETHING EXTRAORDINARY, LIKE A BOY.
LATELY, I'VE BEEN THINKING THAT'S AN ISSUE.

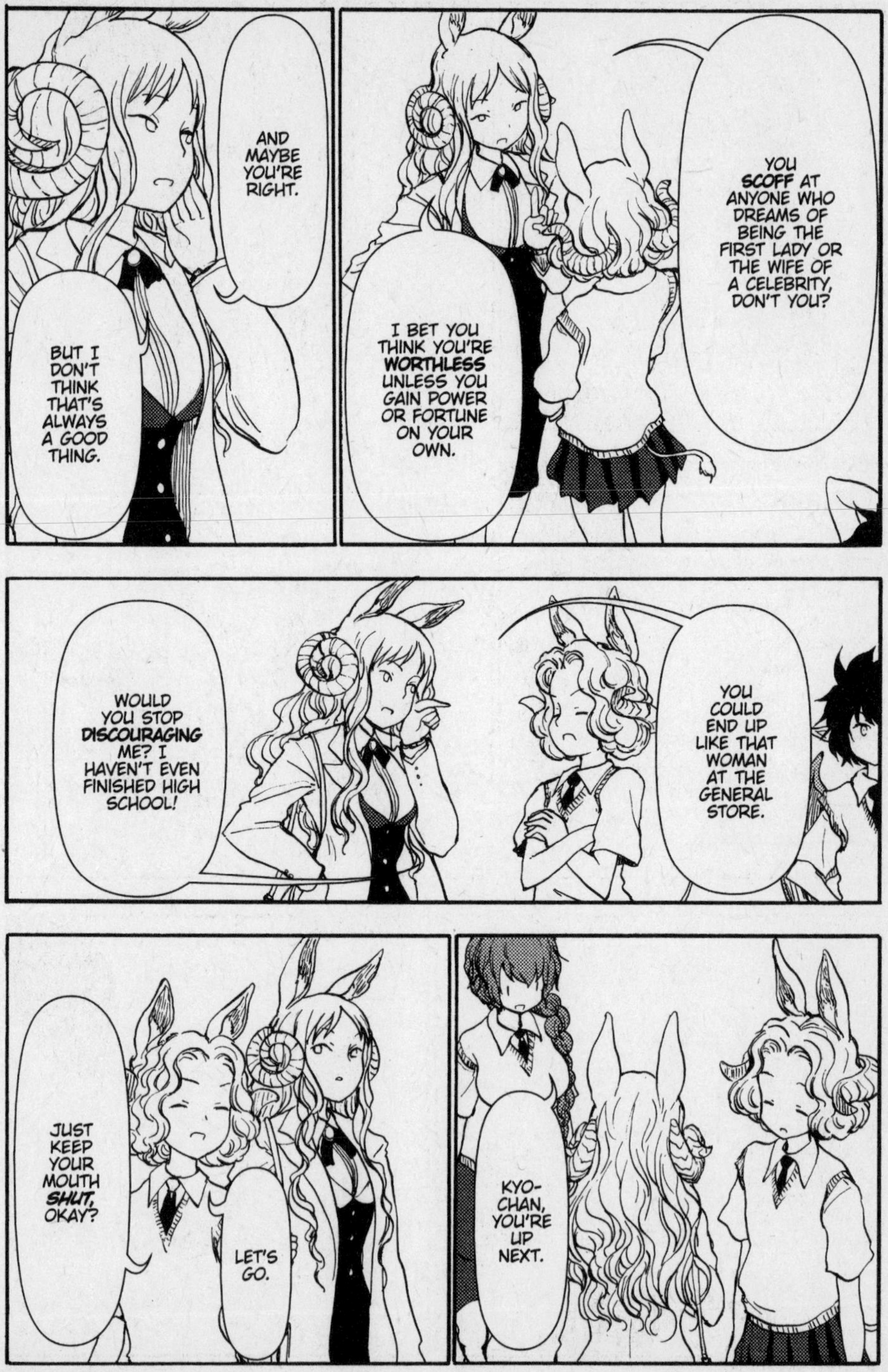
YOU SCOFF AT ANYONE WHO DREAMS OF BEING THE FIRST LADY OR THE WIFE OF A CELEBRITY, DON'T YOU?
I BET YOU THINK YOU'RE WORTHLESS UNLESS YOU GAIN POWER OR FORTUNE ON YOUR OWN.
AND MAYBE YOU'RE RIGHT.
BUT I DON'T THINK THAT'S ALWAYS A GOOD THING.
YOU COULD END UP LIKE THAT WOMAN AT THE GENERAL STORE.
WOULD YOU STOP DISCOURAGING ME? I HAVEN'T EVEN FINISHED HIGH SCHOOL!
KYO-CHAN, YOU'RE UP NEXT.
JUST KEEP YOUR MOUTH SHUT, OKAY?
LET'S GO.

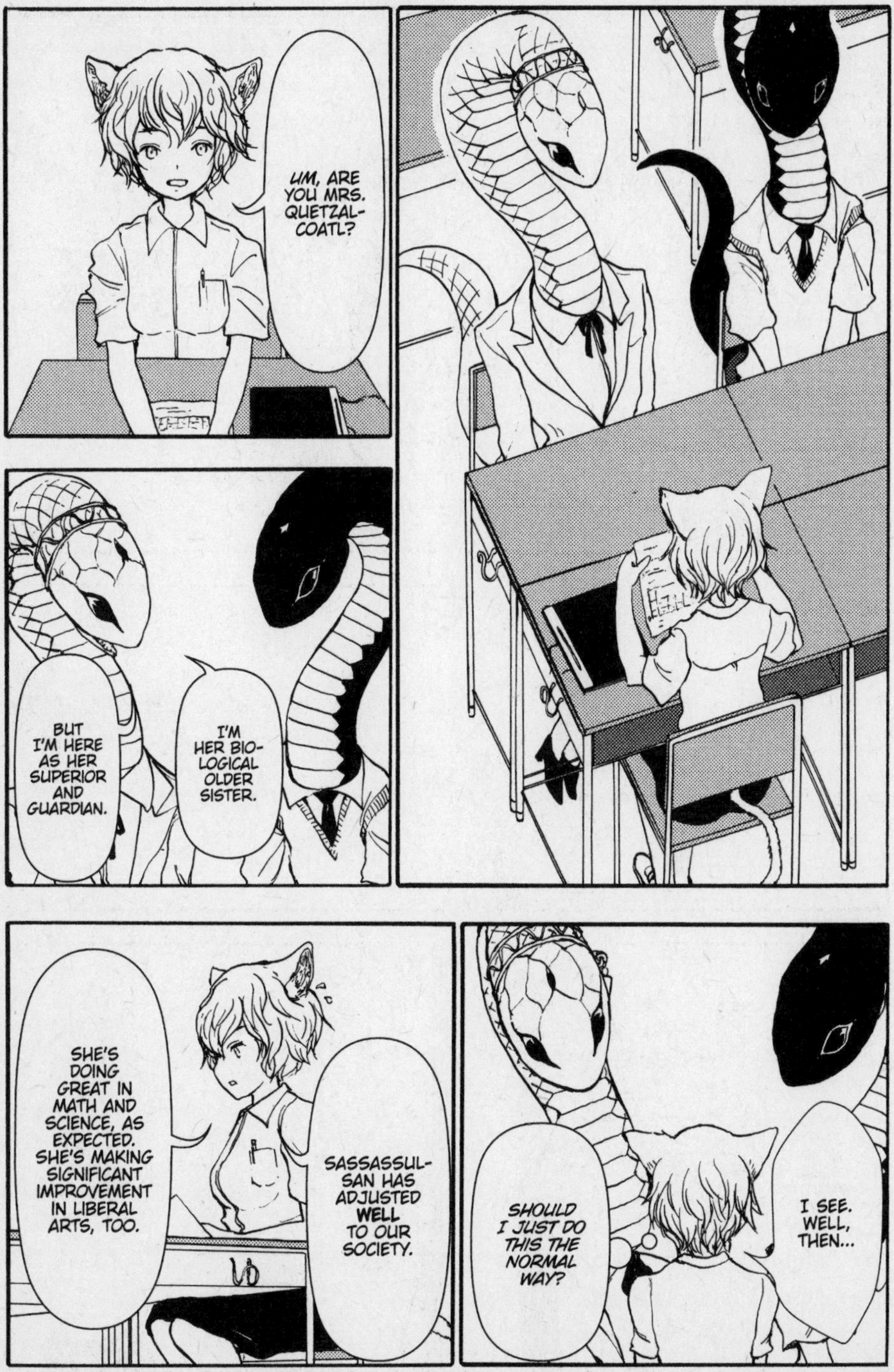
UM, ARE YOU MRS. QUETZAL-COATL?
I'M HER BIO-LOGICAL OLDER SISTER.
BUT I'M HERE AS HER SUPERIOR AND GUARDIAN.
I SEE. WELL, THEN...
SHOULD I JUST DO THIS THE NORMAL WAY?
SASSASSUL-SAN HAS ADJUSTED **WELL** TO OUR SOCIETY.
SHE'S DOING GREAT IN MATH AND SCIENCE, AS EXPECTED. SHE'S MAKING SIGNIFICANT IMPROVEMENT IN LIBERAL ARTS, TOO.

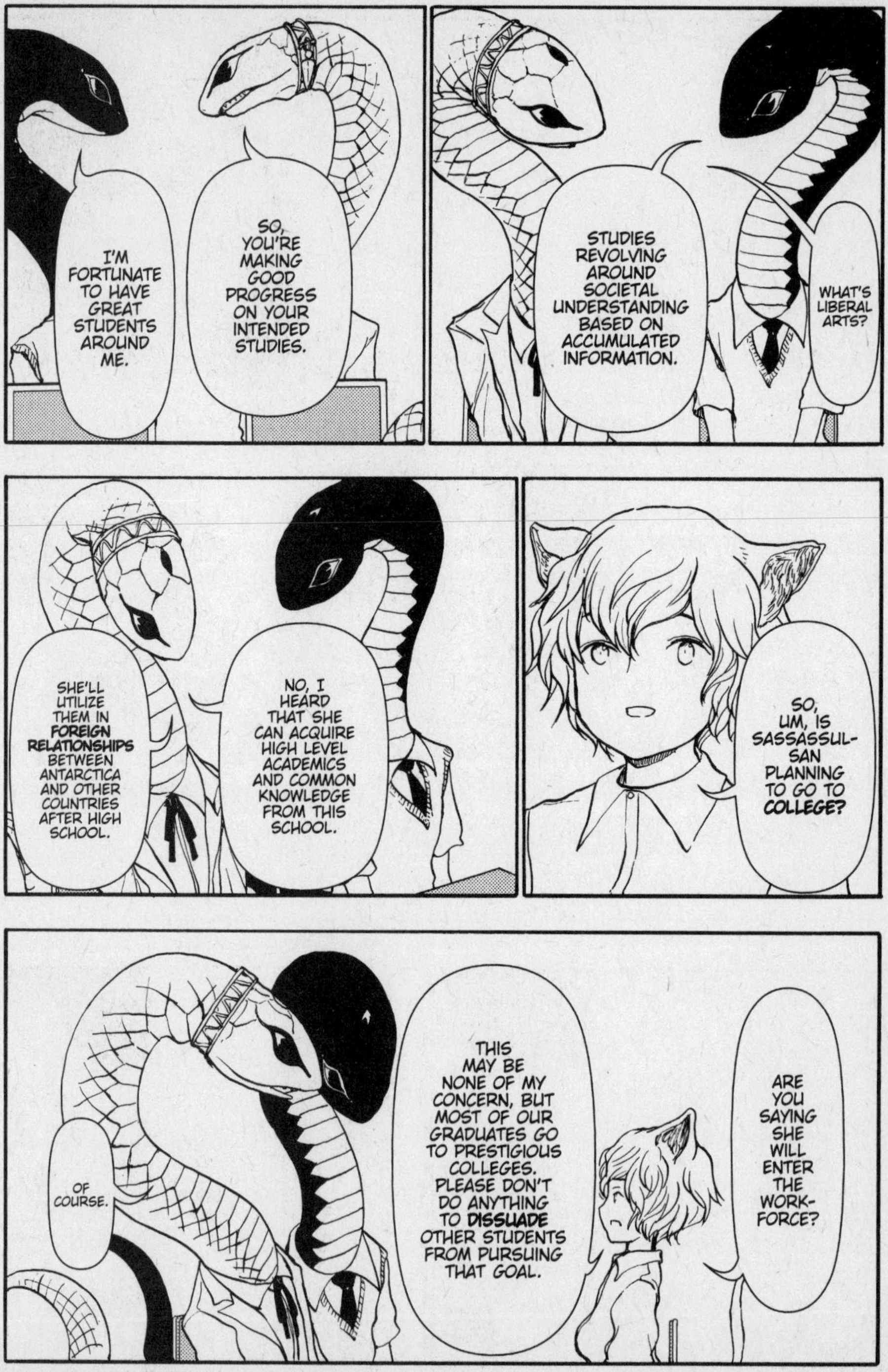
WHAT'S LIBERAL ARTS?
STUDIES REVOLVING AROUND SOCIETAL UNDERSTANDING BASED ON ACCUMULATED INFORMATION.
SO, YOU'RE MAKING GOOD PROGRESS ON YOUR INTENDED STUDIES.
I'M FORTUNATE TO HAVE GREAT STUDENTS AROUND ME.
SO, UM, IS SASSASSUL-SAN PLANNING TO GO TO **COLLEGE?**
NO, I HEARD THAT SHE CAN ACQUIRE HIGH LEVEL ACADEMICS AND COMMON KNOWLEDGE FROM THIS SCHOOL.
SHE'LL UTILIZE THEM IN **FOREIGN RELATIONSHIPS** BETWEEN ANTARCTICA AND OTHER COUNTRIES AFTER HIGH SCHOOL.
ARE YOU SAYING SHE WILL ENTER THE WORK-FORCE?
THIS MAY BE NONE OF MY CONCERN, BUT MOST OF OUR GRADUATES GO TO PRESTIGIOUS COLLEGES. PLEASE DON'T DO ANYTHING TO **DISSUADE** OTHER STUDENTS FROM PURSUING THAT GOAL.
OF COURSE.

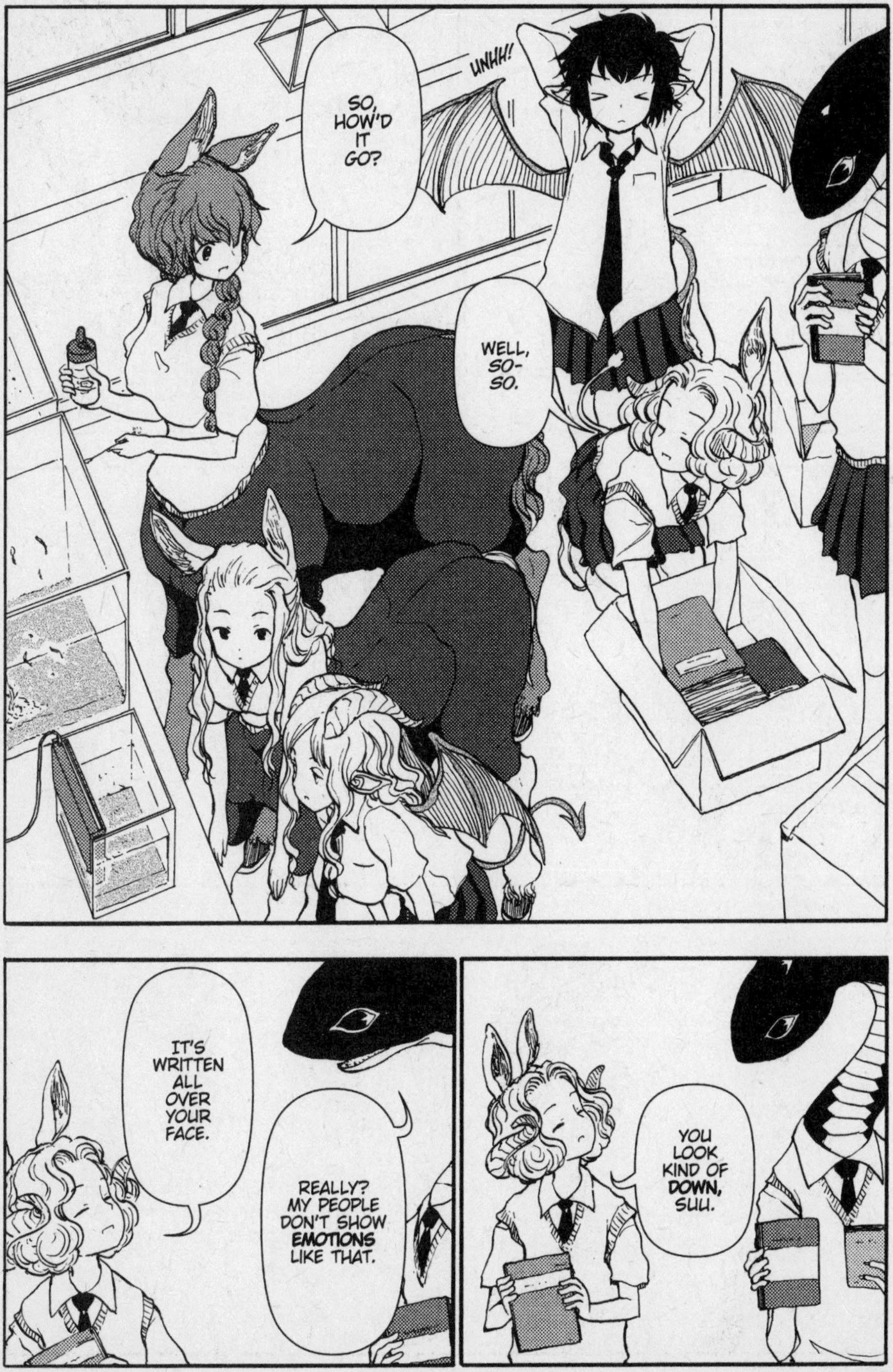
UNHH!
SO, HOW'D IT GO?
WELL, SO-SO.
YOU LOOK KIND OF DOWN, SUU.
REALLY? MY PEOPLE DON'T SHOW EMOTIONS LIKE THAT.
IT'S WRITTEN ALL OVER YOUR FACE.

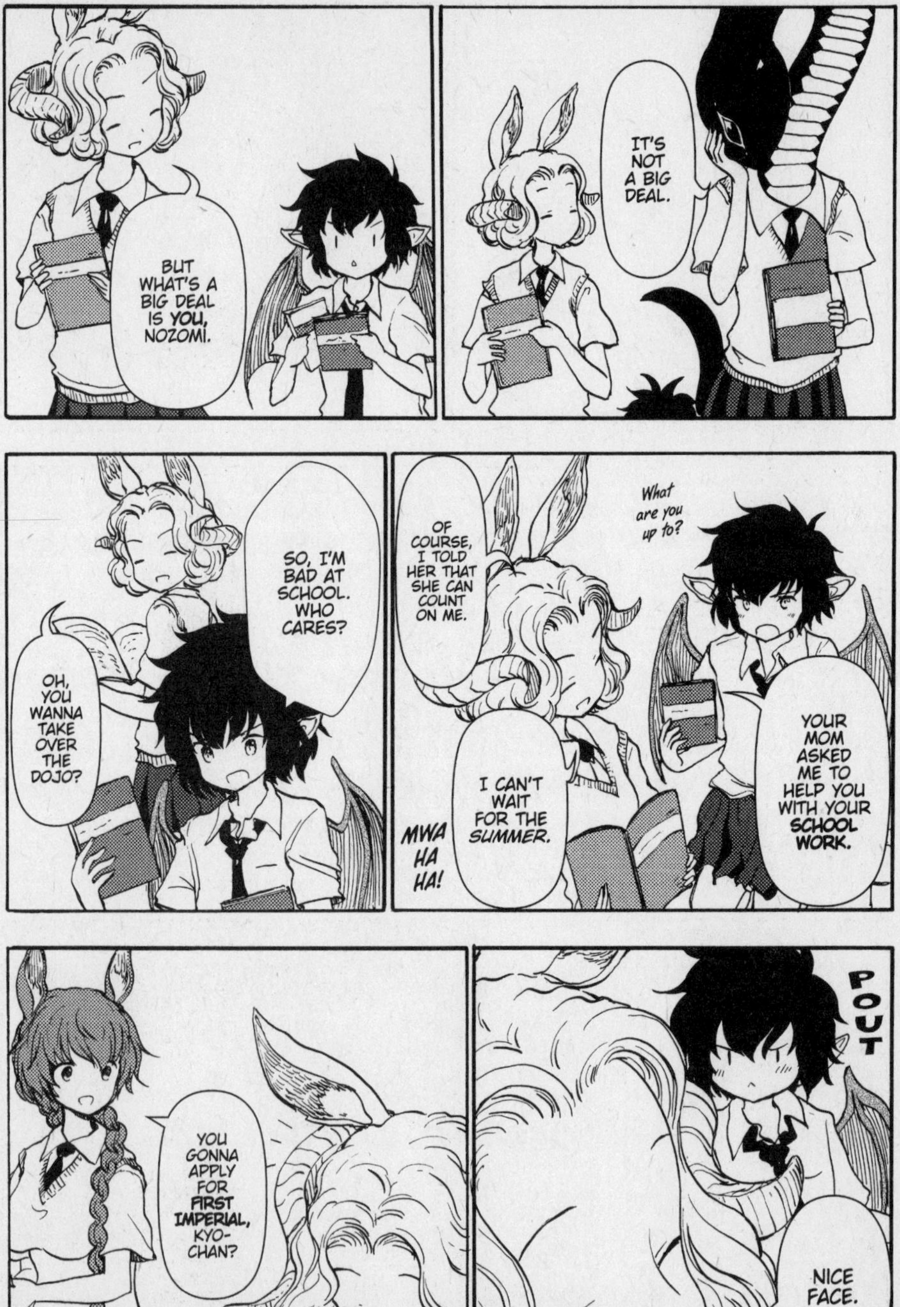
IT'S NOT A BIG DEAL.
BUT WHAT'S A BIG DEAL IS YOU, NOZOMI.
What are you up to?
OF COURSE, I TOLD HER THAT SHE CAN COUNT ON ME.
YOUR MOM ASKED ME TO HELP YOU WITH YOUR SCHOOL WORK.
I CAN'T WAIT FOR THE SUMMER.
MWA HA HA!
SO, I'M BAD AT SCHOOL. WHO CARES?
OH, YOU WANNA TAKE OVER THE DOJO?
POUT
NICE FACE.
YOU GONNA APPLY FOR FIRST IMPERIAL, KYO-CHAN?

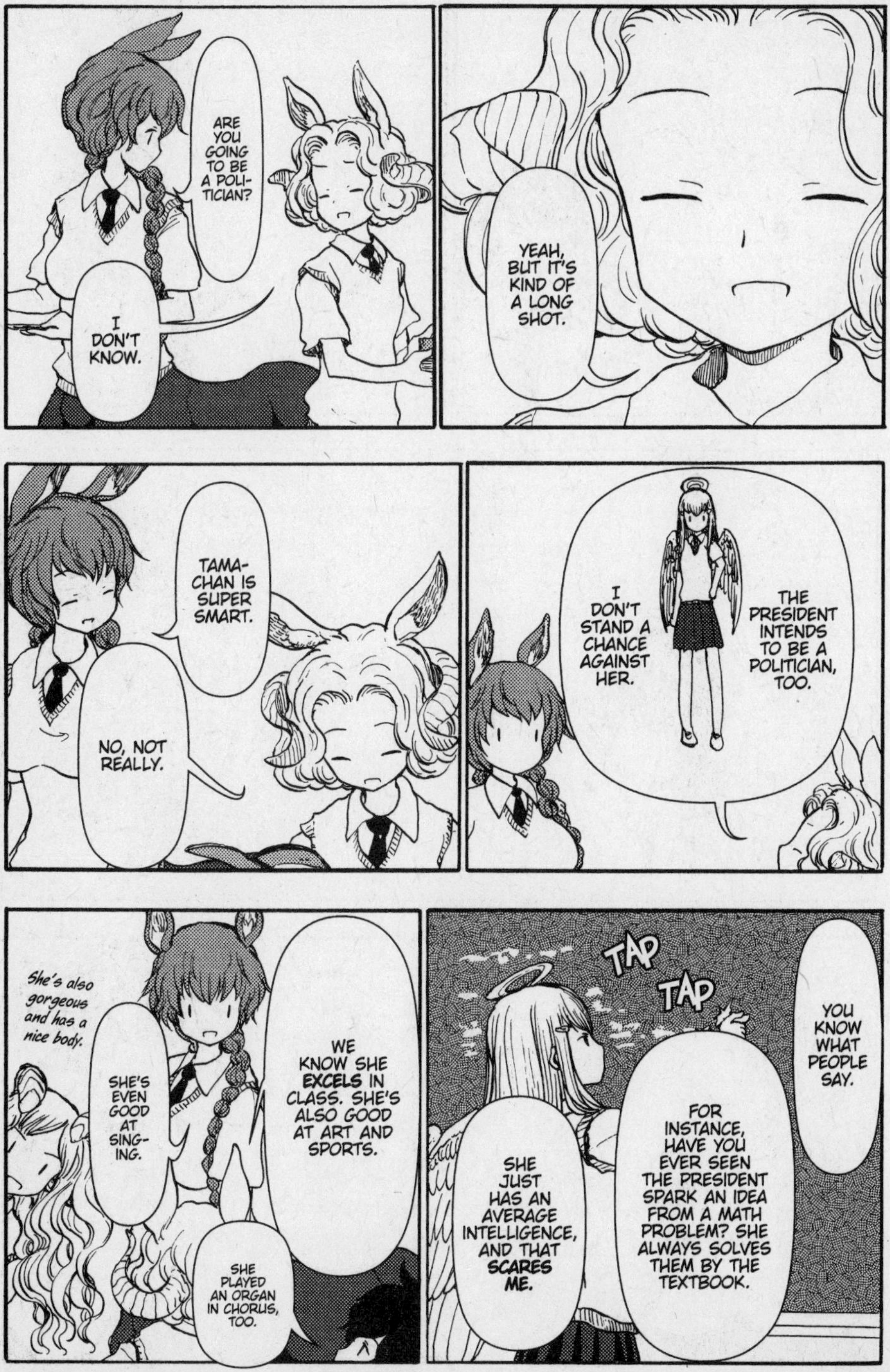
YEAH, BUT IT'S KIND OF A LONG SHOT.
ARE YOU GOING TO BE A POLI-TICIAN?
I DON'T KNOW.
THE PRESIDENT INTENDS TO BE A POLITICIAN, TOO.
I DON'T STAND A CHANCE AGAINST HER.
TAMA-CHAN IS SUPER SMART.
NO, NOT REALLY.
YOU KNOW WHAT PEOPLE SAY.
TAP
TAP
FOR INSTANCE, HAVE YOU EVER SEEN THE PRESIDENT SPARK AN IDEA FROM A MATH PROBLEM? SHE ALWAYS SOLVES THEM BY THE TEXTBOOK.
SHE JUST HAS AN AVERAGE INTELLIGENCE, AND THAT SCARES ME.
WE KNOW SHE EXCELS IN CLASS. SHE'S ALSO GOOD AT ART AND SPORTS.
She's also gorgeous and has a nice body.
SHE'S EVEN GOOD AT SING-ING.
SHE PLAYED AN ORGAN IN CHORUS, TOO.

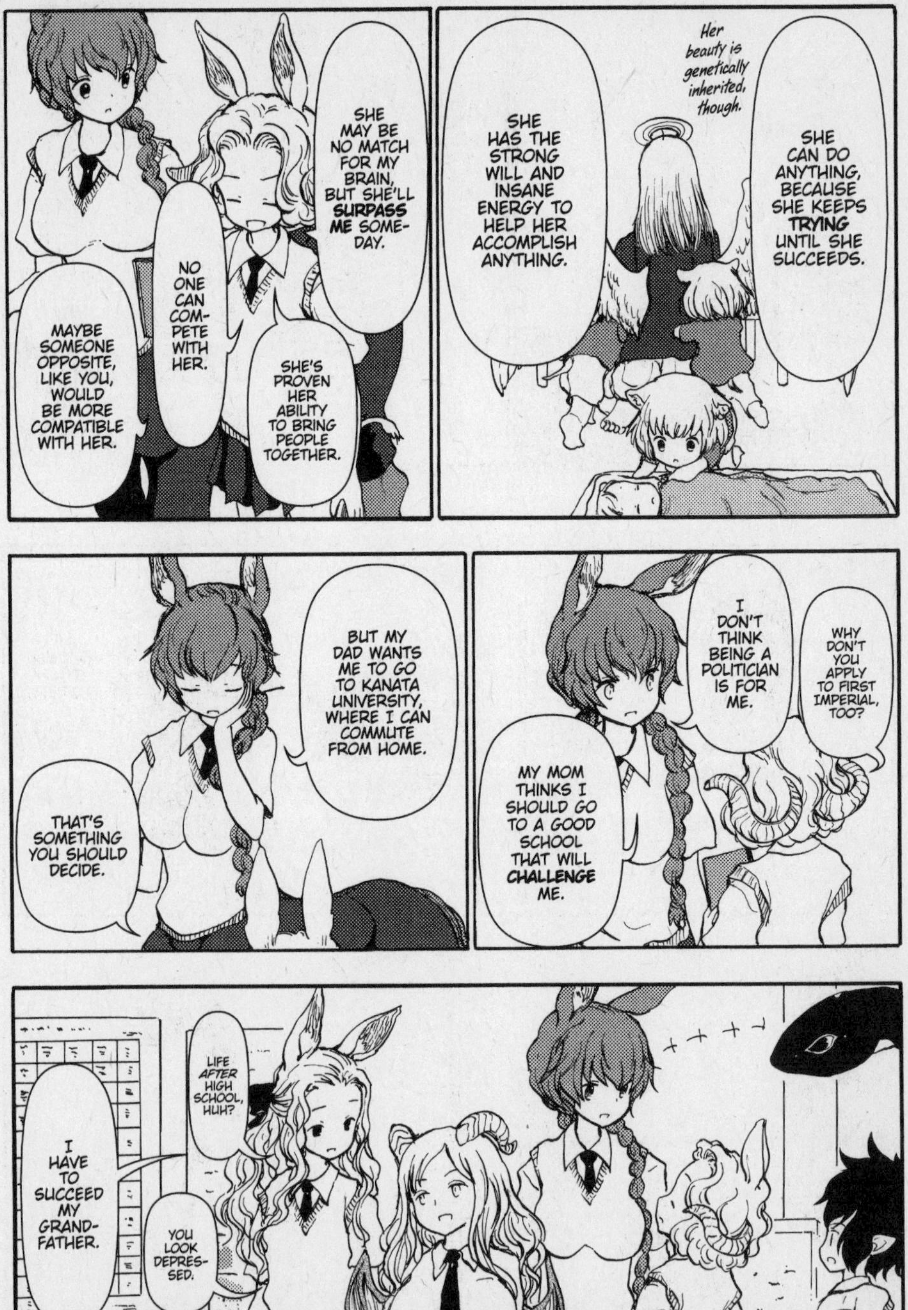
SHE CAN DO ANYTHING, BECAUSE SHE KEEPS **TRYING** UNTIL SHE SUCCEEDS.
Her beauty is genetically inherited, though.
SHE HAS THE STRONG WILL AND INSANE ENERGY TO HELP HER ACCOMPLISH ANYTHING.
SHE MAY BE NO MATCH FOR MY BRAIN, BUT SHE'LL **SURPASS ME** SOME-DAY.
SHE'S PROVEN HER ABILITY TO BRING PEOPLE TOGETHER.
NO ONE CAN COM-PETE WITH HER.
MAYBE SOMEONE OPPOSITE, LIKE YOU, WOULD BE MORE COMPATIBLE WITH HER.
WHY DON'T YOU APPLY TO FIRST IMPERIAL, TOO?
I DON'T THINK BEING A POLITICIAN IS FOR ME.
MY MOM THINKS I SHOULD GO TO A GOOD SCHOOL THAT WILL **CHALLENGE** ME.
BUT MY DAD WANTS ME TO GO TO KANATA UNIVERSITY, WHERE I CAN COMMUTE FROM HOME.
THAT'S SOMETHING YOU SHOULD DECIDE.
LIFE *AFTER* HIGH SCHOOL, HUH?
YOU LOOK DEPRES-SED.
I HAVE TO SUCCEED MY GRAND-FATHER.

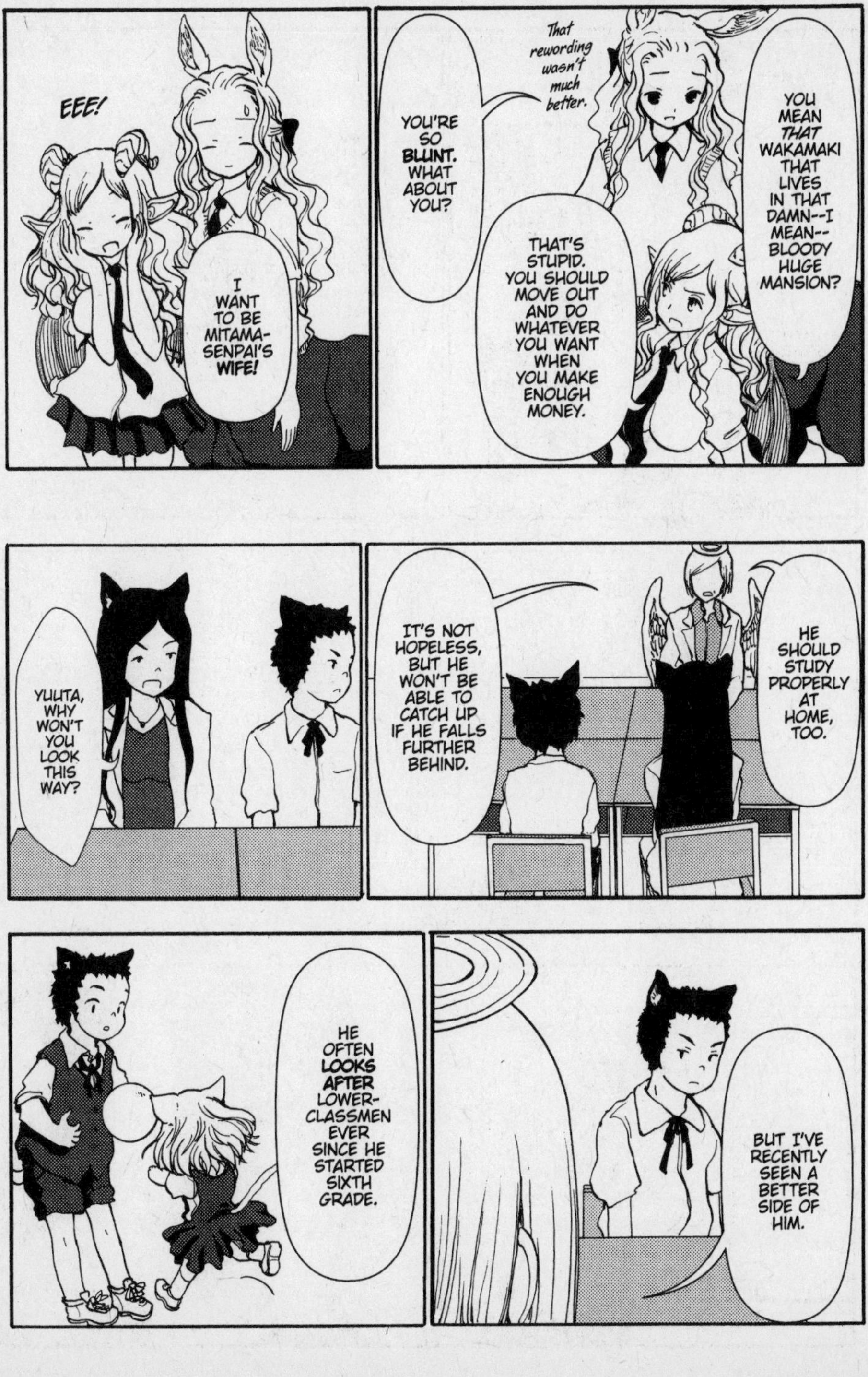
YOU MEAN *THAT* WAKAMAKI THAT LIVES IN THAT DAMN--I MEAN--BLOODY HUGE MANSION?
That rewording wasn't much better.
THAT'S STUPID. YOU SHOULD MOVE OUT AND DO WHATEVER YOU WANT WHEN YOU MAKE ENOUGH MONEY.
YOU'RE SO **BLUNT.** WHAT ABOUT YOU?
I WANT TO BE MITAMA-SENPAI'S **WIFE!**
EEE!
HE SHOULD STUDY PROPERLY AT HOME, TOO.
IT'S NOT HOPELESS, BUT HE WON'T BE ABLE TO CATCH UP IF HE FALLS FURTHER BEHIND.
YUUTA, WHY WON'T YOU LOOK THIS WAY?
BUT I'VE RECENTLY SEEN A BETTER SIDE OF HIM.
HE OFTEN **LOOKS AFTER** LOWER-CLASSMEN EVER SINCE HE STARTED SIXTH GRADE.

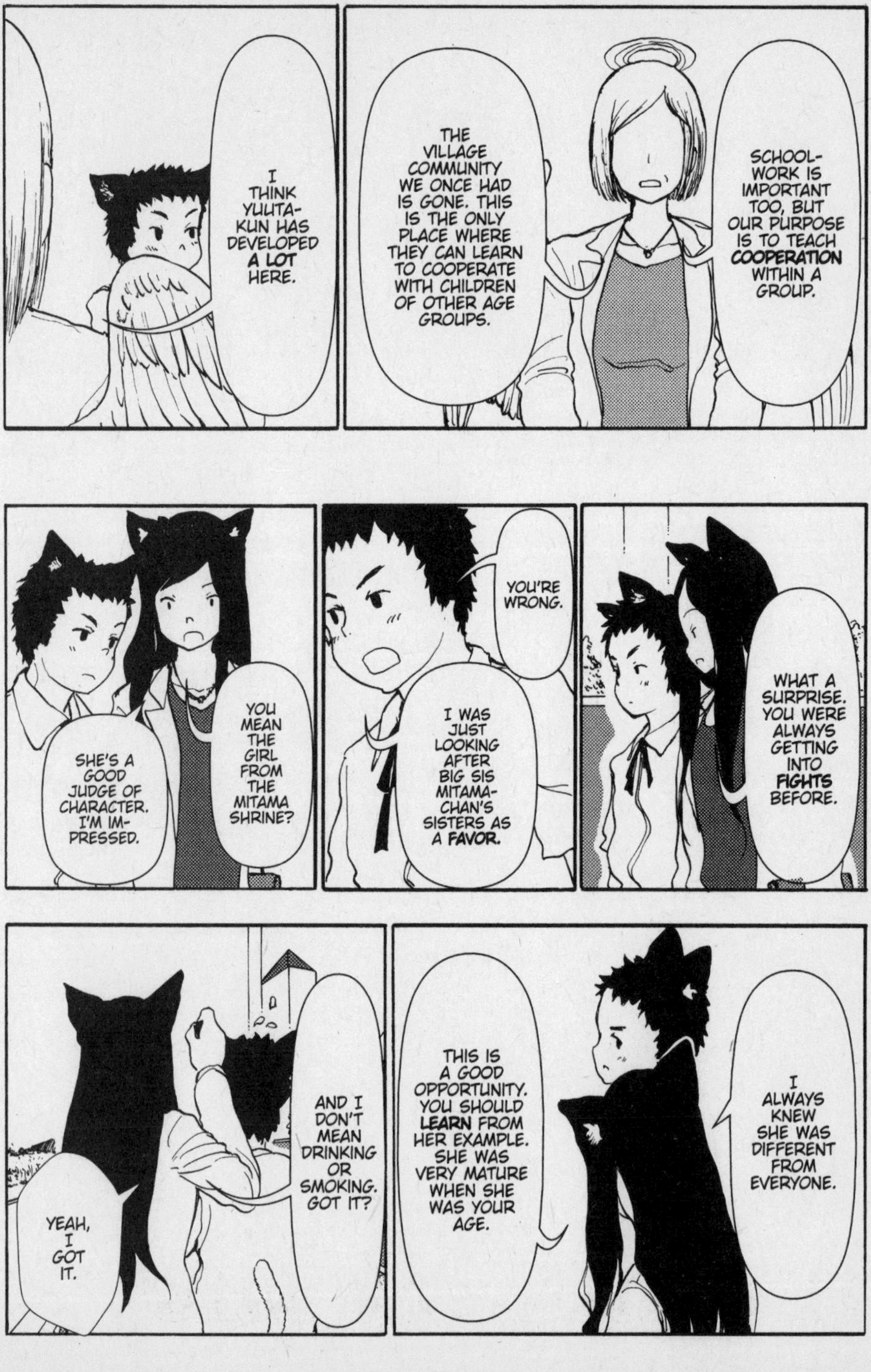
SCHOOL-WORK IS IMPORTANT TOO, BUT OUR PURPOSE IS TO TEACH **COOPERATION** WITHIN A GROUP.
THE VILLAGE COMMUNITY WE ONCE HAD IS GONE. THIS IS THE ONLY PLACE WHERE THEY CAN LEARN TO COOPERATE WITH CHILDREN OF OTHER AGE GROUPS.
I THINK YUUTA-KUN HAS DEVELOPED **A LOT** HERE.
WHAT A SURPRISE. YOU WERE ALWAYS GETTING INTO **FIGHTS** BEFORE.
YOU'RE WRONG.
I WAS JUST LOOKING AFTER BIG SIS MITAMA-CHAN'S SISTERS AS A **FAVOR.**
YOU MEAN THE GIRL FROM THE MITAMA SHRINE?
SHE'S A GOOD JUDGE OF CHARACTER. I'M IM-PRESSED.
I ALWAYS KNEW SHE WAS DIFFERENT FROM EVERYONE.
THIS IS A GOOD OPPORTUNITY. YOU SHOULD **LEARN** FROM HER EXAMPLE. SHE WAS VERY MATURE WHEN SHE WAS YOUR AGE.
AND I DON'T MEAN DRINKING OR SMOKING. GOT IT?
YEAH, I GOT IT.

A Centaur's Life

UNDERSTANDING ANTARCTICANS: PART 8

ALTHOUGH HUMANS ARE HIGHLY INTERESTED, LITTLE IS KNOWN ABOUT THE BREADTH OF ANTARCTICAN KNOWLEDGE AND CIVILIZATION. WE HAVE YET TO CONFIRM WHETHER THE INTELLECTUAL SUBSPECIES IS TRULY AS INTELLIGENT AND LEARNED AS THEIR NAME SUGGESTS. ALSO LACKING IS CONFIRMATION OF THEIR PURPORTED ABILITIES SUCH AS PERFECT MEMORY, EXCELLENT COMPUTING POWER, AND RAPID ACQUISITION OF FOREIGN LANGUAGES. COMPOUNDING THE KNOWLEDGE GAP CREATED BY ANTARCTICAN SECRECY IS THE FACT THAT HUMANS HAVE YET TO FULLY GRASP THEIR WRITTEN OR SPOKEN LANGUAGE. IT'S BELIEVED THAT THE ANTARCTICAN CIVILIZATION MAY HAVE ORIGINATED AS FAR BACK AS 40 MILLION YEARS AGO, AND THAT THEY BEGAN BUILDING THEIR UNDERGROUND CITY AT THAT TIME.

DESPITE THE AGE OF THEIR CIVILIZATION, ANTARCTICANS RELIED ON HUMANS FOR MODERN TRANSPORTATION LIKE AIRPLANES AND MARINE VESSELS, AND DRESSED IN SHABBY ROBES AND FUR COATS (OUTDATED ARMOR AND TRIDENTS FOR THE WARRIOR SUBSPECIES) WHEN THEY BEGAN TO ACTIVELY CONTACT OTHER COUNTRIES IN THE MID-TWENTIETH CENTURY. THAT THEY DID NOT VENTURE INTO OTHER AREAS ASIDE FROM SOUTH AMERICA SUGGESTS THAT THEIR CIVILIZATION DEVELOPED VERY SLOWLY, THOUGH THIS IS NOT UNEXPECTED GIVEN THEIR LIMITED RESOURCES AND POPULATION, NOT TO MENTION THE EXTREME ENVIRONMENT OF THEIR CONTINENT. EVEN HUMANS IN MORE AGREEABLE CLIMATES REMAINED IN THE STONE AGE FOR SEVERAL THOUSAND YEARS, AND THE PRIMITIVE STAGES OF REASONING AND OBSERVATION YIELDED CASES OF EXTRAORDINARY DEVELOPMENT IN SCIENCE AND TECH-NOLOGY (SUCH AS MATHEMATICS AND ASTRONOMY) IN THOSE ANCIENT HUMAN CIVILIZATIONS.

THERE IS A CONVINCING THEORY THAT ANTARCTICANS KEPT HUMANS AWAY FROM THEIR CONTINENT TO HIDE THEIR INFERIOR MILITARY TECHNOLOGY, BUT THE FACT THAT TWENTIETH CENTURY WARSHIPS AND RESEARCH VESSELS WERE UNABLE TO REACH ANTARCTICA SUGGESTS THAT THEY MAY POSSESS ADVANCED DEFENSIVE COUNTER-MEASURES. FAR FROM BEING PRIMITIVE, ANTARCTICANS ARE KNOWN TO HAVE SURPASSED HUMANS IN BIOLOGY, CIVIL ENGINEERING, MATHEMATICS, MEDICINE, AND PHARMACOLOGY AT THE LEAST. WE STILL KNOW VERY LITTLE ABOUT THEIR CIVILIZATION AND LEVEL OF TECHNOLOGICAL ADVANCEMENT. FOR NOW, WE ADVISE TREATING THEM WITH CAUTION AND ADOPTING A STRATEGY OF DIPLOMACY AND APPEASEMENT.

Antarcticans seem to have limited experience with the creative arts. While they show an appreciation for music, they find literature and fine art difficult to understand, especially non-traditional forms such as avant-garde and modern art. Nevertheless, they are passionate about art appreciation and never show signs of boredom. This may be refreshing to those in the fine art world who scorn 'commoners' for lacking interest.

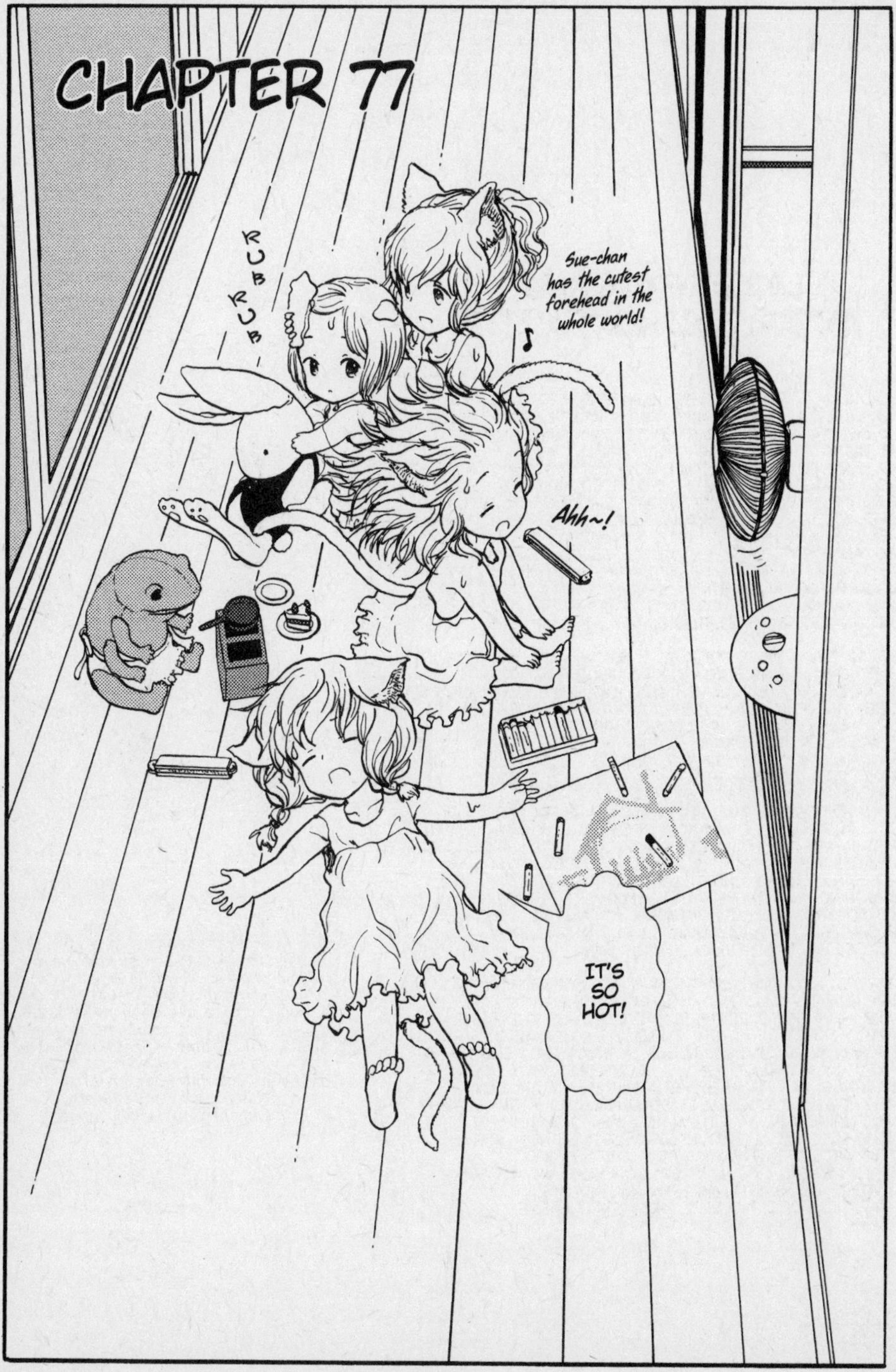
CHAPTER 77
Sue-chan has the cutest forehead in the whole world!
♪
RUB RUB
Ahh~!
IT'S SO HOT!

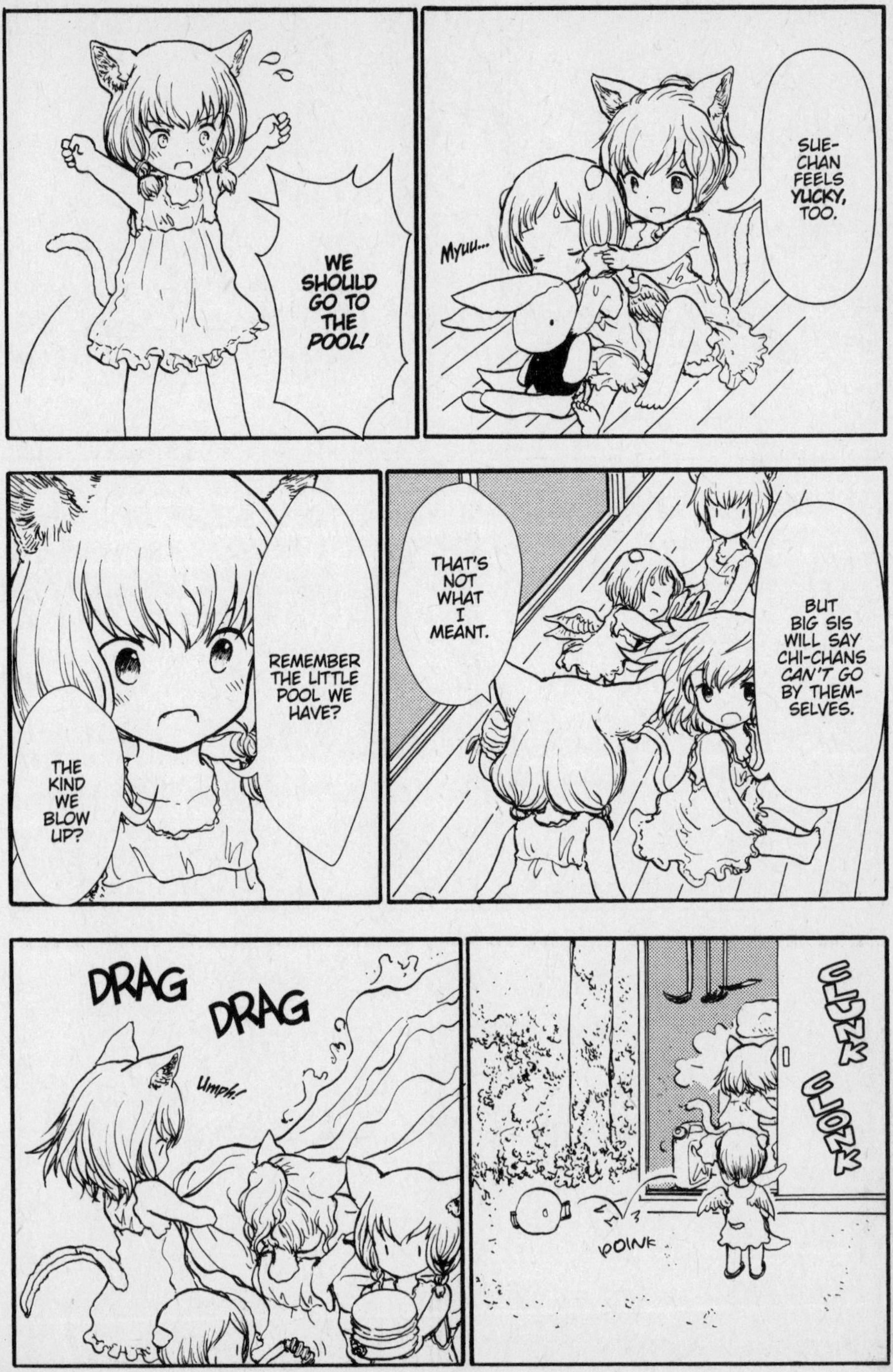
SUE-CHAN FEELS *YUCKY*, TOO.
Myuu...
WE SHOULD GO TO THE *POOL!*
BUT BIG SIS WILL SAY CHI-CHANS *CAN'T* GO BY THEM-SELVES.
THAT'S NOT WHAT I MEANT.
REMEMBER THE LITTLE POOL WE HAVE?
THE KIND WE BLOW UP?
CLUNK
CLONK
POINK
DRAG
DRAG
Umph!

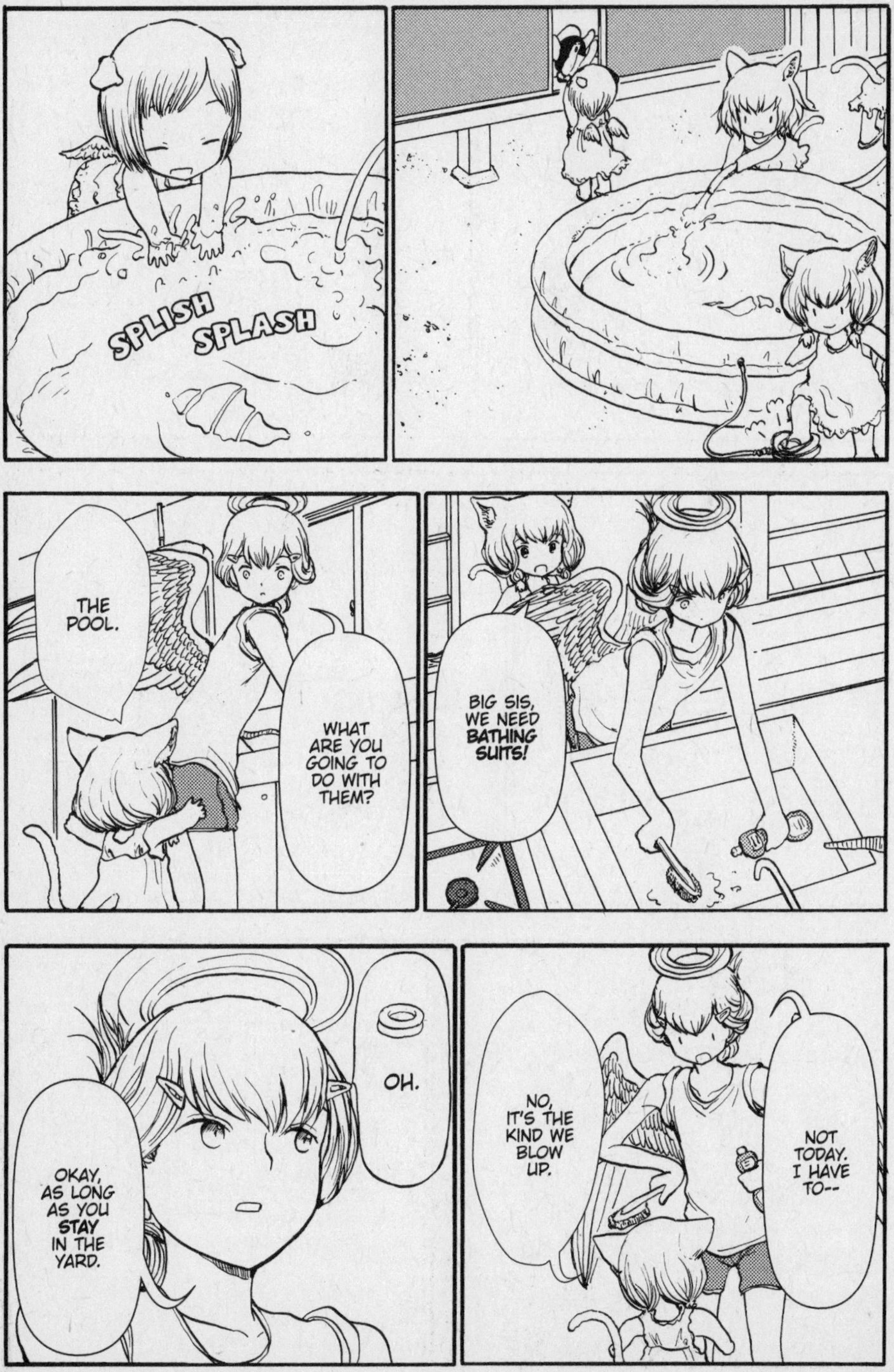
SPLISH SPLASH
BIG SIS, WE NEED BATHING SUITS!
WHAT ARE YOU GOING TO DO WITH THEM?
THE POOL.
NOT TODAY. I HAVE TO--
NO, IT'S THE KIND WE BLOW UP.
OH.
OKAY, AS LONG AS YOU STAY IN THE YARD.

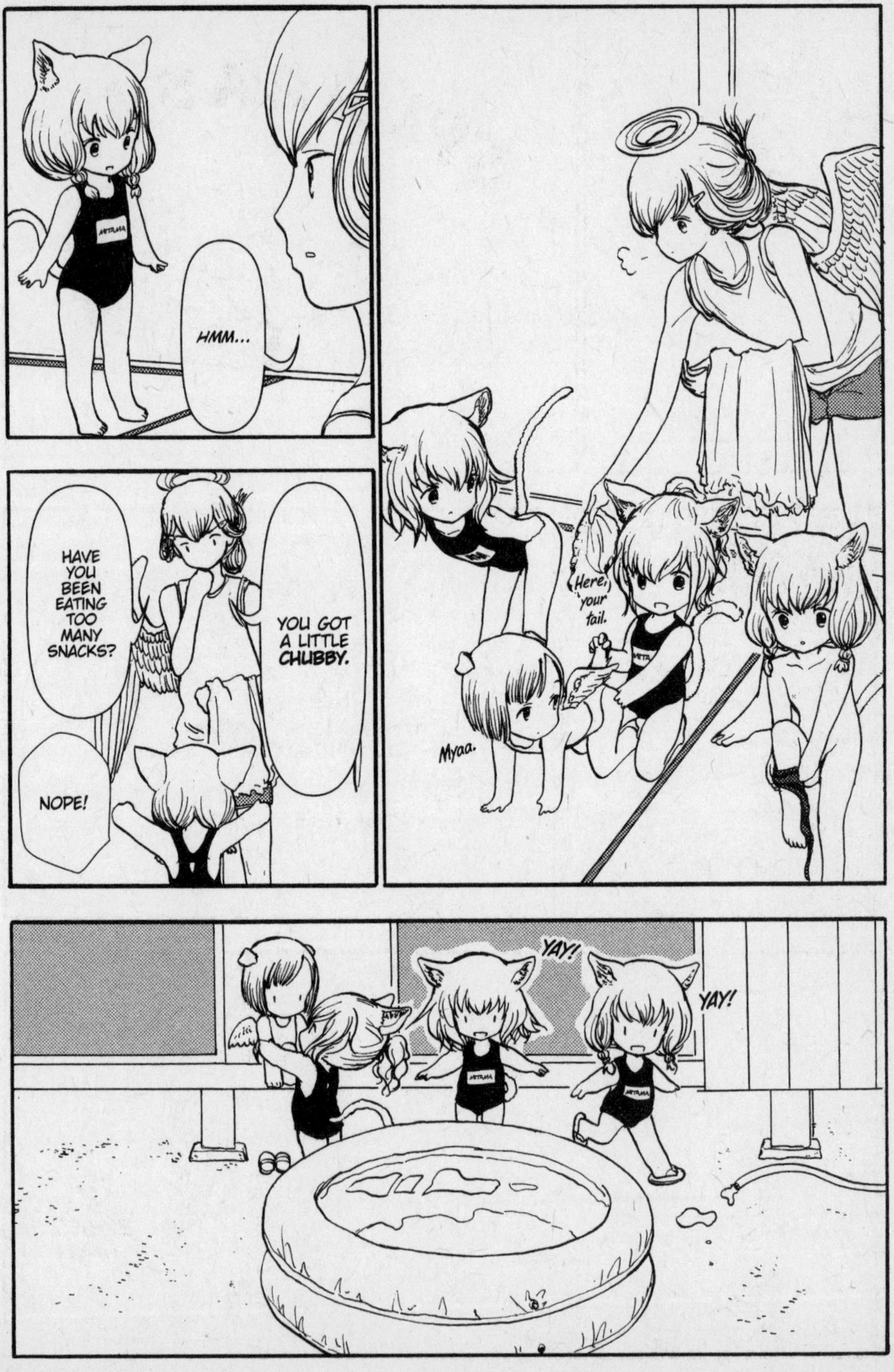
Here, your tail.
Myaa.
HMM...
YOU GOT A LITTLE CHUBBY.
HAVE YOU BEEN EATING TOO MANY SNACKS?
NOPE!
YAY!
YAY!

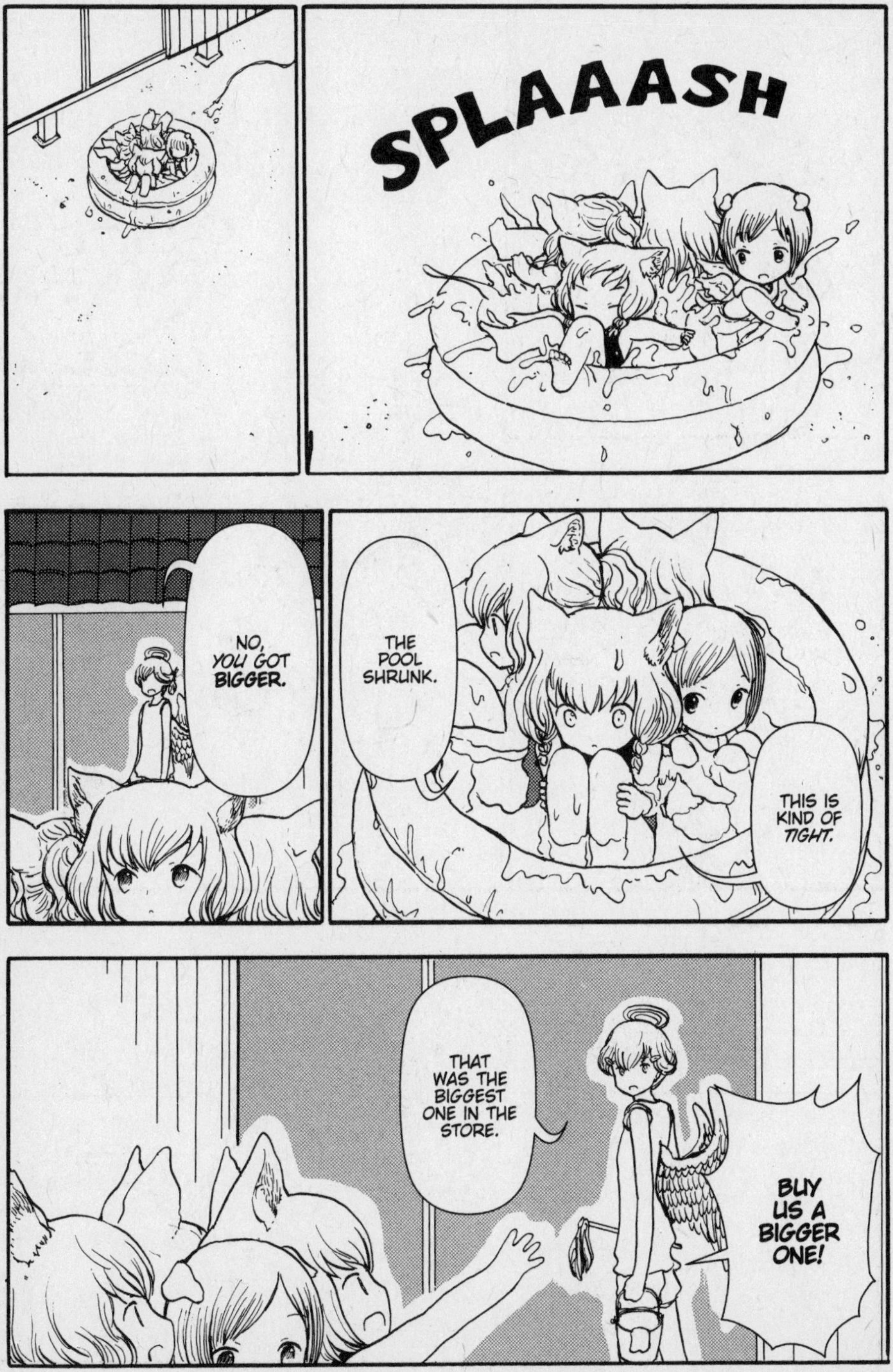
SPLAAASH
THE POOL SHRUNK.
THIS IS KIND OF *TIGHT.*
NO, *YOU* GOT **BIGGER.**
BUY US A BIGGER ONE!
THAT WAS THE BIGGEST ONE IN THE STORE.

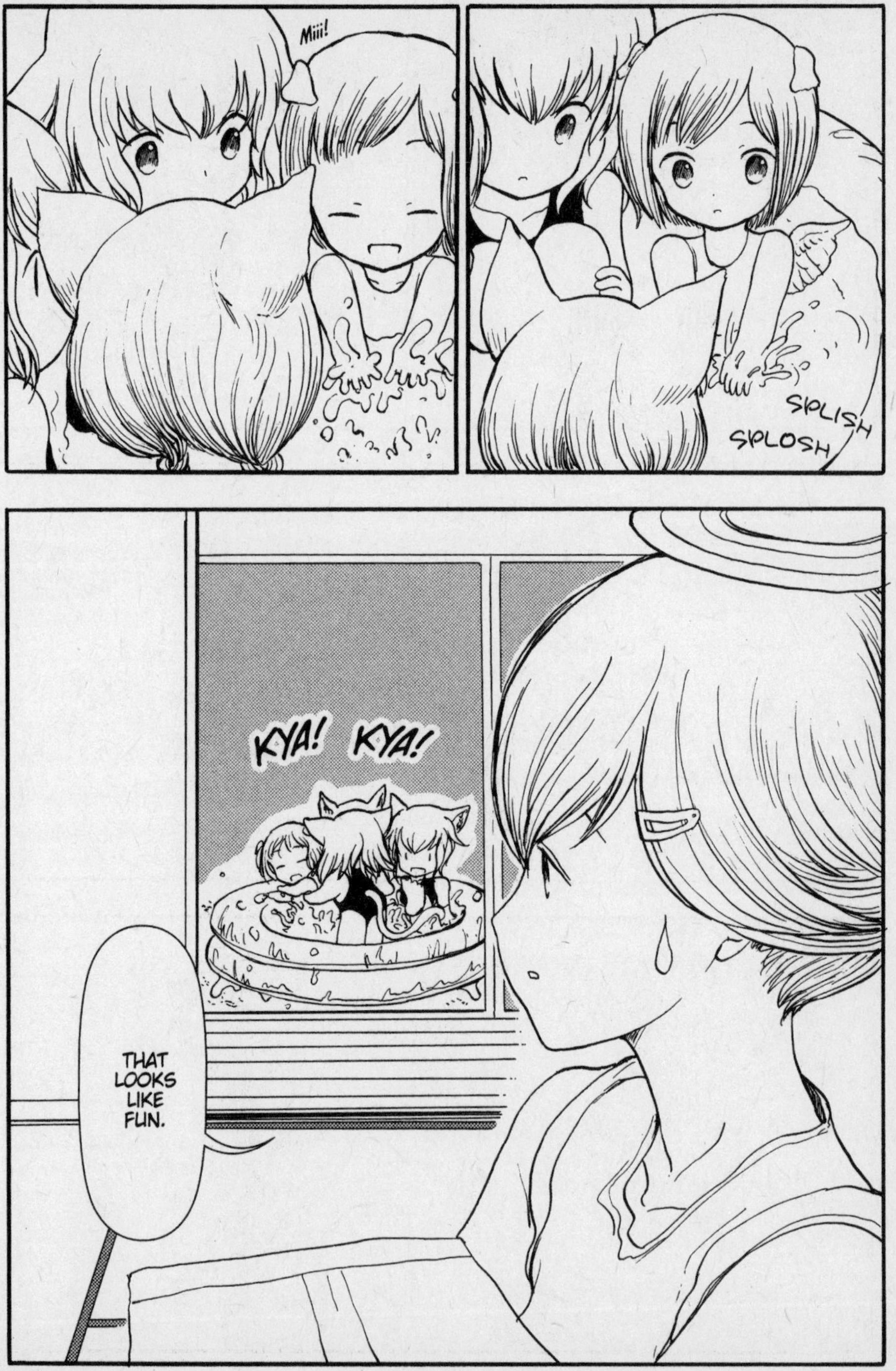
SPLISH
SPLOSH
Miii!
KYA! KYA!
THAT LOOKS LIKE FUN.

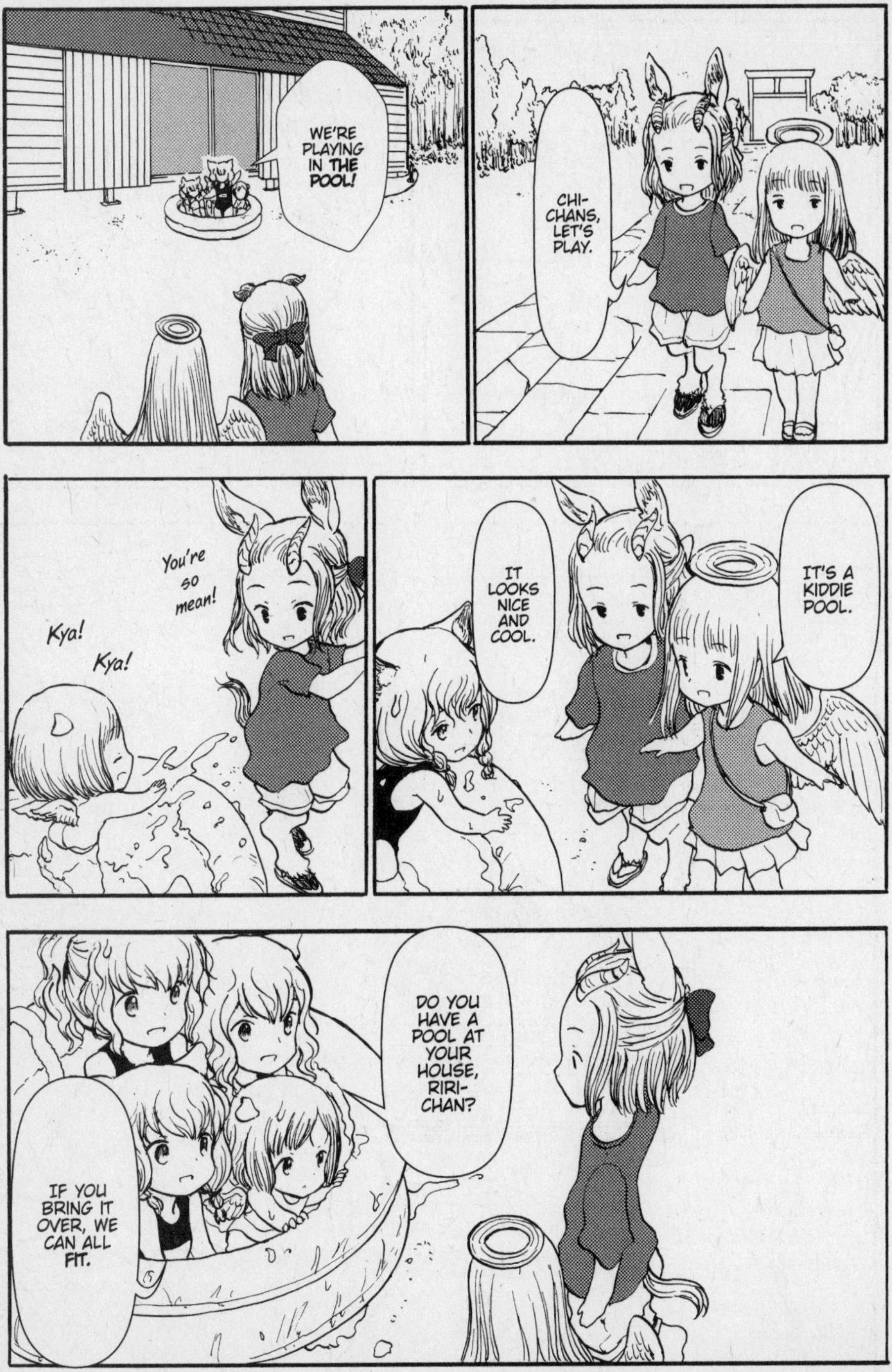
CHI-CHANS, LET'S PLAY.
WE'RE PLAYING IN THE POOL!
IT'S A KIDDIE POOL.
IT LOOKS NICE AND COOL.
You're so mean!
Kya!
Kya!
DO YOU HAVE A POOL AT YOUR HOUSE, RIRI-CHAN?
IF YOU BRING IT OVER, WE CAN ALL FIT.

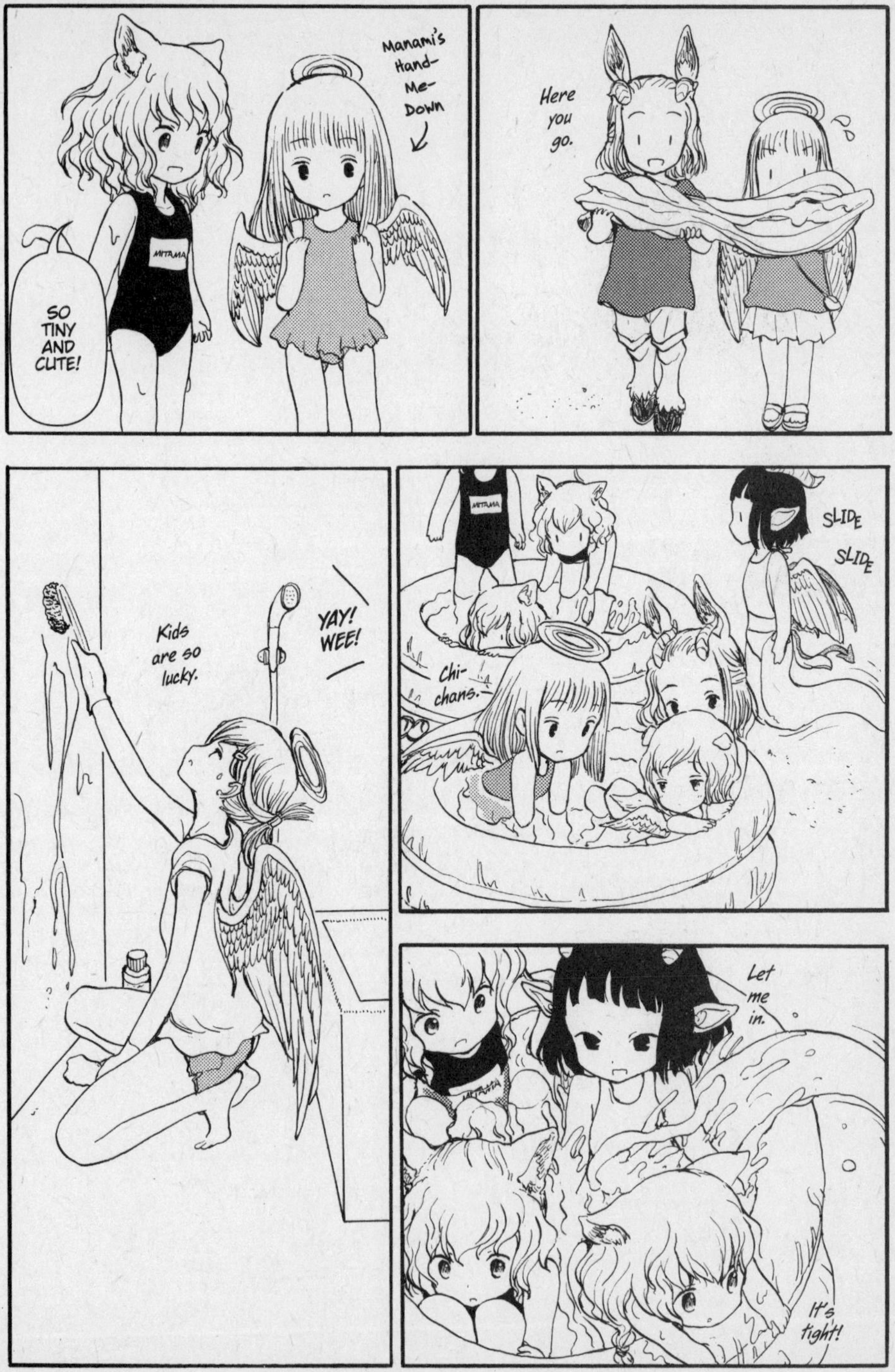
Here you go.
Manami's Hand-Me-Down
SO TINY AND CUTE!
SLIDE SLIDE
Chi-chans.
Let me in.
It's tight!
YAY! WEE!
Kids are so lucky.

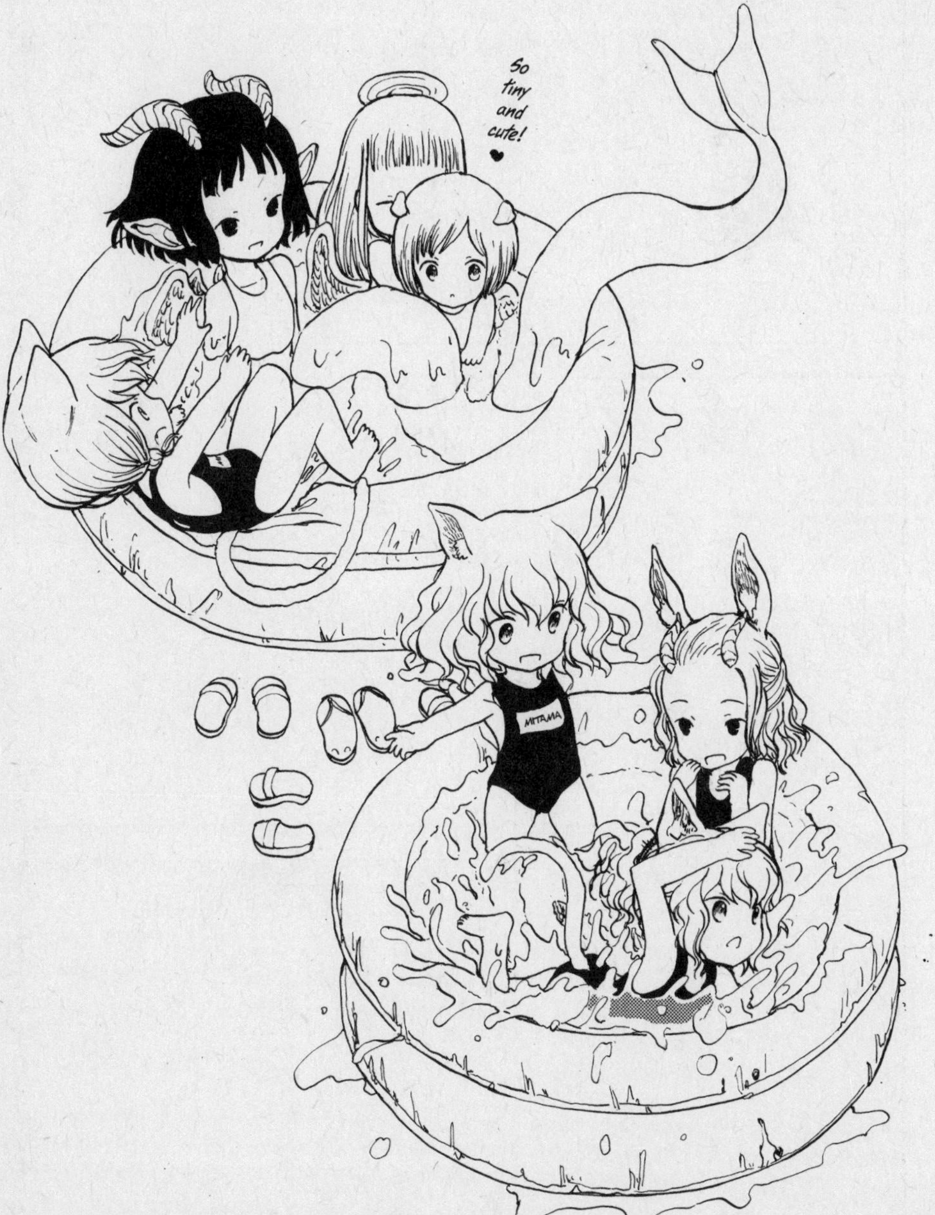
So tiny and cute!
MITAMA

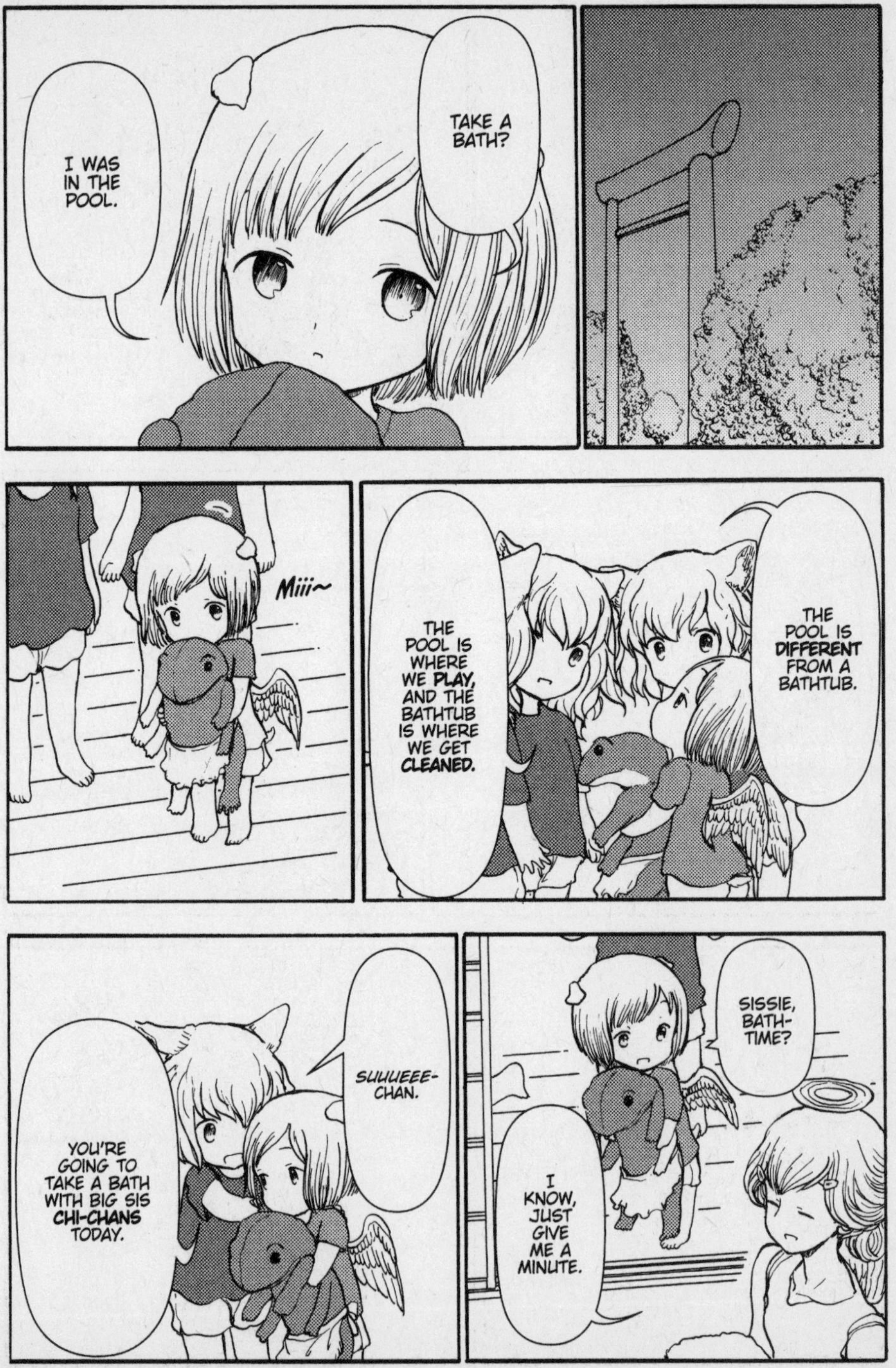
TAKE A BATH?
I WAS IN THE POOL.
THE POOL IS DIFFERENT FROM A BATHTUB.
THE POOL IS WHERE WE PLAY, AND THE BATHTUB IS WHERE WE GET CLEANED.
Miii~
SISSIE, BATH-TIME?
I KNOW, JUST GIVE ME A MINUTE.
SUUUEEE-CHAN.
YOU'RE GOING TO TAKE A BATH WITH BIG SIS CHI-CHANS TODAY.

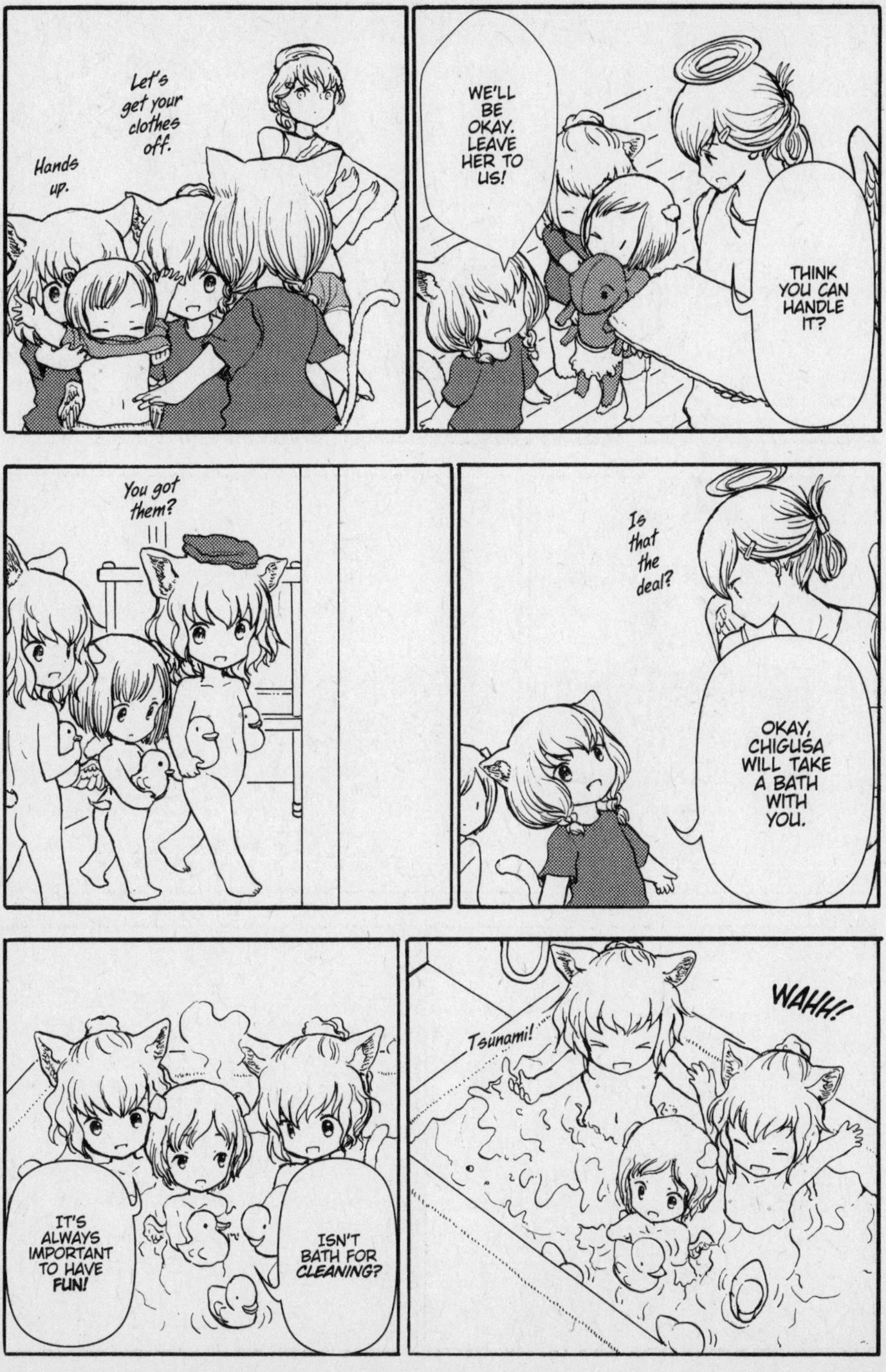
THINK YOU CAN HANDLE IT?
WE'LL BE OKAY. LEAVE HER TO US!
Let's get your clothes off.
Hands up.
OKAY, CHIGUSA WILL TAKE A BATH WITH YOU.
Is that the deal?
You got them?
WAHH!!
Tsunami!
ISN'T BATH FOR *CLEANING*?
IT'S ALWAYS IMPORTANT TO HAVE **FUN!**

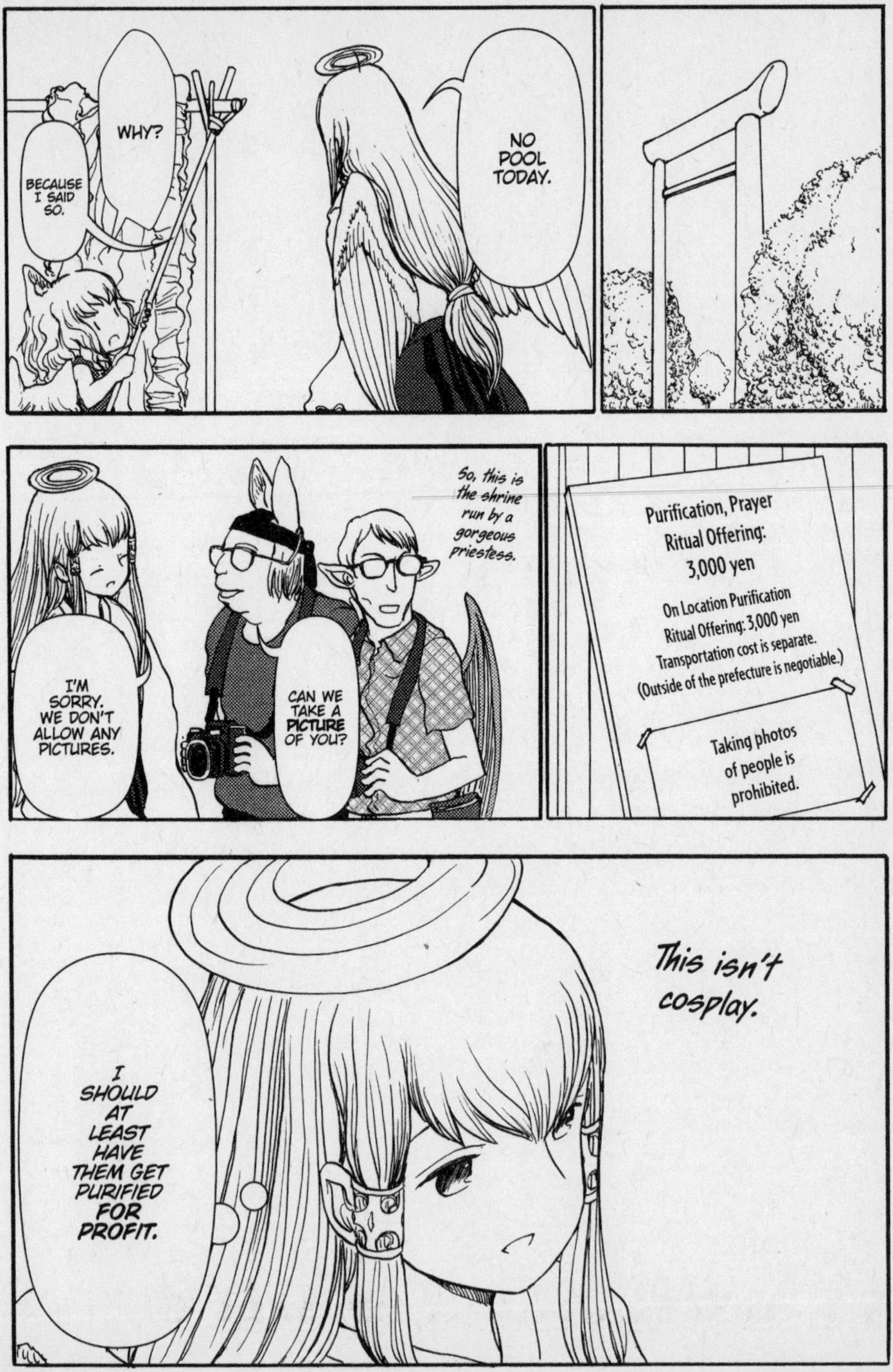
NO POOL TODAY.
WHY?
BECAUSE I SAID SO.
Purification, Prayer Ritual Offering: 3,000 yen
On Location Purification Ritual Offering: 3,000 yen Transportation cost is separate. (Outside of the prefecture is negotiable.)
Taking photos of people is prohibited.
So, this is the shrine run by a gorgeous priestess.
CAN WE TAKE A PICTURE OF YOU?
I'M SORRY. WE DON'T ALLOW ANY PICTURES.
This isn't cosplay.
I SHOULD AT LEAST HAVE THEM GET PURIFIED FOR PROFIT.

A CentaUr's Life

UNDERSTANDING ANTARCTICANS: PART 9

RECENTLY, THE RUINS OF A LOST CITY WERE FOUND IN THE ARABIAN DESERT. THIS IS NOT SURPRISING IN AND OF ITSELF; SINCE ARABIA LIES ON A SINGLE CONTINENTAL PLATE (THE ARABIAN PLATE) THE GEOLOGICAL FORMATIONS ARE QUITE STABLE, AS EVIDENCED BY THE LARGE NUMBER OF ANCIENT, ORGANIC-RICH DEPOSITS THAT BECAME GIANT OIL FIELDS. THIS STABILITY ALSO MEANS THAT ARABIA OFTEN YIELDS WELL-PRESERVED PRIMEVAL RUINS. STILL, NO ONE IMAGINED THAT THE RUINS FOUND DEEP UNDERGROUND WOULD BE 40 MILLION YEARS OLD, OR THAT WHAT THEY WOULD FIND WITHIN WOULD BE QUITE SO ASTONISHING.

THE RUINS WERE A NETWORK OF VERY NARROW PASSAGEWAYS, DECORATED WITH ARTIFACTS THROUGHOUT. ARTWORK THAT ARCHAEOLOGISTS BELIEVED TO BE A DEPICTION OF THE CREATURE BURIED WITHIN THE RUIN SHOWED A REPTILE CRAWLING ON SIX LEGS. THIS IMPLIES A POSSIBLE RELATION TO ANTARCTICANS, BUT THEY SEEM FAR LESS INTERESTED IN STUDYING THEIR ANCESTORS THAN HUMANS ARE. THEIR LACK OF PARTICIPATION LEFT MUCH TO BE INTERPRETED BY OTHERS.
IF THESE RUINS WERE TRULY BUILT BY THEIR ANCESTORS, IT WOULD SHATTER THE THEORY THAT A BIPEDAL RACE PLAYED A ROLE IN THE DEVELOPMENT OF ANTARCTICAN CIVILIZATION AND TOOL USE; THIS ALSO INDICATES THAT THEY MAY HAVE RANGED BEYOND ANTARCTICA DURING THE TIME OF SUPERCONTINENTS, OR PERHAPS LATER.

THE ACCURACY OF THE THEORIES BEHIND THE AGE AND REPTILIAN ANCESTRY OF THE RUINS STILL REMAINS QUESTIONABLE, THOUGH, AND A SIGNIFICANT ERROR IN THE AGE COULD MAKE A DRAMATIC DIFFERENCE. A RELIGIOUS TEXT THAT MENTIONS THE EXISTENCE OF A TRIBE THAT BELIEVED IN A LIZARD TOTEM DURING THE PERIOD OF IGNORANCE COULD SUGGEST THAT THE RUINS WERE WHAT WAS CONSIDERED A SMALL TEMPLE DEDICATED TO A SACRED LIZARD, THOUGH THE RUINS ARE ACTUALLY QUITE LARGE. SUCH SPECULATION IS SUPPORTED BY AN UNUSUAL LACK OF EVIDENCE IN THE ORGANIC MATTER. THERE WERE NO TRACES OF LIFE FOUND, POSSIBLY BECAUSE THE CREATURES HAD BEEN PURIFIED AND BURIED IMMEDIATELY AFTER THE CONSTRUCTION OF THE TEMPLE. THE SPIRITUAL PURPOSE IS STILL UNKNOWN, AND THERE ARE OTHER PARTS OF THE RUINS YET TO BE DISCOVERED. THE EXCAVATION IS STILL UNDERWAY.

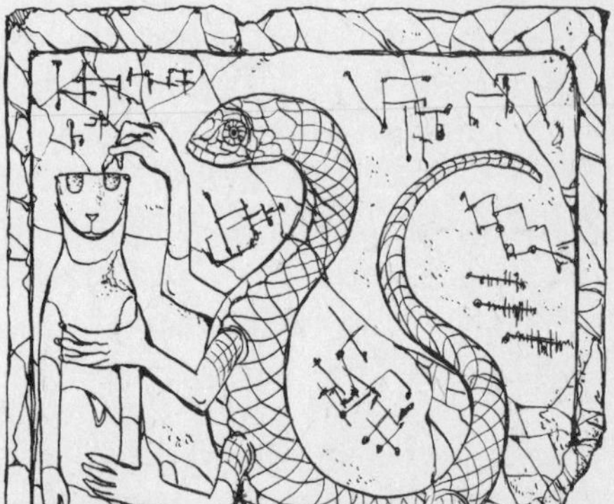

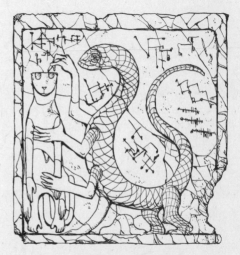

This is an artifact recovered from an Antarctican ruin. It is believed that it depicts a snakefolk tribesman executing a captured monkeyfolk tribesman. It may seem a bit graphic, but it's actually rather typical; the ruins of other civilization have yielded similar artifacts depicting macabre victory celebrations as well. Historians have surmised that they indicate a belief that victory in foreign war is the legacy they leave for their descendants. In that respect, this ruin is not that unusual.

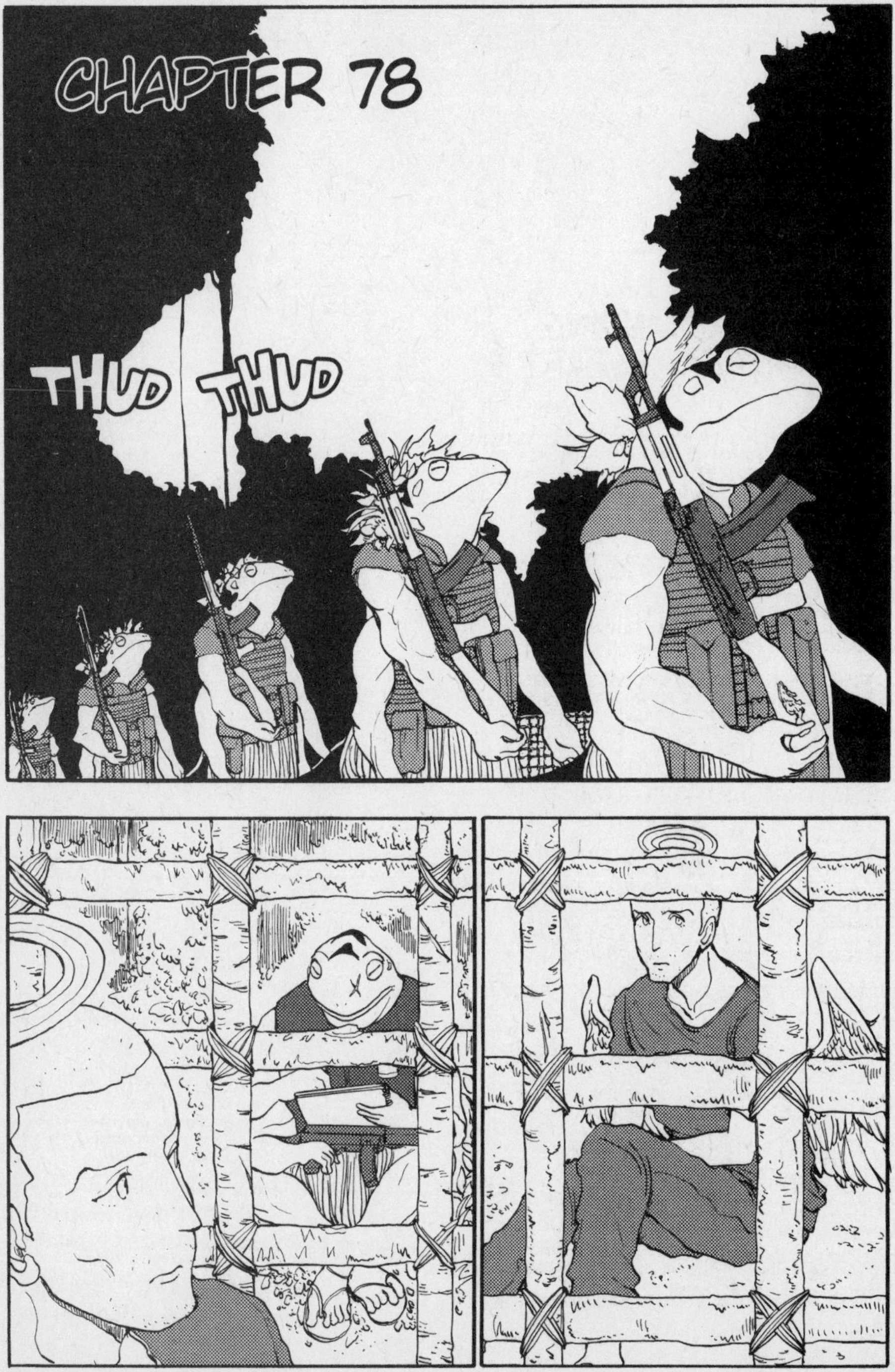
CHAPTER 78
THUD THUD

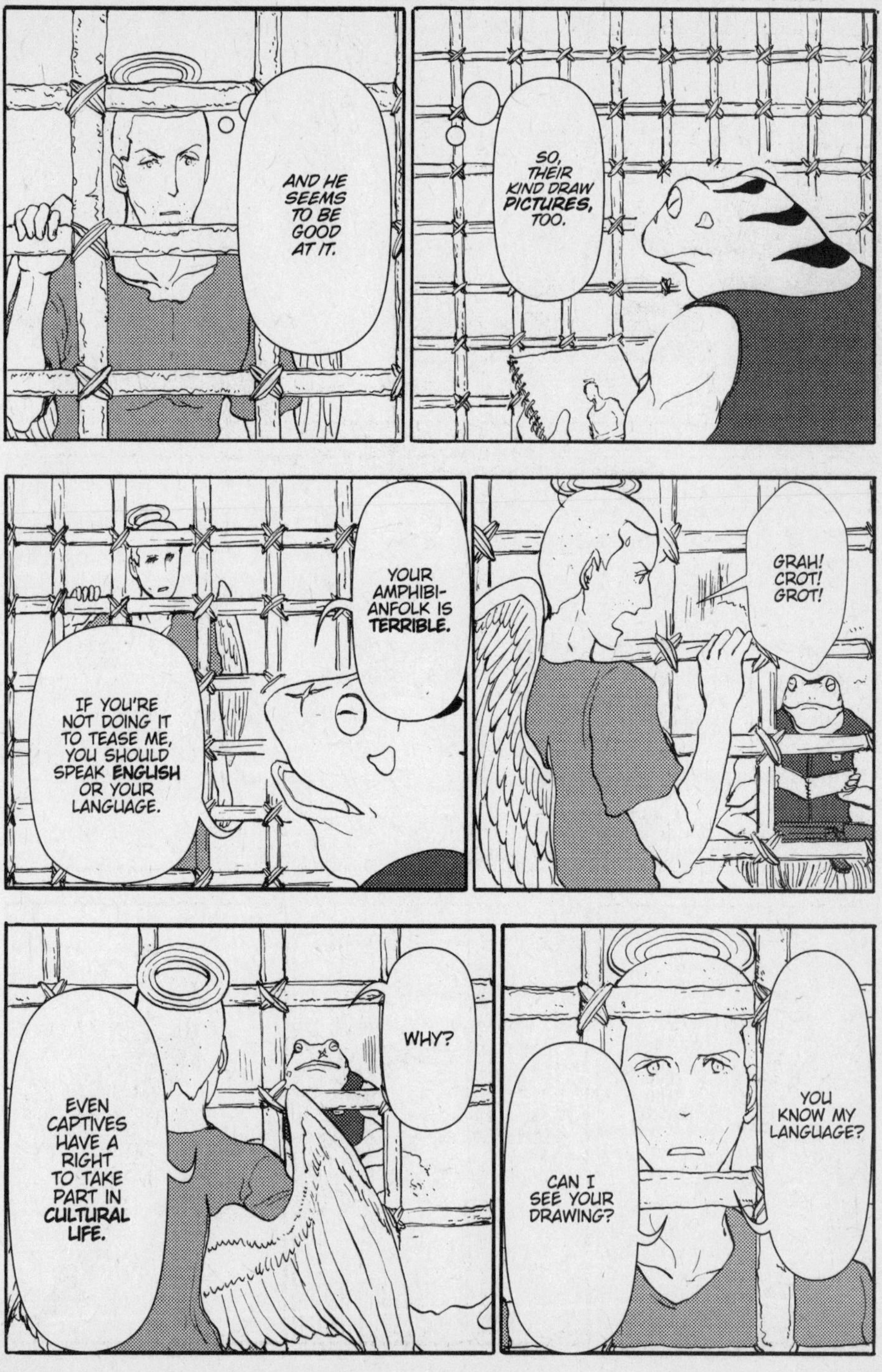
SO, THEIR KIND DRAW **PICTURES**, TOO.
AND HE SEEMS TO BE GOOD AT IT.
GRAH! CROT! GROT!
YOUR AMPHIBIANFOLK IS **TERRIBLE.**
IF YOU'RE NOT DOING IT TO TEASE ME, YOU SHOULD SPEAK **ENGLISH** OR YOUR LANGUAGE.
YOU KNOW MY LANGUAGE?
CAN I SEE YOUR DRAWING?
WHY?
EVEN CAPTIVES HAVE A RIGHT TO TAKE PART IN **CULTURAL LIFE.**

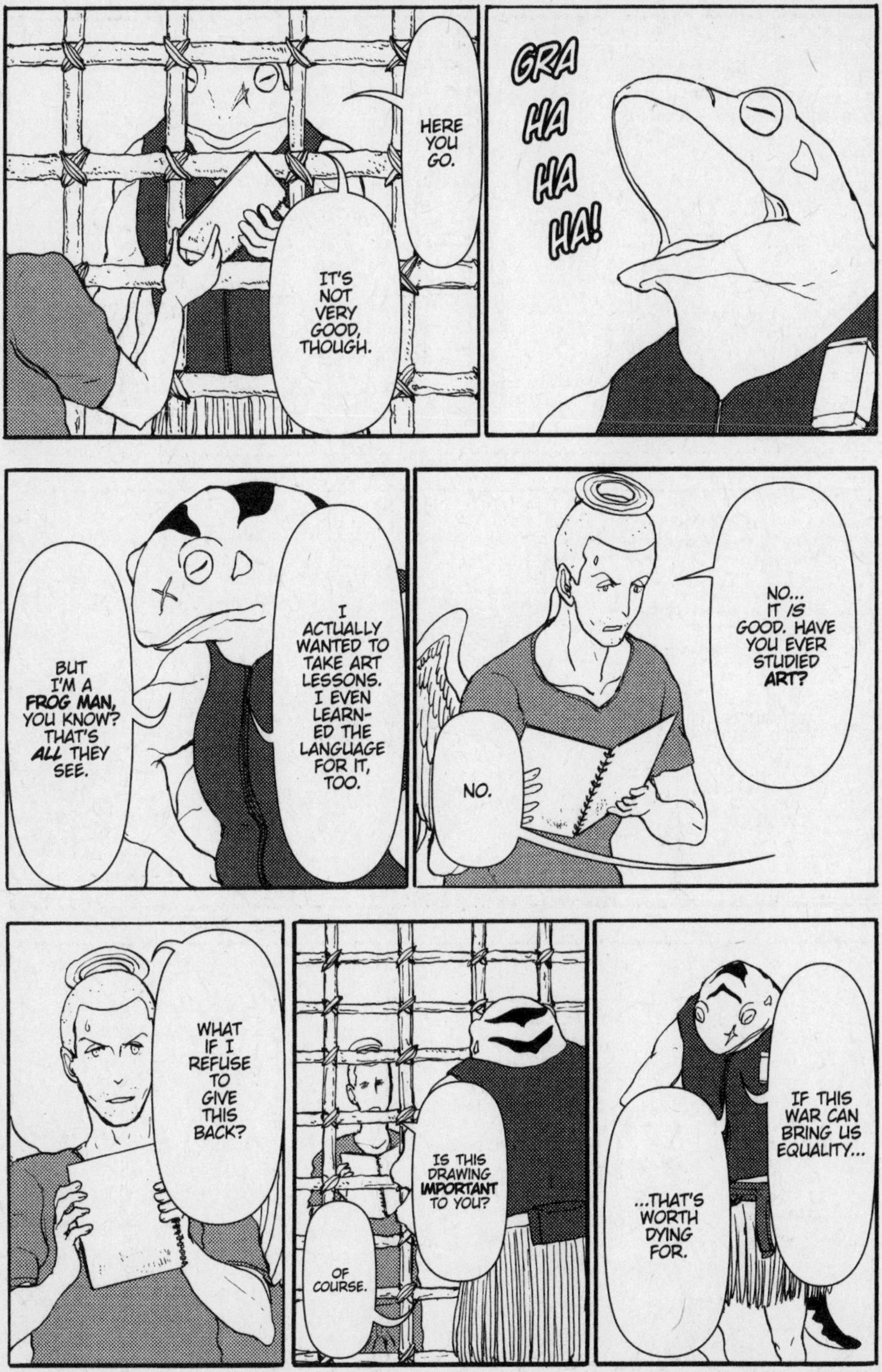
GRA HA HA HA!
HERE YOU GO.
IT'S NOT VERY GOOD, THOUGH.
NO... IT *IS* GOOD. HAVE YOU EVER STUDIED **ART?**
NO.
I ACTUALLY WANTED TO TAKE ART LESSONS. I EVEN LEARNED THE LANGUAGE FOR IT, TOO.
BUT I'M A **FROG MAN,** YOU KNOW? THAT'S ***ALL*** THEY SEE.
IF THIS WAR CAN BRING US EQUALITY...
...THAT'S WORTH DYING FOR.
IS THIS DRAWING **IMPORTANT** TO YOU?
OF COURSE.
WHAT IF I REFUSE TO GIVE THIS BACK?

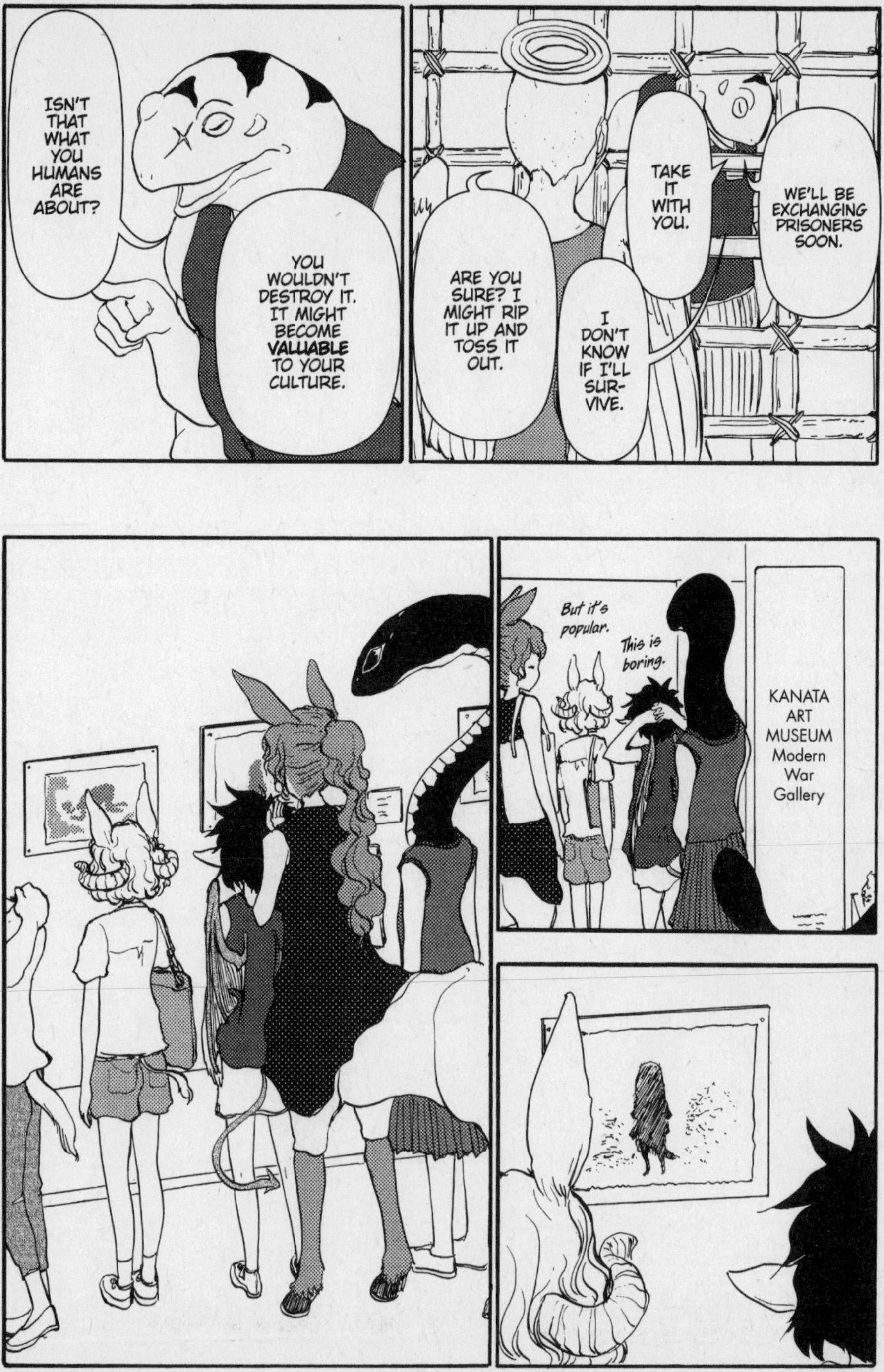
WE'LL BE EXCHANGING PRISONERS SOON.
TAKE IT WITH YOU.
I DON'T KNOW IF I'LL SUR-VIVE.
ARE YOU SURE? I MIGHT RIP IT UP AND TOSS IT OUT.
YOU WOULDN'T DESTROY IT. IT MIGHT BECOME **VALUABLE** TO YOUR CULTURE.
ISN'T THAT WHAT YOU HUMANS ARE ABOUT?
KANATA ART MUSEUM Modern War Gallery
This is boring.
But it's popular.

A Centaur's Life

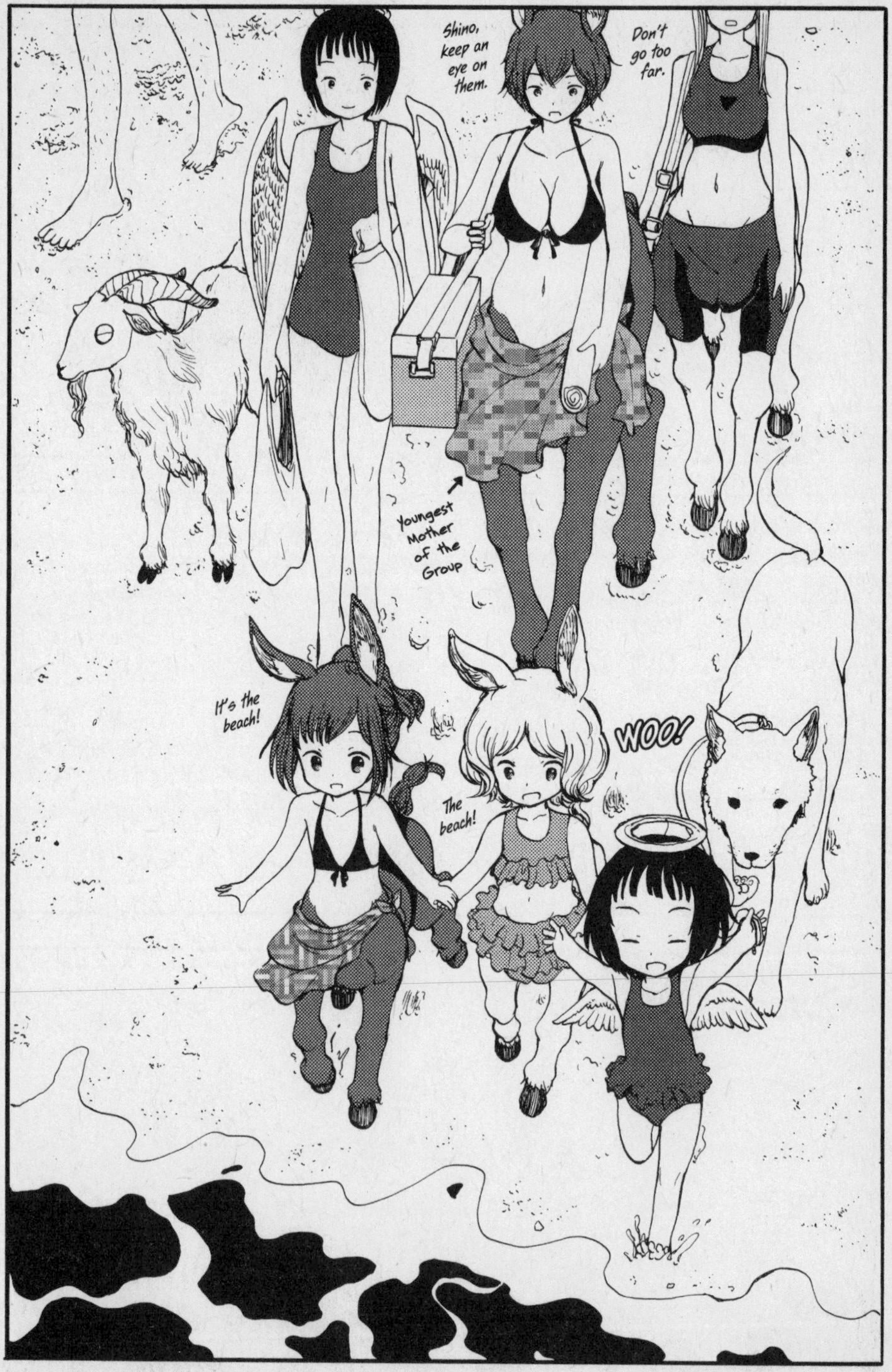
Don't go too far.
Shino, keep an eye on them.
Youngest Mother of the Group
WOO!
The beach!
It's the beach!

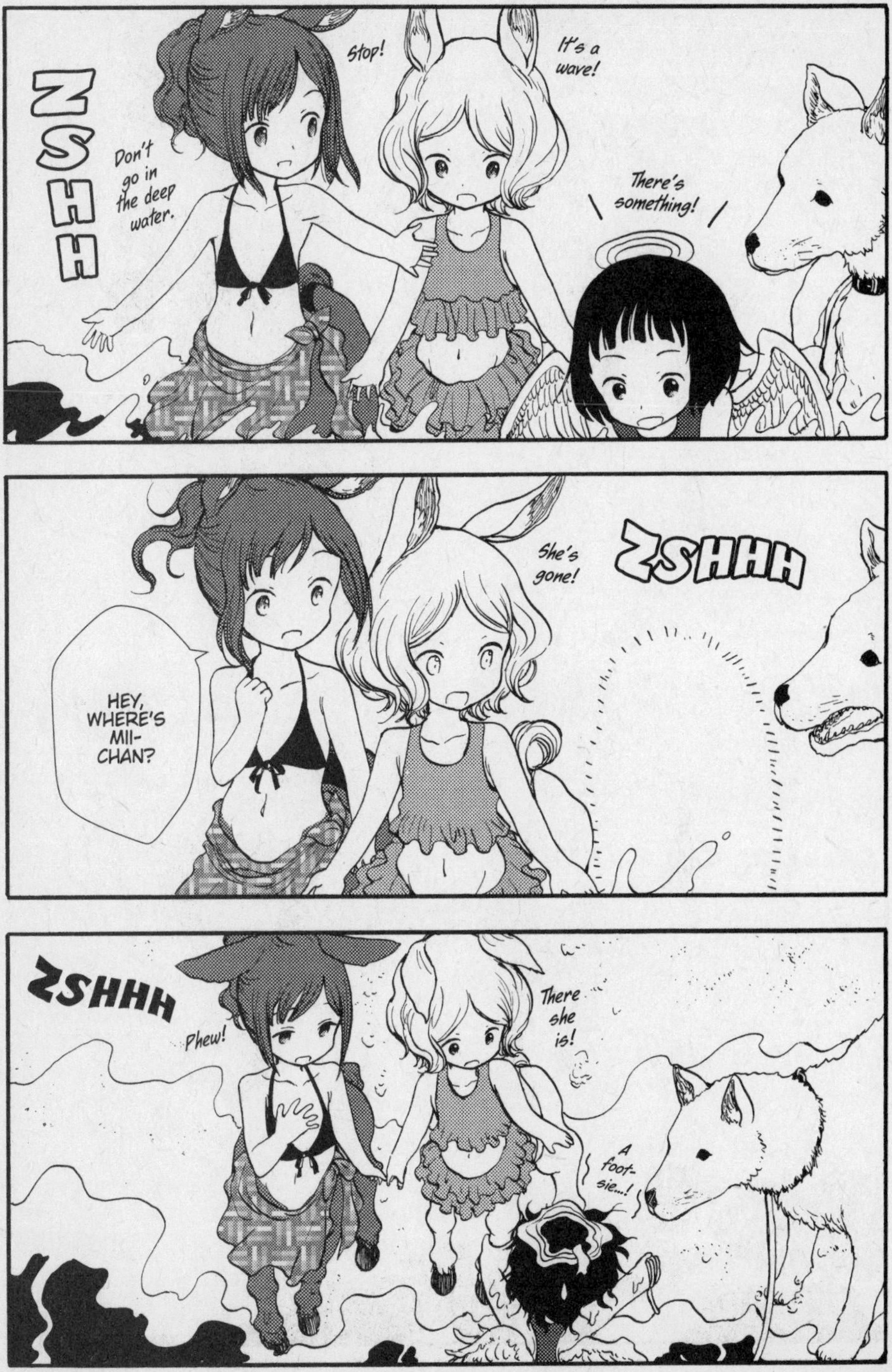
It's a wave!
There's something!
Stop!
Don't go in the deep water.
ZSHH
ZSHHH
She's gone!
HEY, WHERE'S MII-CHAN?
There she is!
A foot-sie...!
Phew!
ZSHHH

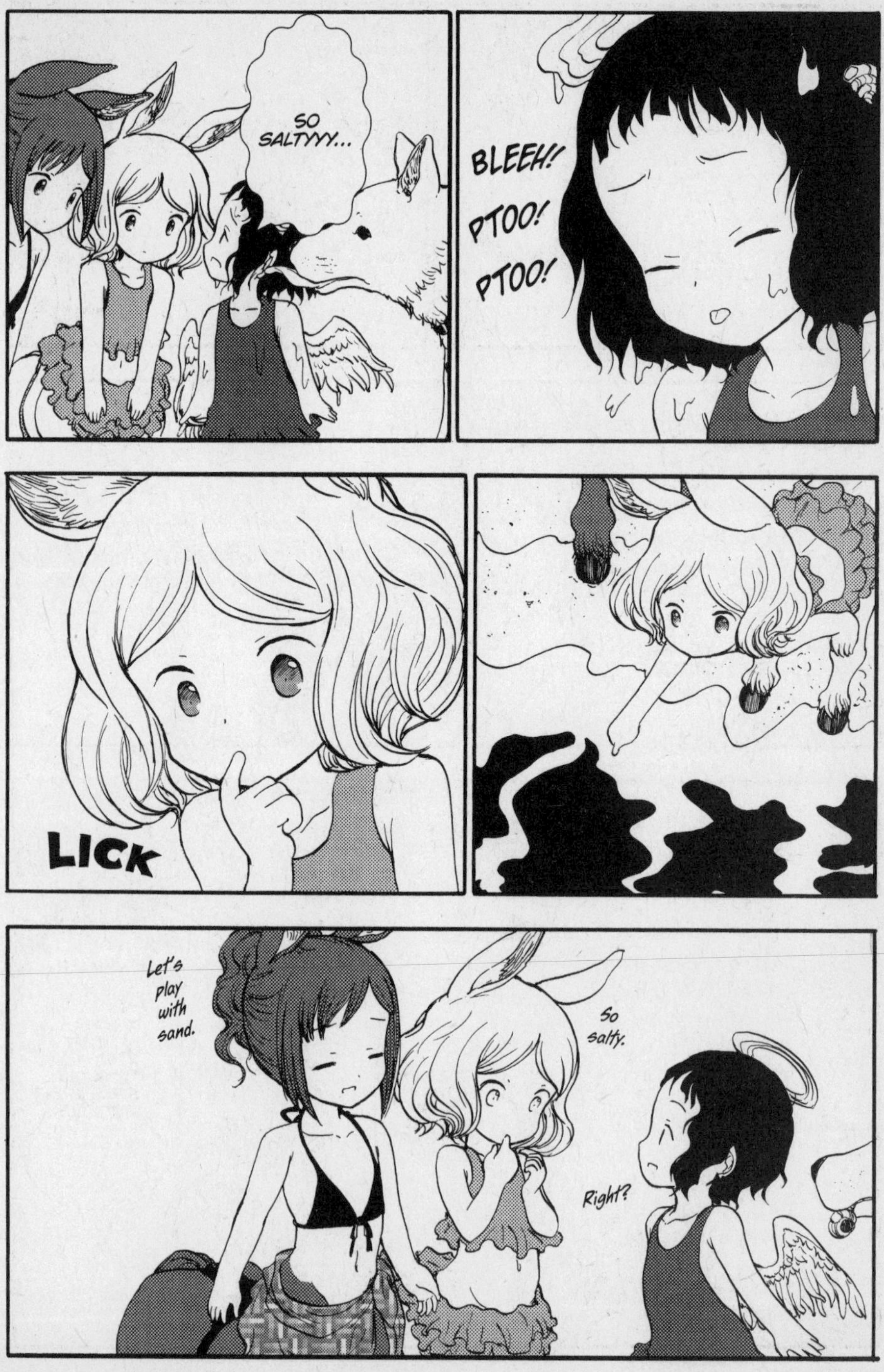
BLEEH!
PTOO!
PTOO!
SO SALTYYY...
LICK
So salty.
Right?
Let's play with sand.

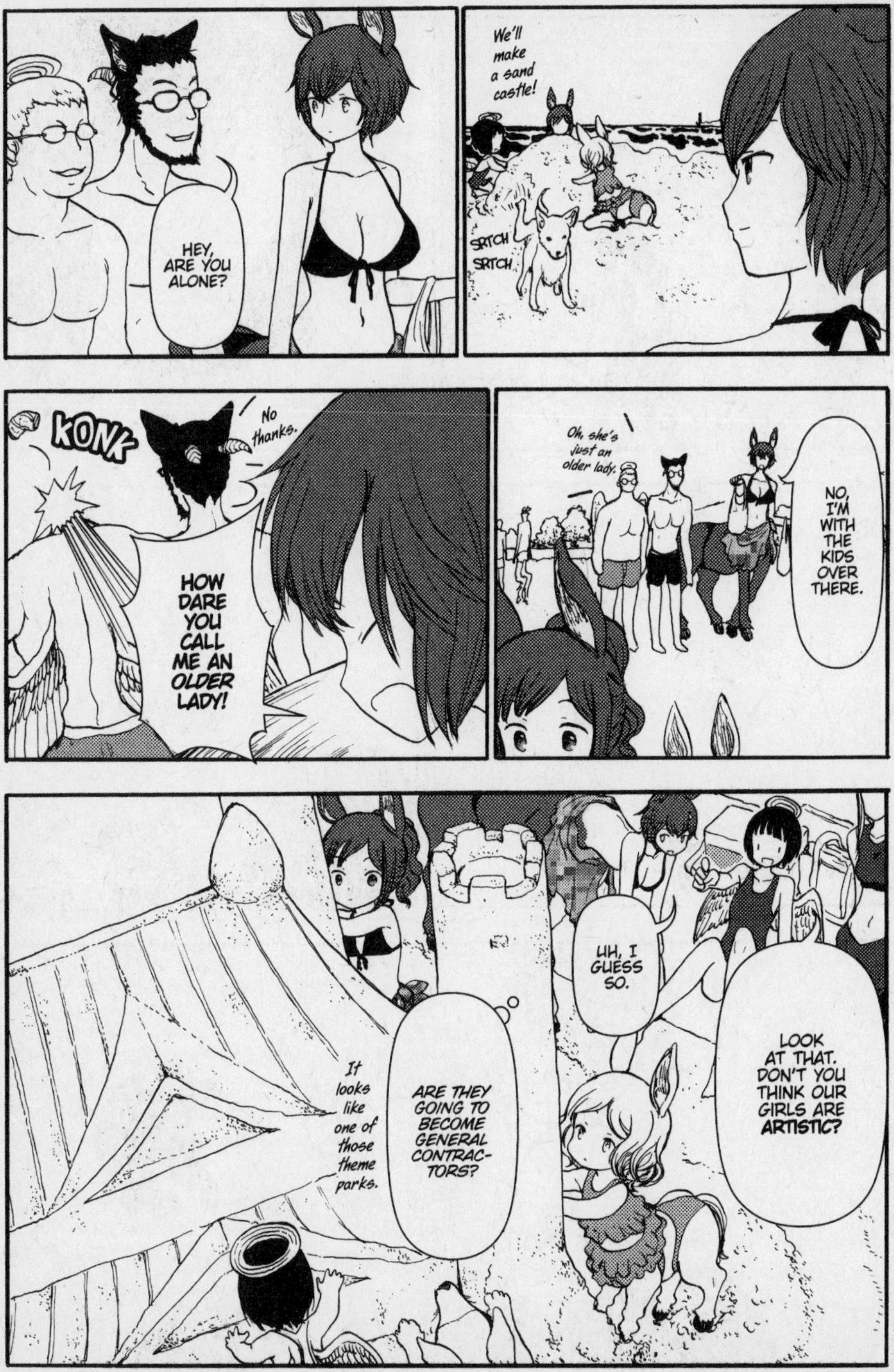
We'll make a sand castle!
SRTCH SRTCH
HEY, ARE YOU ALONE?
NO, I'M WITH THE KIDS OVER THERE.
Oh, she's just an older lady.
No thanks.
KONK
HOW DARE YOU CALL ME AN OLDER LADY!
LOOK AT THAT. DON'T YOU THINK OUR GIRLS ARE ARTISTIC?
UH, I GUESS SO.
ARE THEY GOING TO BECOME GENERAL CONTRAC-TORS?
It looks like one of those theme parks.

THE PLIGHT OF THE PEASANTS

Industry prospers in times of peace, and the Edo Era was no different; but the lot of the peasant was still a difficult one, especially in Kanata.

According to historical records, Hidachi was an abundant region specializing in silk production. Accounts from this period indicate that the plains here were reputed to be so vast that the roads across it seemed endless. Geologically speaking, the plain's dark, rich topsoil is only a thin layer covering poor red soil beneath, but the lack of evidence of frequent landslides, volcanic eruption, and river flooding imply that it was still ideal for stable agriculture. Nevertheless, there was little irrigation development in central Hidachi at this time, including the area where Kanata City stands today. Instead, people built paddy fields for rice cultivation at the foot of the hills, and settlements still exist nearby to this day. Centaurs were unable to plow the water-filled rice fields for obvious physical reasons, but evidence points to extensive dryland farming as well, making Hidachi the largest wheat-producing region in Japan until modern times.

Despite these agricultural successes, the regional economy struggled due to problems with trade. The major limiting factor boils down to inadequate access to seaports, of which there were only two in Hidachi at the time. The nearest port to Kanata, Nakaminato, was still quite a distance away and could only be reached overland, making trade less feasible. The other port was even further, but could be accessed by Lake Kasumigaura and the Sanzuse River. In fact, this port was commonly used in earlier times when whole route was under the control of the Oda clan, but these holdings fragmented when the daimyo was killed at the end of the Sengoku period. Stymied by logistical boundaries on one hand and changing political boundaries on the other, Kanata lost connection to major economic zones and was forced to become largely economically self-sufficient.

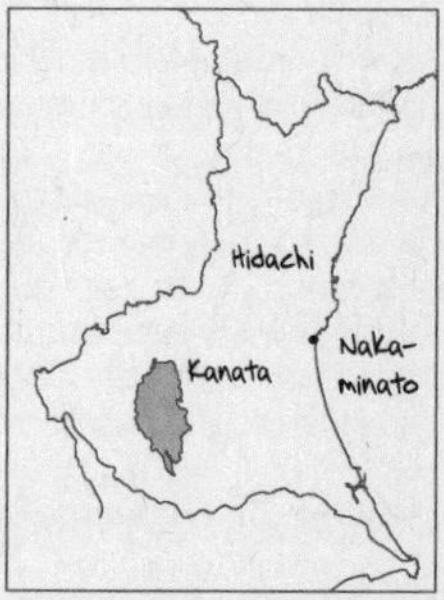
Hidachi
Kanata
Naka-
minato

The taxes of the Edo period were yet another burden on the peasants of Kanata. Most taxes were levied annually in rice, with the worth of wheat and other crops being converted to rice as previously discussed, and not converted to cash until arriving in Osaka. This may seem like a step backward at first glance, given that taxes in the previous period were paid directly in cash, but we cannot draw conclusions about this apparent regression without examining the larger picture. In this case, the answer lies in currency—copper coins, to be precise. Copper coins were issued in Japan several times during the even earlier Heian period, but there were merely symbolic. Instead, coins imported from the neighboring country Chuuka were regularly circulated as currency. These imports declined in the Sengoku period, though, resulting in a shortage. Lower-quality coins entered circulation to compensate, but their use dropped dramatically when most daimyo refused to accept them as tax payment, causing them to lose their value. Thus, the shortage of viable currency led to the reinstitution of rice taxes.

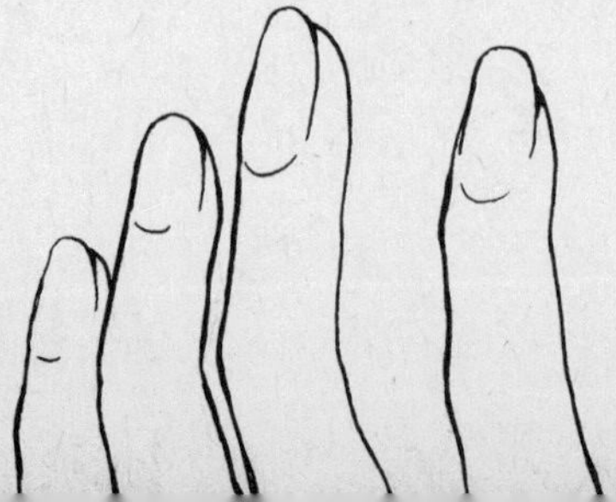

LEARN ABOUT OUR TOWN! KANATA CITY'S PAST, PRESENT, AND FUTURE.

With taxes once again being levied in rice, the country encouraged rice production and even banned some other cultivation, commercial crops in particular. Even traditional silk production collapsed, as peasants lacked the technology to produce silk thread themselves. Indeed, most silk clothing made in the early Edo period was produced using imported raw silk, and it wasn't until popularity surged in the next era that the industry rebounded. With the decline in raw silk production rendering mulberry orchards unnecessary and other cash crops banned, peasants faced major economic difficulties and could only earn money by selling their meager crop surpluses. Despite this fact, the peasantry was still expected to shoulder a heavy tax burden, pay crop storage fees out-of-pocket, and provide unpaid labor for transportation services called sukegou.

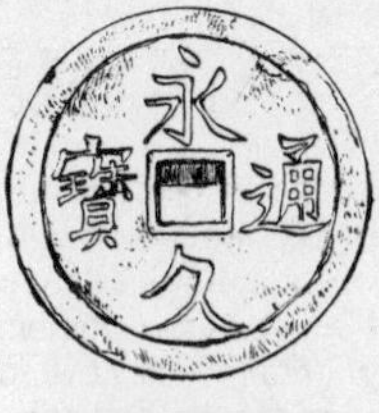
永
通
久
寶

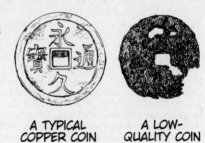

A TYPICAL COPPER COIN

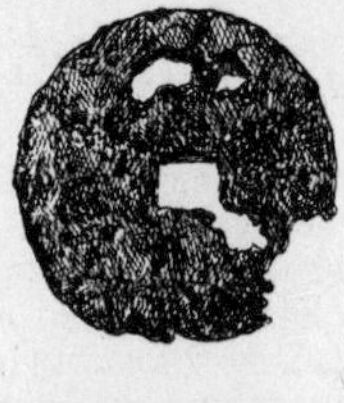

A LOW-QUALITY COIN

Historians argue that it was this sukegou system that later brought the peasants of Kanata to the breaking point. But what was it?

After the Bakufu took power, they built a road system (with Edo as a hub) and set up post stations along the routes. Post stations were staffed with mounted couriers to deliver official items for low or no charge, much like post stations in the earlier Heian period. However, unexpected spikes in volume often exceeded the capacity of the dedicated system, which is where sukegou came into play. Nearby villages were forced to supply men and horses to the post stations, and the burden spread to increasingly distant communities as the volume continued to rise. Villages provided these resources at their own expense, meaning that remote villages gave many more hours of unpaid work than their closer counterparts. During the busy farming season, villages that were already short on manpower simply couldn't spare anyone for sukegou, and they were forced to pay a tax penalty instead.

Villages in Kanata were far from the nearest post station, but were still expected to provide unpaid workers for sukegou. This demand, in addition to a tax burden that they already considered unfair, ultimately pushed the peasants of Kanata too far; when their discontent reached its limit, the Bakyuu Sukegou Riot erupted.

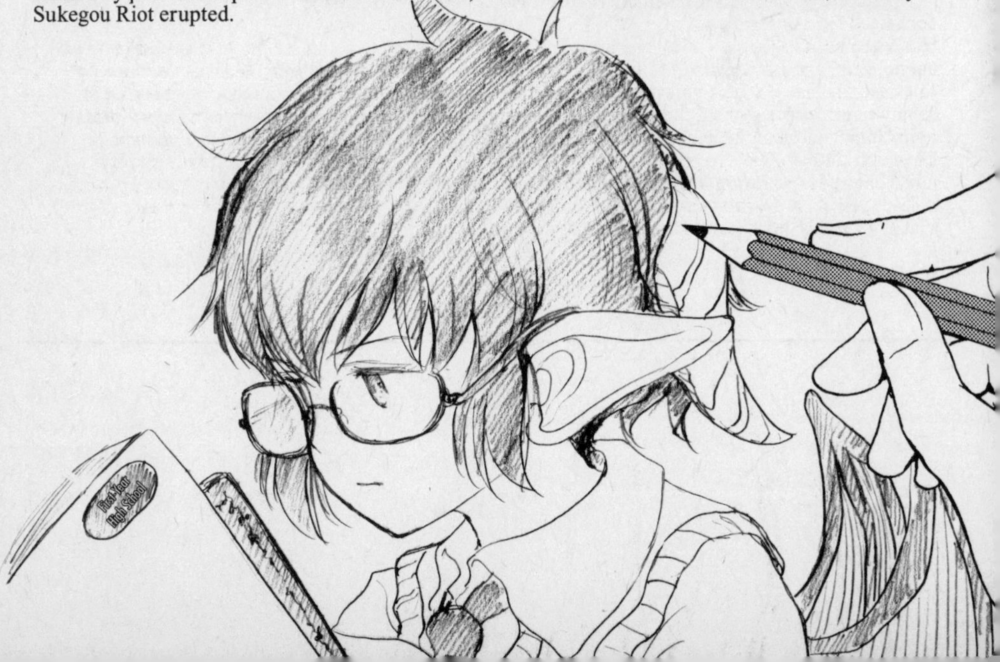
First Year
High School

SEVEN SEAS ENTERTAINMENT PRESENTS

A Centaur's Life

story and art by KEI MURAYAMA

VOLUME 11

TRANSLATION
Elina Ishikawa

ADAPTATION
Holly Kolodziejczak

LETTERING AND RETOUCH
Jennifer Skarupa

LOGO DESIGN
Courtney Williams

COVER DESIGN
Nicky Lim

PROOFREADER
Patrick King

ASSISTANT EDITOR
Jenn Grunigen

PRODUCTION ASSISTANT
CK Russell

PRODUCTION MANAGER
Lissa Pattillo

EDITOR-IN-CHIEF
Adam Arnold

PUBLISHER
Jason DeAngelis

CENTAUR NO NAYAMI VOLUME 11
© KEI MURAYAMA 2015
Originally published in Japan in 2015 by TOKUMA SHOTEN PUBLISHING
CO., LTD., Tokyo. English translation rights arranged with TOKUMA SHOTEN
PUBLISHING CO., LTD., Tokyo, through TOHAN CORPORATION, Tokyo.

Seven Seas books may be purchased in bulk for promotional, educational, or
business use. Please contact your local bookseller or the Macmillan Corporate
and Premium Sales Department at 1-800-221-7945, extension 5442, or by
e-mail at MacmillanSpecialMarkets@macmillan.com.

Seven Seas and the Seven Seas logo are trademarks of
Seven Seas Entertainment, LLC. All rights reserved.

ISBN: 978-1-626924-46-8

Printed in Canada

First Printing: March 2017

10 9 8 7 6 5 4 3 2 1

DISCARD

FOLLOW US ONLINE: www.gomanga.com

READING DIRECTIONS

This book reads from *right to left*, Japanese style. If
this is your first time reading manga, you start
reading from the top right panel on each page and
take it from there. If you get lost, just follow the
numbered diagram here. It may seem backwards at
first, but you'll get the hang of it! Have fun!!

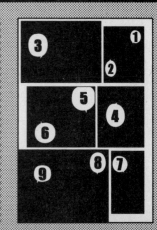